LF

Attributions and
Psychological Change

Attributions and Psychological Change

*Applications of attributional theories
to clinical and education practice*

edited by

Charles Antaki

Department of Psychology, University of Lancaster

and

Chris Brewin

Department of Psychiatry, University of Leeds

1982

ACADEMIC PRESS

A Subsidiary of Harcourt Brace Jovanovich, Publishers
London   New York
Paris   San Diego   San Francisco   São Paulo
Sydney   Tokyo   Toronto

ACADEMIC PRESS INC. (LONDON) LTD.
24/28 Oval Road
London NW1

United States Edition published by
ACADEMIC PRESS INC.
111 Fifth Avenue
New York, New York 10003

British Library Cataloguing in Publication Data

Attributions and psychological change.
1. Attributions (Social psychology)
I. Antaki, Charles   II. Brewin, Chris
155.2   HM291.A/
ISBN 0-12-058780-7
LCCN 81-71575

Phototypesetting by Oxford Publishing Services
Printed and bound in Great Britain by
T.J. Press (Padstow) Ltd.

List of Contributors

Charles Antaki   Department of Psychology, University of Lancaster, Lancaster LA1 4YF, England

Daniel Bar-Tal   School of Education, Tel-Aviv University, Ramat-Aviv, Israel

Chris Brewin   Department of Psychiatry, University of Leeds, Leeds LS2 9LT, England

Daphne Blunt Bugental   Department of Psychology, University of California, Santa Barbara, California 93106, USA

Lee A. Chaney   Department of Psychology, University of California, Santa Barbara, California 93106, USA

Dean Janoff   Department of Psychology, University of California, Santa Barbara, California 93106, USA

Mary Anne Layden   Department of Psychology, Beaver College, Glenside, Pennsylvania 19038, USA

Christopher Peterson   Department of Psychology, Virginia Polytechnic Institute and State University, Blacksburg, Virginia 24061, USA

Anthony E. Reading   Department of Psychological Medicine, King's College Hospital Medical School, London SE5 9RS, England

Colin G. Rogers   Department of Educational Research, University of Lancaster, Lancaster LA1 4YF, England

Janet L. Sonne   Patton State Hospital, 3102 E. Highland Avenue, Patton, California 92369, USA

Richard Totman   Department of Experimental Psychology, Sussex University, Brighton BN1 9QG, England

Fraser Watts   MRC Applied Psychology Research Unit, 15 Chaucer Road, Cambridge CB2 2EF, England

J. Mark G. Williams   University Department of Psychiatry, Royal Victoria Infirmary, Newcastle-upon-Tyne, England

To our parents

Preface

How do people account for their own everyday experiences and the experiences of others? In what way do these accounts help or hinder people in coming to terms with disappointment, in mastering new skills and in adapting to new situations? Attribution theory proposes that ordinary explanation can be thought of as a process by which people attribute events and experiences to one or more causal factors, and it has suggested several ways in which such factors can be classified. Recently it has become clear that causal attributions not only describe the present and the past but also have important implications for the future through their effect on people's emotions and on their expectations of success and failure. Attributional theories are about the influence of attributions on thoughts, feelings and behaviour, and they have a number of important observations to make about how maladaptive responses are generated and how they might be changed.

This book has been compiled in response to the growing interest in attributional theories shown by applied psychologists over the last decade. We present a number of papers which describe the contribution that an attributional approach has already made, or can potentially make, to psychotherapy, to medicine and to education. The book is designed primarily for practitioners, but, although the emphasis is less on theory and more on practical applications, many of the chapters have important theoretical implications. No prior knowledge of attributional research is assumed, and in the early part of the book its historical development and theoretical background are critically examined. Later chapters are concerned with specific applications and show a range of original research, reviews of previous work, and analyses of psychological practice in attributional terms.

Interest in the psychology of attributions has developed as part of the movement towards more cognitive theories of behaviour that has been taking place both in the laboratory and in the world outside it. Some laboratory theories of learning and motivation, especially behaviouristic ones, have had a powerful influence on clinical and educational practice; more recently, the advent of social learning theory with its emphasis on cognitive processes has been closely associated with the use of modelling as a therapeutic technique. Social learning theory has also insisted that people's expectations are a crucial determinant of their behaviour, and it has been largely due to the work of Bernard Weiner that the importance of causal attributions in producing these expectations has been recognized. Weiner has demonstrated the usefulness of his theories in educational practice by directing much of his research to understanding the causes of success and failure in the classroom. Many of his ideas have subsequently been taken up and elaborated in the recent reformulated version of the learned helplessness theory of depression.

There have been a number of other applications of attributional theory to clinical and educational settings, and many of these are described in the following chapters. This readiness on the part of practitioners to think in attributional terms probably comes from two main sources. First, it is a theory about people's psychological accounts, and this alone might be enough to engage the interest of applied psychologists who deal with people who are searching for the causes of their experiences.

The second reason is that many applied psychologists have always believed that cognitive factors are of great importance in understanding people's behaviour, and that helping people to change involves finding out how they perceive and appraise the world they live in. This emphasis on cognitive factors, exemplified in the work of George Kelly, Albert Ellis and Aaron Beck, has prepared the way for the cognitive propositions of attributional theories.

Attributional theory offers just one of a number of possible cognitive approaches to psychological practice. It should be emphasized that the approach does not invalidate or supersede other cognitive approaches. Neither is attribution-based therapy a completely new form of therapy. What is claimed, however, is that attributional theory is one way of understanding why psychological change occurs and, because it is a general theory, it is equally applicable to the clinic and classroom. In addition, a cognitive theory based upon causal attributions has three particular advantages. Firstly, the focus is on a specific class of cognitions which are identifiable, measurable and classifiable. Secondly, clinical practice is grounded in a body of experimental evidence produced in the laboratory, where the theoretical concepts can be further refined in parallel to developments in the field. Thirdly, a number of quite specific predictions can be derived from the theory which can be tested with individual clients.

In conclusion, we remind the reader that the applications of attributional theory are still in their infancy. This book is not an evaluation of such applications, for which enough evidence is simply not available, but should rather be read as a source of ideas and principles which can illuminate and inform professional psychological practice in many different contexts. The strengths and weaknesses of attributional theory are discussed in these pages both from a theoretical and an empirical standpoint, but a final evaluation of its worth must depend on the success with which the theory can be used by applied psychologists.

We would like to acknowledge the secretarial help we have had in preparing this book for publication; in Lancaster from Sylvia Sumner, Anne Parker and Hazel Satterthwaite, and in Leeds from Sheila Turner. Their help was patiently given and very gratefully received. Thanks are also due to Martin Lea for his excellent work on the index.

January 1982   Charles Antaki
                                                  Chris Brewin

Contents

II
Psychotherapeutic Applications

III
Medical Applications

IV
Educational Applications

I
Introduction to the Applications of Attribution Theory

1
A Brief Introduction to
Attribution and Attributional Theories

Charles Antaki

A. INTRODUCTION

Imagine that things haven't been going well at work recently. You haven't managed to get things done on time, and what you have managed to scrape through hasn't been up to standard. Things are coming to a head. A colleague stops you in the corridor and asks you whether you're feeling quite yourself. You overhear two others mention your name and one of them remarks to the other that you might not be up to the job any more. This morning in your mail is a memo from the boss saying she wants to see you. At your interview with her she opens the conversation by frankly saying that she's seen your work suffer, and that she suspects the explanation may be something to do with things at home.

By now you may well be wondering yourself quite what is up. People are attributing your current difficulties at work to ill-health, incapacity and family stress. But, you might say to yourself, all that's happening is that your work is going through the usual chaos that this time of the year brings. Or that it may look bad, but it's no worse than anyone else's work. Or that you're giving up cigarettes, this time for good, and it's bound to cause some temporary disruption. Or you might agree with the worst things that people are saying—that you can't cope any more, you're over the hill, and you might as well move over and let a younger person through.

3

I hope the story has been entirely imaginary—but I think that it should illustrate what could happen if things in one's life began to move out of their usual and comfortable orbit. In a case like this one, the importance of people's explanations of what's happening to them and around them—the theme of this book—is, I hope, fairly clear; you, your colleagues and your employer will all be searching for an explanation of your behaviour, and all of you will guide your actions by the explanations you finally arrive at. If your colleagues thought that the reasons for the poor work was that you were going downhill, the careerists would shun you (though, hopefully, the caring ones would befriend you); if they saw that it was the temporary effect of cigarette starvation they might tut-tut, but do nothing more than begrudge any extra work it meant for themselves; if they were told quietly that the reason was that your spouse had just left you, they might all rally round and offer whatever help they could. If you yourself thought it was a temporary reaction to something in the office that would soon go away, you might carry on, entirely undisturbed. But if you thought that it was a signal of your declining abilities, on the other hand, you would be risking some degree of distress which, whatever the real cause of the problem at work, might only make things worse. The explanations one has of such things in one's everyday life have powerful effects on one's feelings, plans, moods, hopes and well-being.

There are, of course, more colourful examples of what can happen when explanations are a matter of concern. The effects can be not merely uncomfortable but psychiatrically dangerous, as in the following vivid case quoted by Valins and Nisbett (1972). In the Vietnam war, a new arrival to the front line was, apparently, at much greater risk of psychiatric upset than an established veteran; and the cause of his problems was not so much the fear of the enemy but his treatment at the hands of troops on his own side. Older hands at the front treated the new arrival with derision and contempt—making him prey to what the Army psychiatrists called the "f—ing new guy" syndrome. New arrivals did not know, and could not be familiar with, the unwritten rules of the company they were joining and so were regarded by veterans as potentially dangerous people with whom to go into combat. Unaware of this, the new arrival would attribute the cause of his maltreatment to something to do with his own particular incompetence, something specially inadequate about himself which made the more experienced troops treat him with contempt. What the psychiatrists did when treating such a soldier was to steer him away from the unduly self-punitive explanation and onto the more realistic explanation—that the cause of the treatment he was getting was the quite indiscriminate attitude of the other soldiers to *any* new arrival.

The psychiatrists realised that the soldier's problems in the front line were mediated, and could be changed, by the explanations he had for what was going on. Acknowledging and changing people's conscious and unconscious explanations of events has been a part of changing behaviour for as long as people have counselled one another; today, among social psychologists and clinicians, a particular theory of how explanations are formed and how they affect behaviour has begun to come to prominence. Throughout this book, contributors use the framework of *Attribution Theory* to analyse explanations and to show how they lead to, or are implicated in, a variety of psychological disorders and behavioural problems. Broadly, all the contributors are concerned with people's explanations conceived of as causal analyses of, or attributions for, behaviour; and what I shall try to do in this chapter is to offer a brief guide to the very broad church of attribution theory.

In the first section below I shall give a brief historical guide to the development of models of how people *arrive* at attributions; in the second part of the chapter I shall concentrate on theories of *what effects these attributions have* on people's feelings and behaviour. I shall use a consistent terminology to distinguish the one sort of enterprise from the other. In the past, when authors referred to attribution theory as a general approach, what they meant was theories of the first sort—theories about how people worked out the causes of someone's behaviour (and the term was used even though there was no *one* theory of this sort). But these were theories about one half of the interesting things about attributions: how people arrived at them. The theories reserved judgement, for the most part, on how these attributions would actually affect people's lives. Other theories, with slightly different pedigrees, rose up to fill the gap; when these appeared, the phrase "attribution theory" had too narrow a range of usage to comfortably take them in, and the phrase *attributional theory* (Arrowood, cited by Kelley, 1978) was invented to fit the bill. I shall follow this very useful division between attribution theory and attributional theory, and present a brief guide to each sort in turn.

B. ATTRIBUTION THEORY: A BRIEF HISTORY

How do people decide why their fellows behave as they do? What information do they work on? How do they put the information together? Do they use the same process when they come to wondering about their own actions? These are the prime questions that attribution theory tries to answer. Or, rather, these are the questions that a number of attribution theories try to answer; there is no one theory standing alone and in splendid isolation from the rest of social psychology. There are a number of models of the process of ordinary explanation all sharing, and going together to make, the name of attribution theory. What binds them all together is the strong thread of argument that says that ordinary explanations are *causal*—that people seek to find the cause of behaviour. Almost equally strong is the thread of methodological preference for investigating these causal explanations with the tools of the experimental psychologist. The package of models that these threads bind together has grown enormously during the last 20 years, putting some strain on the reliance on causes and the laboratory methods; but the basic models at the centre of the package are still fundamentally the same.

I cannot hope to do more in this chapter than sketch the basic models briefly; it would be barely possible in a short chapter even to list the full bibliography of work done in the name of attribution theory; there were, as Kelley and Michela (1980) report, about 900 pieces of work in attribution theory up to 1980, more than enough to completely take up the chapter in a simple list of references. Kelley and Michela themselves do an excellent job of surveying the field economically and lucidly, and fuller treatment with much intelligent comment is to be found in Harvey and Weary's (1981) short book.

The Beginnings of Attribution Theory

The history of attribution theory begins in the study of person perception. Person perception theorists in the 1950s were concerned with what people thought about one another: what they would judge another person to be like, how quickly they would form their judgements, what they would base them on, how much they would be influenced by their own needs and desires and so on. Attribution theory developed from this when theorists began to direct greater attention to people's ascription not of qualities but of *causes*. The rationale for the change was Heider's (1958) proposition that a major, if not *the* major job of the perceiver in understanding the world, social as well as physical, was to find the underlying causes of the things that he or she saw happening within it. Accepting this, the task of the social psychologist became to describe how people search for the causes of social behaviour—in effect, to treat the ordinary person as if he or she were a psychologist.

What Heider did was to break down ordinary explanations into two sorts—personal and environmental causes. According to his analysis, people explained an action either by attributing its cause to something to do with the person who performed it or by attributing it to some external source. The sight of a man running full pelt down the street might be explained by attributing it to some external event causing the man to panic and run—a fire, say, or riot police—or by attributing it to some personal desire to cause a scene, to frighten people or simply to run. The distinction between a cause which is "internal" to the person and one that is "external" is of course one that glosses over a good many things about causality and the nature of human action; but Heider's first consideration was to identify what the ordinary explainer, not the sophisticated psychologist or philosopher, used in his analyses. Much as they might gloss over important qualifications and subtleties that the philosopher would be concerned about, these notions had, according to Heider, that immediately familiar feel that guaranteed their validity as the ordinary explainer's accounts.

Heider did indeed pursue the complications of his analyses in *The Psychology of Interpersonal Relations,* and the book is a much richer source of ideas than I can do justice to here, or indeed than attribution theorists themselves have recognized (as Harris and Harvey (1981) point out); but what Heider's analysis did, from the point of view of psychological posterity, was to drive a wedge into the mass of ordinary explanations and cleave it neatly into two sorts. His personal/environmental attribution distinction has been greatly influential, and is a staple of even the most recent work. Some theorists, however, now acknowledge that it survives to trouble, as well as to guide, our thinking about explanations; I shall look into this later on in the chapter (see Section D).

What Heider had done was to suggest a language that people's causal perceptions might be cast in; further work formalized the sequence of operations that the perceiver might go through to arrive at Heider's personal and environmental attributions.

Two Models of the Attribution Process

The first formalization of Heider's principles of ordinary explanation was Jones and Davis' (1965) theory of correspondent inference. This was a theory about the way in which people arrived at a dispositional explanation of a given behaviour—how people decided that what a person did was due to some long-lasting trait the person possessed. After Heider, Jones and Davis proposed that the task of the explainer was to discount the operation of situational or external constraints of the person's behaviour; the more such external constraints could be discounted, the more the behaviour was likely to be due to the other major explanatory concept, internal, or dispositional, cause.

Jones and Davis proposed that the perceiver's task could be achieved by the operation of two comparatively simple formulae, the computation of the number of unique consequences, or *non-common effects,* of an action and of their *desirability*. The first step was to compute the range of the likely effects of the agent's actions and the effects of whatever actions he or she had forgone. The less the two sets of effects overlapped, i.e. the fewer effects that were common to both actions, the less surely could the perceiver decide which of the effects of the chosen action had been specially significant in making the agent's mind up. The more overlap between the effects of the action chosen and the action forgone, however, the greater became the significance of those effects which were unique and followed from only one of the actions. However, the usefulness of the non-common effect, as Jones and Davis called it, would depend on how socially desirable it was. If the thing that discriminated between the two courses of action was something that would attract anyone to one choice rather than another, then an observer could form no very informative picture of what the actor's particular dispositions must be.

The second major statement about how people arrived at Heider's internal and external attributions for others' behaviour was Harold Kelley's suggestion of a mental computation along the lines of a logical analysis (Kelley, 1967). Where Jones and Davis had concentrated on how the perceiver came to attribute people with internal dispositions for the behaviour they performed, Kelley was concerned with how the perceiver might decide whether the cause of the action was a personal disposition or something about the actor's environment, or indeed some interaction between the two sets of causes. Where Jones and Davis worked on the paradigm case of a perceiver confronted with one single piece of behaviour he or she had to draw inferences from in isolation, as it were, Kelley worked with the case where the perceiver knew (or could find out, or guess) not just about the single case, but the history of the behaviour and the actor's part in it.

What Kelley did with these two elaborations of the Jones and Davis model was to propose that the perceiver collected the information that he or she needed to explain the actor's behaviour from three sources. The perceiver collected, consciously or unconsciously, information about how often the actor had done that action in similar circumstances elsewhere in the past (what Kelley called *consistency information*); how often the actor performed the same sort of action in different circumstances (*distinctiveness information*) and finally how many other people did that sort of thing in those sort of circumstances (*consensus information*). All this information bore on one question—did the behaviour covary uniquely with the actor? In other words, did one see the action if and only if that particular actor was there to perform it? If one found in one's collection of facts that the actor had a long history of doing this sort of thing in other places, that these circumstances always produced this reaction from him or her and that no-one else behaved this way, one could reasonably attribute the cause of the person's behaviour to some inner cause and not take much account of the surroundings.

In general, the promise of research on Kelley's model was that it could allow the specification of the ways in which people pick up and put together the social information that is involved in making explanations. It has already yielded a good deal of information about how people *misuse* the data they pick up (cf. the example of the front line soldier earlier on), and this has been a very fruitful line of enquiry into the limitations of ordinary explanations and the ways that our cognitive processes are likely to lead us astray (Ross, 1977).

The Differences between Actors' and Observers' Attributions

So far we have seen two models of how the *observer* processes information to arrive at a causal judgement about someone else's behaviour. Jones and Nisbett (1972) proposed that there were differences between the attributions of observers and those of the actors they observed. Using Heider's analysis again, they described observers' attribution as dispositional and actors' attributions as situational. In other words, they noted that a person tended to explain his or her own actions as being due to the demands or opportunities of the situation, but saw other people's actions as being due to their dispositions.

They proposed two reasons for the difference, one class of reasons to do with the informational and perceptual difference between actors and their observers, the other class to do with more ego-involving motivational reasons. They paid more attention to the informational and perceptual reasons for the difference, and stressed that it was the perceptual differences that might be the most significant. The informational difference was simply that actors knew more about the history of their actions than their observers usually did, and always knew more about their attitudes towards it, their intentions and their motivation. The perceptual differences that Jones and Davis proposed had a more radically psychological flavour; they suggested that actors and observers might differ in their explanations not only because they had different information available to them, and not only because actors might *want* to attribute the environment with the responsibility for their actions, but also because of the simple perceptual difference in the scene confronting actors and observers. As Jones and Nisbett put it, "for the observer, behaviour is figural against the ground of the situation. For the actor it is the situational cues which are figural and that are seen to elicit behaviour" (1972, p. 93).

It was at this point that attribution theory became more than the formalization of commonsense of which it might have stood accused previously (if it was an accusation). Jones and Davis's perceptual proposition was not a commonsensical one; it attributed one cause of explanations to something that was not part of our ordinary, and usually rational understanding of explanations. The principle they were working from was a perceptual psychological principle borrowed from Gestalt psychology (the figure-ground principle), quite different from common-sense notions. It was here the mainstream attribution principles came closer to work that was being done on explanations by other psychologists who, although not following Heider's recommendation to start with uncovering the psychology buried in ordinary words and expressions, nevertheless concerned themselves with how people understood the events in which they found themselves.

Self-perception

Attribution theory seems to have as a guiding light the notion that people and their cognitive processes are *rational*, and has been taken to task for it by some writers (e.g. Langer, 1978; Kidd and Amabile, 1980; Lalljee, 1981; Shotter, 1981). Attribution theory models, like Kelley's and Jones and Davis's, certainly look as though they are formalizations of a thoroughly rational sequence of well-ordered thoughts. Indeed Kelley makes a point of taking as his model for ordinary explanation the clear-thinking, systematic detective work of a scientist. What these models do is to direct our attention to how rational information may be used well or badly by the mind—but what if there are irrationalities hidden away in our explanations? Jones and Nisbett came closest to showing how irrational tendencies might be at work by suggesting that literal point of view might make a difference. Other psychologists, not working in a framework that assumes—to some degree at least—a rational method of explanations gave freer rein to irrational forces.

Bem (1967), for example, suggested that in some circumstances your faith in your own explanation of what you were feeling could be completely unfounded. In his theory of self-perception, he proposed that people's explanations of their actions could sometimes be no more than guesses based on their overt behaviour, and not conclusions based directly on private information within themselves. You might, he suggests, suddenly ask yourself, after a lifetime of the habit, why you ate brown bread, and your answer "because I like it" could just as easily be a deduction from the fact that you're always eating it as from any more private and immediate knowledge. This suspicion of internal causes of behaviour came from Bem's behaviourist background, and promoted a radical re-think of the way we attribute causes of some of the things we find ourselves doing.

Bem's proposition is important not only because it identifies something about ordinary explanations that our ordinary commonsense might miss, but also, and more pertinently for this book, because it suggests to us that *Kelley's and Jones and Davis's models can describe not only the judgements of an observer, but also the judgements of an actor.* So far we have been concentrating on models of what we must be thinking in order to reach a conclusion about why some other person is behaving as they are. If Bem is right, then the processes of information-processing will also be the ones that we use to understand our own actions—like the observer, we will wonder about non-common effects and their desirability (as in Jones and Davis's model) or about consistency, consensus and distinctiveness (as in Kelley's model). The times when we will use these observers' tools will be, according to Bem, the times when our own internal evidence for why we are doing something is weak or ambiguous. As we shall see in Chapter 2, when it comes to talking about our own ordinary explanations for some actions and feelings, this poverty of internal evidence can be quite common and potentially dangerous.

Summary of Basic Attribution Principles

We have seen that attribution theory has at its centre three complementary, but not formally linked, principles. Kelley's best-known principle, to put it briefly, is that an attribution is arrived at by a search (but not necessarily a conscious one) for the causal candidate which is most closely associated historically with the event being explained. Jones and Davis's principle, again put briefly, is that people use information about a person's choices and their consequences to arrive at a decision about his or her personal dispositions. Jones and Nisbett's main principle is that the differences between an actor's explanations and an observer's may be due to informational differences or, less rationally, to differences in what they are attending to. Jones and Nisbett's secondary principle is that motivational (selfish) reasons can also account for the actor/observer difference. There is a further principle which focuses on the actor's attributions: Bem suggests that, in some cases, actors cannot rely on their own private information in explaining what they are doing or what is happening to them; in such cases they use what they can see and hear themselves do, just as an observer would.

Attribution Theory: Models of Decision Making

Attribution theory, taken as the theory of how people reach a decision about what causes their own and other people's behaviour, has the immediate promise of helping understand why, and how, people come to conclusions about causes in a variety of important decisions. Recent attribution work in psychological laboratories has been much occupied with just this problem, and the analyses of such social psychologists as Ross (1977), and Monson and Snyder (1977) are addressed to the problem of accuracy of perception and the reasons for inaccuracy. Accuracy, inaccuracy and the possibility of bias in the decision-making processes are themes of the application of attribution theory to everyday judgements.

Frieze *et al.* (1979) include in their book a number of real life *decision processes* that attribution theory can illuminate or provide a model for. These can be as apparently rational as the deliberations of a jury (McGillis, 1979) or judgements made by parole boards (Carroll, 1979) or as intuitive or emotional as the reactions of battered wives (Frieze, 1979), or the perceptions of lonely people (Peplau *et al.*, 1979). What attribution theory, in the sense of the models we have seen so far, can do is to give a way of decribing these different decision processes and so make them more tractable to improvement. If one could show a parole board, for example, what information they *actually* based their judgements on (rather than what they *said* they did), and how their judgements could be biased simply by the workings of the human cognitive system, then one might be able to improve the decision making process and make it more open to public accountability. In a less public domain, consider how it could help to open up the decision making process of someone who has decided that he or she was "lonely" (Peplau *et al.*, 1979). People do worry about the causes of such uncomfortable experiences (Harvey *et al.*, 1978), but the explanation they arrive at may not always be the correct or appropriate one. Peplau *et al.* identify two major sources of inaccuracy in people's explanations of why they are lonely: people underestimate the power of the situations they find themselves in and they underestimate the degree to which the situation might change or be changeable. Knowing this about people's explanations of loneliness would help by suggesting to people that the interaction between personal characteristics and the situation is what produces loneliness; and both, it could be pointed out, are modifiable.

Knowing how explanations are arrived at is also a help to the clinician who wants to operate on the client's attributions so as to produce a change in the interpretation, or labelling, of his or her experiences. Since the famous experiment by Schachter and Singer (1962) a great deal of effort has gone into devising ingenious ways of influencing people's labelling of their internal states by operating on their attributions. In the Schachter and Singer experiment, people were persuaded to think that their state of arousal (which was actually caused by a drug) was "euphoria" or "anger" equally easily, simply by putting them into a situation where they were sitting next to someone who acted in a happy or angry way and who made them do happy or angry things. Nisbett and Schachter (1966) interpreted this as people changing the label they would ascribe in their internal states by changing the attribution they made for its cause: if arousal could be attributed to something external (like the drug) then the subject in the experiment reported no particular feeling of happiness or anger; but if the subject was not told that the drug would produce arousal, then the only thing he could attribute feelings to were true emotions. Although it is true to say that Schachter's early work has been the subject of some controversy recently (Eiser, 1980; Manstead and Wagner, 1981), the logic of his procedures was a great stimulus in the development of a technique called misattribution (Ross et al., 1969) which is more fully covered in the next chapter.

Attribution theory can take us to the point of providing us with a description of the process of arriving at an attribution, but then leaves the question of what effect this explanation has on feelings and behaviour to speculation. The suggestions of Peplau et al. about what the lonely person will feel and how he or she will act go beyond attribution theory and become a small attributional theory. Attributional theories are explicitly about the link between the attribution one makes for an event and one's reaction to it and behaviour towards it; in the next section we shall take a brief look at two of the main examples.

C. ATTRIBUTIONAL THEORIES

In the chapter so far, the models of causal attribution I have been talking about have been models of how people process information to arrive at a judgement about the causes of their own or other people's behaviour. Obviously psychologists are not simply interested in such models for their descriptions of mental processes (though that is an attraction); they are also concerned with how the products of those processes are used to guide people's conduct. Heider (1958) was himself as concerned, if not more concerned, with the influence of attributions on feelings and behaviour as on the exact way in which attributions were formed.

Attributional Theories: Models of Cognitions Affecting Behaviour

As in attribution theory proper, there is no one complete and systematic attributional theory. That is, there is no one single set of propositions to which all enquirers into the relation of attribution to behaviour can refer. As in attribution theory proper, there are a number of complementary but unlinked principles which guide research; the two attributional models I sketch in this section are self-sufficient theories, while others stand on the platform of the general attribution principles I described in the first part of the chapter. The two theories below receive much attention in Daniel Bar-Tal's and Chris Peterson's chapters in this volume and I shall need to touch on them only briefly here.

Weiner's attributional theory of motivation. Weiner's theory, as elaborated in his 1979 paper, has a very wide range of application. The central idea, to put it simply, is that a person's motivation to something is a function of how well he has done the same thing in the past and to what he attributes his success (or lack of it). Weiner takes Heider's internal–external cause division and cross-cuts it with two others: *stability* (a cause can be long-lasting, like habitual laziness, or likely to change or go away overnight, like a causal mood) and *control* (a cause can be brought under someone's control or it cannot—effort, say, is something one can change, but luck is not). Once one has these three dimensions one can see what people can attribute their successes and failures to, and one can make predictions about how that attribution is going to affect their future work. The *stability* of the attribution, according to Weiner, determines one's expectations of future success: "If one attains success . . . and . . . the conditions of causes of that outcome are perceived as remaining unchanged, then success . . . will be anticipated with a great degree of certainty" (1979, p. 9). The *location* of the attribution (internal to the actor or to be found in the task, the circumstance and so on) is thought to influence self-esteem and affect in general, though the influence is acknowledged to be a complex one (1979, p. 14). The attribution of *control* affects how the actor reacts towards people he or she interacts with; for example, the less controllable someone's misfortune is seen to be, the more one will help him or her (unlike the first two dimensions of attributions, control is more applicable to attributions of others' behaviour than it is to one's own).

To take an example of Weiner's dimensions in operation, imagine a schoolgirl attributing her success in biology to something unstable, uncontrollable and external (her teacher's temporary generosity, for example). With this pattern of attributions one might expect her to think less well of her abilities and try less hard (since she does not believe in her own capacities) when it came to a class test or an independent project. If, on the other hand, she attributed her success to something stable, controllable and internal (her own facility for the subject, say) then we might predict a quite different future for her. Weiner (1979) reports a good deal of evidence from studies done elsewhere (usually by other attribution workers not directly testing his thesis) supporting the idea that there is a strong relationship between the attributions one makes for success and one's behaviour in a large variety of achievement situations. Bar-Tal in Chapter 6 takes up the story and elaborates the theory and its attributional component.

The attributional reformulation of learned helplessness theory of Abramson et al. The central idea of the attributional reformulation of learned helplessness is rather similar to the central idea of Weiner's theory of achievement and motivation: that one's attributions for past successes and failures affects how one deals with new opportunities for achievement. The difference is that the theory of Abramson *et al.* describes a model of a clinical syndrome— depression—where Weiner's describes a model for failures in achievement. People, according to Abramson *et al.*, whose record of success and failure on some particular task (or, on a larger canvas, in life) is such that they perceive no relation between their efforts and their rewards, risk feeling too helpless to do anything about their circumstances and so, the argument runs, court clinical depression. The attributional component of the Abramson *et al.* model is the involvement of attributions as mediators of the person's beliefs about the cause of the outcomes. When it came to formulating an attributional theory of how these were effective, it was found that Heider's initial conception of the simple internal–external split was not enough—like Weiner, Abramson *et al.* needed two more dimensions. They used the additional dimension of *stability* that Weiner had identified and added their own dimension of *globality*. The stability of the attributed cause is its likelihood of staying constant, and its globality is the range of events it will cover. Attributing one's success on a task to one's own ability, for example, is to attribute it to a stable cause; but to specify that one's ability is limited only to this particular task is to limit the globality of the attribution. Like Weiner, Abramson *et al.* suggest that the basic internality dimension has its influence on such affective reactions as self-esteem; the other two dimensions in their analysis were linked more particularly to depressive factors. The stability of the attribution would affect the permanence of depression; the globality of the attribution would affect its range and extent. A person who made attributions that were internal, stable and global for failures was someone who was at most risk of being depressed.

The therapeutic possibilities of the reformulation are complicated by theoretical and practical problems, as Peterson's chapter later in the book reveals. Peterson has some sharp things to say about the purely information-processing aspect of attribution theory and its relevance to clinical intervention; he sees the need for another look at the question of how cognitions affect behaviour and recommends a greater respect for the complexity of ordinary explanations (see Chapter 6).

The intricacy of the picture which I have sketched in outline in this section is elaborated in Chapter 2. The objections to an easy application of both attribution theory and attributional theory are numerous, both on the methodological and on the conceptual level (see especially Totman's chapter for an analysis of the conceptual underpinnings of attributional applications). Before we turn to a discussion in Chapter 2 of methods of applying attribution and attributional principles, I want in the last section of this chapter to enter a *caveat* about the use and potential misuse of the two most important concepts in attribution theory and in attributional theories: the Heiderian concepts of personal and environmental causation or, as they are nowadays called, internal and external attributions.

D. THE USE OF THE INTERNAL/EXTERNAL CAUSE DISTINCTION

Throughout the chapter so far I have used the terms internal and external attribution as if their meaning was unambiguous and their use by the theorists I cited universally agreed and uncontentious. Unfortunately, this is not the case. In recent years, Heider's original conception of the personal–environmental split in attribution of cause has been hotly debated, elaborated by some into broader taxonomies, and dismissed by others as being misleading. This has implications for the use of the terms in psychological practice and in the writings of the contributors to this book.

The worst possibility is that applied workers are working with concepts which are thought by academic researchers to be outdated. This sometimes happens when concepts from theoretical research are borrowed verbatim by applied practitioners, who may not have the time to keep up with the latest developments and may simply not know that theory has moved on, and that the models they have borrowed have become undermined by new research. This rather gloomy picture is not quite the case, but there are some causes for anxiety. In mainstream attribution theory, the internal–external distinction has undergone some development and revision not always noted by applied workers in the misattribution or personal control framework.

For Kelley, Heider's concepts meant dispositional properties of entities, which could be either internal (self) or external (Kelley, 1967); they were both "causal agents" (Kelley, 1972) in the production of behaviour. For Jones and Davis (1965) the concept of internal cause was more speficically intention and disposition. For Jones and Nisbett (1972) external causes were "situational requirements" and internal attributions were "stable personal dispositions" (1972, p. 80). The central theme among these three theorists was that an internal attribution made a claim about something longstanding about the actor, and an external attribution made a claim, at its most general, about something to do with the circumstances in which the actor found himself. Two kinds of objections were raised against this apparently simple distinction. Methodologically, it was difficult to find ways of measuring the two sorts of attribution unambiguously; conceptually, there were some who said that the distinction was misleading and did not pay enough respect to the complexities of ordinary explanations.

The measurement problem is one of terminological confusion compounded by psychometric imprecision. Van der Pligt (1981) catalogues the large variety of ways in which researchers have tried to record their subjects' internal and external attributions; even in the comparatively smallish area of actor–observer differences, he shows that there is a profusion of methods of recording and measurement. Among the variety, he notes, there is a lack of any thorough attempt to validate, make reliable or otherwise purify the rating scales used as a matter of course by almost all attribution researchers.

The conceptual problem identified by other writers almost certainly contributes to the more technical measurement problem Van der Pligt identifies since, if the basis of the units of measurement is faulty, then perfecting their calibration on a recording instrument will be impossible. Among the objections raised are that causal attribution is simply not the only, or even the major, mode of ordinary explanations—people explain by giving reasons rather than causes (Buss, 1978) and can explain by describing (Antaki and Fielding, 1981) or by excusing and justifying (Tedeschi and Riess, 1981) neither of which need involve causal attribution; that people are more concerned about the distinction between means and ends than they are with the distinction between internal and external causality (Kruglanski, 1975); that explanation is a social phenomenon that can take place non-verbally or otherwise without recourse to "rationality" (Shotter, 1981) but the form of which is determined not by the need to identify causes but to pursue interactional goals (Lalljee, 1981); and, most radically of all, that the internal–external distinction is one that reflects not so much ordinary people's psychology but the psychology of the psychologists who, for various unacknow-ledged reasons, ascribe it to their laboratory subjects (Harré, 1981).

The more recent of these objections against the internal–external con-cepts have yet to be met, and may indeed prove to be unfounded; but there is no doubt that, at the very least, there is considerable variety in the ways in which Heider's personal and environmental causes are now referred to. "Internal" and "external" are probably the most popular terms, but "dispositional" versus "situational", and "entity" versus "situation" are common pairs as well. Ross (1977) brought some order to the area by suggesting that we adopt a uniform definition of the terms so as to at least make usage consistent. His suggestion is worth noting.

Ross suggested that we use internal attributions to mean "Explanations that do not state or imply any dispositions on the part of the actor beyond those typical of actors in general" (1977, p. 177). In other words, Ross uncovered the legal convenience of "the reasonable person" which had been implicit in previous definitions of internal and external causes. If the hypothetical "reasonable person" familiar from legal argument would have done what the actor did, then one could not attribute any par-ticularly dispositional cause for the action: an internal attribution "is dispositional because it resorts to an individual difference or distinguish-ing personality variable" (ibid., p. 177). Conversely, an external attribution was what one would arrive at if one decided that in that situation the reasonable person would act in that way; or, as Ross put it, "a situational attribution . . . invokes a widely accepted and generally applicable S–R law" (ibid., p. 177). Just as a jury might accept that a wife assaulted her husband because she had been provoked to the point where any reasonable person would be likely to react violently, so would an attributor decide that an actor's actions were externally caused if anyone in that situation would have done the same thing.

Ross's suggestion for uniform usage of the internal and external con-cepts is well taken. The concepts of internal and external locus of cause are common to every chapter in this volume, so, to ensure a degree of uniformity in the way in which they are used, contributors use Ross's definitions unless they have their own special terms or use the terms peculiar to the theories of Weiner or Abramson et al.

E. SUMMARY

In this chapter I have given necessarily brief sketches of two complicated pictures, attribution theory and attributional theory, and I hope I have shown that the models in the two pictures have lent themselves to two rather different kinds of practical application. On the one hand, there are the information-processing models of Kelley and Jones and Davis, and on the other and there are the behavioural theories of Weiner and Abramson *et al.*; the one kind of model allows the practitioner to base his or her intervention on a working model of the way his or her client *forms* attributions; the other gives the practitioner guidance on what *affective and behavioural consequences follow* from the client believing in the attributions once formed. In the next chapter we shall see how these two different families of models find applications in the use of attributions as tools for, and goals of, psychological change.

ACKNOWLEDGEMENTS

The author is grateful to Chris Brewin and Steve Duck for reading and making useful comments on an earlier version of the chapter.

REFERENCES

Abramson, L., Seligman, M. E. P. and Teasdale, J. (1978). Learned helplessness in humans. *Journal of Abnormal Psychology* **87**, 49–74.

Antaki, C. and Fielding, R. G. (1981). Research on ordinary explanations. *In* C. Antaki (ed.), *The Psychology of Ordinary Explanations of Social Behaviour*. London and New York: Academic Press.

Bem, D. (1967). Self perception theory. *In* L. Berkowitz (ed.), *Advances in Experimental Social Psychology (Vol. 6)*. London and New York: Academic Press.

Buss, A. R. (1978). Causes and reasons in attribution theory: a conceptual critique. *Journal of Personality and Social Psychology* **36**, 1331–1321.

Carroll, J. S. (1979). Judgements made by Parole Boards. *In* I. H. Frieze, D. Bar-Tal and J. S. Carroll (eds), *New Approaches to Social Problems*. San Francisco: Jossey-Bass.

Eiser, J. R. (1980). *Cognitive Social Psychology*. London: McGraw Hill.

Frieze, I. H. (1979). Perceptions of battered wives. *In* I. H. Frieze, D. Bar-Tal and J. S. Carroll (eds), *New Approaches to Social Problems*. San Francisco: Jossey-Bass.

Harré, R. (1981). Expressive aspects of descriptions of others. *In* C. Antaki (ed.), *The Psychology of Ordinary Explanations of Social Behaviour*. London and New York: Academic Press.

Harris, B. and Harvey, J. H. (1981). Attribution theory: from phenomenal causality to the intuitive social scientist and beyond. *In* C. Antaki (ed.), *The Psychology of Ordinary Explanations of Social Behaviour*. London and New York: Academic Press.

Harvey, J. H. and Weary, G. (1981). *Perspectives on Attributional Processes*. Iowa: Wm. C. Brown Co.

Harvey, J. H., Wells, G. L. and Alvarez, M. D. (1978). Attribution in the context of conflict and separation in close relationships. *In* J. Harvey, W. J. Ickes, and

R. F. Kidd (eds), *New Directions in Attribution Research, Vol II.* New Jersey: Erlbaum Associates.

Heider, F. (1958). *The Psychology of Interpersonal Relations.* New York: Wiley.

Jones, E. E. and Davis, K. (1965). From acts to dispositions. *In* L. Berkowitz (ed.), *Advances in Experimental Social Psychology.* Vol. 2. London and New York: Academic Press.

Jones, E. E. and Nisbett, R. E. (1972). The actor and the observer. *In* E. E. Jones, D. E. Kanouse, H. H. Kelley, R. E. Nisbett, S. Valins and B. Weiner (eds), *Attribution: Perceiving the Causes of Behavior.* New Jersey: G.L.P.

Kelley, H. H. (1967). Attribution theory in social psychology. *In* D. Levine (ed.), *Nebraska Symposium on Motivation.* Lincoln: University of Nebraska Press.

Kelley, H. H. (1972). Attribution in Social Interaction. *In* E. E. Jones, D. E. Kanouse, H. H. Kelley, R. E. Nisbett, S. Valins and B. Weiner (eds), *Attribution: Perceiving the Causes of Behavior.* New Jersey: G.L.P.

Kelley, H. H. (1978). A conversation with Edward E. Jones and Harold E. Kelley. *In* J. H. Harvey, W. J. Ickes and R. F. Kidd (eds), *New Directions in Attribution Research,* New Jersey: Erlbaum Associates.

Kelley, H. H. and Michela, J. L. (1980). Attribution theory and research. *Annual Review of Psychology* **31,** 457–501.

Kidd, R. F. and Amabile, T. M. (1981). Causal explanations in social interaction: some dialogues on dialogue. *In* J. H. Harvey, W. J. Ickes and R. F. Kidd (eds), *New Directions in Attribution Research,* Vol III. New Jersey Erlbaum Associates.

Kruglanski, A. (1975). The endogenous-exogenous partition in attribution theory *Psychological Review* **82,** 387–406.

Lalljee, M. (1981). Attribution theory and the analysis of explanations. *In* C. Antaki (ed.), *The Psychology of Ordinary Explanations of Social Behaviour.* London and New York: Academic Press.

Langer, E. J. (1978). Rethinking the role of thought in social interaction. *In* J. H. Harvey, W. J. Ickes and R. F. Kidd (eds), *New Directions in Atrribution Research,* I. New Jersey: Erlbaum Associates.

Manstead, A. S. R. and Wagner, H. L. (1981). Arousal, cognition and emotion: an appraisal of two-factor theory. *Current Psychological Reviews* **1,** 35–54.

McGillis, D. (1979). Biases and jury decision making. *In* I. H. Frieze, D. Bar-Tal and J. S. Carroll (eds), *New Approaches to Social Problems.* San Francisco: Jossey-Bass.

Monson, T. C. and Snyder, M. (1977). Actors, observers and the attribution process: toward a reconceptualisation. *Journal of Experimental Social Psychology* **13,** 89–111.

Nisbett, R. E. and Schachter, S. (1966). The cognitive manipulation of pain. *Journal of Experimental Social Psychology* **2,** 227–236.

Peplau, L. A., Russell, D. and Heim, M. (1979). The experience of loneliness. *In* I. H. Frieze, D. Bar-Tal and J. S. Carroll (eds), *New Approaches to Social Problems.* San Francisco: Jossey-Bass.

Ross, L. (1977). The intuitive psychologist and his shortcomings. *In* L. Berkowitz (ed.), *Advances in Experimental Social Psychology,* Vol 9. London and New York: Academic Press.

Ross, L., Rodin, J. and Zimbardo, P. G. (1969). Towards an attribution therapy. *Journal of Personality and Social Psychology* **12,** 279–288.

Schachter, S. and Singer, J. E. (1962). Cognition, social and physiological determinants of emotional state. *Psychological Review* **69,** 379–399.

Shotter, J. (1981). Telling and Reporting. *In* C. Antaki (ed.), *The Psychology of*

Ordinary Explanations of Social Behaviour. London and New York: Academic Press.

Tedeschi, J. T. and Reiss, M. (1981). Verbal strategies in impression management. *In* C. Antaki (ed.), *The Psychology of Ordinary Explanations of Social Behaviour.* London and New York: Academic Press.

Valins, S. and Nisbett, R. E. (1972). Attribution processes in the development and treatment of emotional disorders. *In* E. E. Jones, D. E. Kanouse, H. H. Kelley, R. E. Nisbett, S. Valins and B. Weiner (eds), *Attribution: Perceiving the Causes of Behaviour.* New Jersey: G.L.P.

Van der Pligt, J. (1981). Actors' and observers' explanations: divergent perspectives or divergent evaluations? *In* C. Antaki (ed.), *The Psychology of Ordinary Explanations of Social Behaviour.* London and New York: Academic Press.

Weiner, B. (1979). A theory of motivation for some classroom experiences. *Journal of Educational Psychology* **71**, 3–25.

2
The Role of Attributions in
Psychological Treatment

Chris Brewin and Charles Antaki

A. INTRODUCTION

In the last chapter we saw that attribution theory meant two things: theories about how people form attributions and theories about how those attributions affect their feelings and behaviour. Both kinds of attribution theory have been taken up and used in applied settings. In this chapter we shall describe the development of attributional treatments and therapies, especially those in psychotherapeutic practice, and we shall critically examine how those treatments relate to the attribution and attributional theories on which they are based.

Most successful psychological treatments end up by altering the patient's or client's view of the cause of their symptoms or problems. Clients treated with behaviour therapy may come to see symptoms as caused by a faulty learning process or an inappropriate response to feelings of anxiety. Psychoanalytic interpretations will often encourage clients to reattribute their feelings to certain early experiences which are thought to play a causal role in later disturbance. It would not be surprising if, having had successful treatment, clients tended to adopt the causal model used by their therapists. An intriguing possibility, however, is that the adopting of a particular causal model actually contributes in its own right to successful treatment.

It has often been suggested that therapies may owe their effectiveness more to non-specific aspects of the therapeutic environment than to the

23

specific procedures which are unique to each type of treatment. The relationship between therapist and client has been examined with this possibility in mind, as well as the way entering therapy arouses the client's expectations of change. The purpose of this chapter is to look at another non-specific factor, the way in which therapy changes clients' explanations of their symptoms and difficulties. Recent advances in attributional theories described by Antaki in Chapter 1 suggest that attributions may affect responses to therapy in quite specific ways. These findings allow the possibility that attribution change may account for much of the effectiveness enjoyed by a wide range of therapies, whether behavioural, cognitive or psychodynamic. In this chapter the emerging role of attributions in therapeutic practice will be described. First, however, an important distinction needs to be made between two ways in which attribution change may be employed. One way is to use it as a therapeutic tool, with the direction of change being determined by some external, non-attributional goal. The other way is to let attributional change itself be the goal, determining the direction of the change by reference to the empirical connections between attributions and behaviour proposed, for instance, by Abramson *et al.* (1978) and Weiner (1979). Examples of these two approaches are now discussed.

B. ATTRIBUTION CHANGE AS A THERAPEUTIC TOOL

Changing people's explanations for their problems is an implicit part of many therapies, if only because most therapies have an underlying aetiological theory which the therapist regards as plausible. Giving an acceptable account of a person's problems is also a frequent precursor of initiating therapy, as the therapist may be concerned to give a rationale for treatment which will have the client's support. Therapies differ, however, in the importance which is attached to this aspect of treatment. For some the aim of treatment will be to convince clients to view their problems as stemming from certain experiences, whose nature will be determined by the aetiological theory, while for others improvement will be expected to follow quite different aspects of the therapeutic situation, such as exposure to a phobic stimulus or the acquisition of certain skills. Nevertheless it is a characteristic of many therapies that clients are seen as wrongly perceiving the cause of their problems, and therapists seek to replace these perceptions with more accurate ones.

An example of this use of attribution change is given by Davison (1966). His client, a man in his forties, had experienced twitches over his eye, heart and solar plexus. The client was worried about "pressure points" over his eye which he had come to believe were spirit-induced, and he felt that this spirit was interfering in his decisions. The client was admitted to hospital with a diagnosis of paranoid schizophrenia. Therapy consisted in convincing the client that his "pressure points" were a response to tense situations and could be brought under control using muscular relaxation. Once the client accepted this explanation he started to refer to his symptoms as "sensations" and abandoned his belief in spiritual causation.

Davison's case is similar to that of Johnson *et al.* (1977) who analysed a patient's delusional behaviour in explicitly attributional terms. Johnson *et al.* were confronted with a man who attributed his apparently spontaneous sexual arousal to stimulation by an external entity he could best describe as a "warm form". Therapy consisted of getting him to reattribute his arousal to the stimulation provided by his leg movements. Both these cases involved the substitution of more "normal" explanations for the less personally and socially acceptable ones previously adhered to. Both the new attributions, furthermore, were based on careful observation of the client's behaviour and were presumably dictated by the therapists' formulation of the problem. The nature and direction of the reattribution rested therefore on observation, on a particular theoretical model, and on a desire to "normalize" the clients' experience.

It is likely that many clients have worrying symptoms reattributed in this way by friends, relatives or their general practitioner. It is common for people with unwanted symptoms like irrational fears, violent feelings towards other members of the family or temporary impotence to feel they are abnormal in some way and to worry about the significance of the symptoms. The opportunity to learn that such symptoms are common, and that their attribution to personal inadequacy or abnormality was incorrect, may come as an enormous relief. Once again, the nature and direction of such reattribution rests on the correction of apparent misperception and misunderstanding.

In the cases considered so far the reattribution process has been based on the premise that the client, in making his or her original attribution, did not have access to some salient piece of information, such that the "pressure points" coincided with situational stress in Davison's case, or that temporary feelings of violence or episodes of impotence are quite common. This may be called "common-sense reattribution". Often, however, there may be no obvious neglect of information but the therapist may feel that his or her interpretation of the data is more accurate than that of the client, that the data are best seen in a particular way. Psychoanalytic treatments, for instance, are based on theories about the origin of symptoms in childhood experience, whether real or imaginary, and their aim is often to get clients to reattribute their problems in ways consistent with theory. This is achieved by the use of "interpretations", which guide clients towards a new understanding of their problems. A frequently mentioned goal of this kind of therapy is "insight", which appears to refer to the success with which the client has adopted the therapist's explanatory framework. The assumption is that it will be beneficial to clients to view the cause of their problems in a manner consistent with the facts as seen by the therapist.

A further discussion of the amenability of psychoanalytic treatments to attributional analysis can be found in the second half of this chapter. There are other more recent approaches to treatment which have made more explicit use of reattribution to achieve their aims. One of these approaches has attempted to capitalize on the different attributions of actors and observers, described in Chapter 1, to analyse problems in interpersonal relationships. The eventual goal is to improve relationships by altering attributions for the behaviour of the other person or persons until such attributions are mutually acceptable. The other approach, known as "misattribution therapy", attempts to get people to relabel their feelings of arousal in a harmless way by encouraging them to attribute the arousal to a neutral source.

Changing Attributions for Other People's Behaviour

Many causes of ordinary distress are one's beliefs about what other people are doing. Often even the simple difference in two people's understanding of the same thing will be enough to trigger unhappiness and recrimination. The issue they fight over may be trivial, but the explanations one gives the other may strike him or her as unfeeling and unempathic. That can be enough in its own right to start an argument. We know from Jones and Nisbett's (1972) principle of actor and observer differences and the great body of experimental work that has been done on it that two people will indeed differ about the explanations they have for each other's behaviour: actors will tend to attribute their own behaviour more to situational factors while observers will tend to attribute the behaviour of actors to those actors' personal dispositions or characteristics. We also know that these differences can come about not for the reasons each side will attribute to the other—meanness, lack of feeling, refusal to be reasonable and so on—but for less coloured and more sober reasons like the amount of information each person has, their knowledge of the other person, and even their focus of attention. If a married couple find themselves disagreeing over why one of them did something or other, it might help to take the heat out of the situation if both of them realized that these more neutral factors were involved in the divergence of their explanations. The Jones and Nisbett formulation of what might be happening in a difference of opinion over someone's behaviour offers a very useful guide to the therapist who is concerned with clients' relationships. The issue is whether or not the disagreement between the two parties can be helped, or even resolved, by showing each person the degree to which mechanical, unintentional, unnoticed processes go to make up the difference. If the difference is not really a substantive one, then such processes are liable to be important and making the couple aware of them is likely to be helpful.

A piece of research that starts from this position is Storms' (1973) study where actors and audience were confronted with a radically different view of an event from the one they would have been used to. Briefly, Storms arranged for two people to have a conversation and be videotaped at the same time. The angle of the cameras was important—they were pointed over the shoulder of each participant. When the tape was played back, it showed each participant either the scene as it had appeared to him, or the scene as it had appeared through the other person's eyes. Storms took measurements of how a number of people saw the conversation: those who were not involved but simply watched it take place; those who participated in the conversation and had not seen the videotape playback; and the participants after they had seen the videotape, either showing their own view again, or showing the view through the other person's eyes. What Storms found was that there was indeed the actor–observer difference in the accounts given by the two participants—each said that the conversation was dictated more by the characteristics of the other person and by the situation than by their own characteristics (clearly they could not both be right). This pattern was also found for those who were shown the tape of their own point of view. However, for the group who were shown what the other person saw, their attribution became significantly less situational—that is, they attributed what happened less to the characteristics of the other person and the situation. One cannot say that they explained things more in terms of their own dispositions, though, since this was measured separately and there was no significant difference between these actors and the ones who had only seen the situation for their own point of view. Nevertheless, Storms' experiment was an interesting test of the Jones and Nisbett hypothesis that mere point of view could make a difference in people's account of what had happened.

Regan and Totten (1975) and later Gould and Sigall (1977) found that a simple verbal instruction to be empathic with the actor could produce a shift in observers' attributions and make them more like actors—that is, more situational and less dispositional. Their manipulation was a figurative, rather than a literal, interpretation of Jones and Nisbett's proposition that point of view affects attribution. As a verbal instruction, it looks at first sight easier to translate into therapeutic practice. But in fact it was the more elaborate videotaping interpretation that was picked up by clinicians as being the method likely to yield the best results.

Wright and Fichten (1976) reminded us that videotape had played a part for a number of years in marital therapy, and they brought the various threads of its use into an analysis of marital conflict that drew heavily on attributional principles. They advocated the use of videotape, but were concerned that there should be more research done first on the actual processes that were going on in the therapy situation with this new technique of mechanical re-orientation.

The re-orientation technique still has to be used by clinicians, however, and the research into the perceptual basis of the actor–observer paradox still has to be fully done. Until it is, perhaps the more useful work applying the actor–observer model will be the work done on the role of attributions in personal relationships. Orvis et al. (1976) reported an attributional analysis of the explanations couples had of areas of conflict between them and showed that the difference in attributions that Jones and Nisbett had identified in the laboratory could also be found in couples' real-life conflicts. More to the point, perhaps, they found that couples tended not simply to differ in their neutral attributions of cause, but also to blame one another for the same events and to exonerate themselves from responsibility. This does raise the possibility that the attribution approach is not, however, necessarily the best way to look at couples' disagreements which have a recriminative flavour; it has been pointed out that the strength of attribution theory is its analysis of strictly causal explanations, and it is not well-armed to deal with explanations that can be couched in more florid language and use concepts like blame, responsibility, guilt, exoneration and justification which are not understandable in purely causal-attribution terms (Antaki, 1981; Tedeschi and Reiss, 1981; Semin, 1981; Harré, 1981). Nevertheless, the lead of Orvis et al. has been followed in one empirical study (Harvey et al., 1978) and in three analytical treatments (Kelley, 1979; Newman, 1981; Harvey et al., in press) and may provide some interesting insights into the ways attributions are used in relationships, both in forming them and in breaking them off.

Misattribution Therapy

The roots of misattribution therapy are in Schachter's work in the early and mid-1960s on the cognitive labelling of physiological arousal. The classic Schachter and Singer experiment of 1962 showed that people could be made to label drug-induced arousal in different ways according to the external cues they were given. Briefly, subjects in the experiment were asked to state whether they felt happy or angry. Their internal feelings were in fact entirely due to the effect of a drug—the same drug for all subjects—but they reported feeling happy or angry according to whether they were exposed to the experimenter's confederate acting in a "happy" or "angry" way. Schachter and Singer, and commentators since, have interpreted the results of the experiment as supporting the view that the emotions we feel may (at least sometimes) be no more than the guesses we make at what we must be feeling. Although the Schachter and Singer experiment is now seen to be not without its faults (Eiser, 1980; Manstead and Wagner, 1981) and attempts to replicate it have not been entirely successful, Schachter's paradigm was married to an attribution theory account with some enthusiasm.

The first step along the way was a joint paper by Schachter and an attribution theorist (Nisbett and Schachter, 1966) in which the term attribution was first used in the context of labelling. Previously, (Schachter and Singer, 1962; Schachter, 1966) Schachter had not talked particularly of attributions, but of explanations; this paper marked the emphasis on the influence of causal attributions although, interestingly, Nisbett and Schachter did not use the general categories of "internal" and "external" attributions widely used in mainstream attribution theory (see Chapter 1).

The next step towards clarifying just how much people's explanations could be manipulated by altering the information they were given about their internal states was the work done by Valins (Valins, 1966; Valins and Ray, 1967). In his first experiment Valins (1966) showed that subjects would be influenced in their liking for pictures by what was reported to them as being the relayed and amplified sound of their own heart beat. Pictures that were accompanied by a discernible increase in heart rate were reported as more attractive than those unaccompanied by an increase. In fact the heartbeat the subject heard was a tape recording and the experiment was designed so that over a number of trials every picture had as much chance of (apparently) stimulating a reaction as any other picture. Once again the interpretation of these results was that subjects were searching for a reasonable explanation of what was going on. Their heart rate was going up; they were being exposed to a reasonably attractive picture; surely the cause of the increased heart rate must have been something to do with the picture—therefore the picture must have been more attractive than the others.

Soon after this came Valins and Ray's (1967) paper on the treatment of mild "phobias". As in the Valins experiment, the idea was to get subjects to infer their feelings from their heart rate. People who were fearful of snakes were shown a series of slides of either snakes or of a card saying "shock". When the "shock" slide came up the subjects were given a mild electric shock. Throughout the presentation of slides the subject was played what was ostensibly an amplification of his own heartbeat. The shock slides were accompanied by a detectable increase in heart rate while the snake slides were not. In fact, of course, the heartbeats were bogus. The point was to see whether people would infer their feelings from their heart rate; the supposition was that hearing that their heart rate did not change would be taken by people as evidence that in fact they were not afraid of snakes. Certainly Valins and Ray found in their laboratory tests afterwards that people in this condition were less wary of snakes than people who had been through the same experience but who thought that the "heartbeats" were in fact just extraneous noise. The internal information about their reaction to snake slides was negative, and therefore they presumably inferred that they were not afraid of snakes.

The clinical application of this sort of finding looked clear enough. Unfortunately, as Brehm (1976) has pointed out, Valins and Ray's original experiment has not enjoyed uniformly successful replication; in fact, after a survey of the literature Brehm concludes that "the most important finding was that the Valins and Ray results were repeatedly not replicated" (Brehm, 1976, p. 161). The paradigm of presenting people with outside clues from which they could infer their internal states did not, however, falter with the failure to replicate the Valins and Ray results. The first paper to make use of the term "attribution therapy" (Ross et al., 1969) was very much in this tradition.

Like the previous studies, Ross et al. confronted undergraduates with a rather artificial laboratory task and manipulated their beliefs about their internal states. Subjects were first made fearful by getting them to antici-pate possible electric shock. The manipulation was achieved by giving them one set or another of initial instructions about how a certain stimulus (a noise, in this case) would make them react. One half were told it would, among other things, make their ears ring (reactions unrelated to fear) while the other half were told that the noise would induce palpita-tions and other fear-mimicking reactions. While being exposed to the noise, both groups were given the opportunity to work on two tasks, one of which would bring them monetary reward, the other of which would rescue them from having to be given an electric shock. The subjects who were told that the effects of the noise were to produce palpitations etc. now had some external stimulus to attribute their fearfulness to, and so presumably thought themselves less afraid of the shock—they spent less time on the shock-avoidance task and more time earning money on the other task. The other subjects, not able to attribute their palpitations to the noise, apparently decided that they must be afraid of the shock and tried to avoid it by completing the shock-avoidance task. The change in the attribution of arousal produced a change in behaviour.

Up until this study, no-one had actually articulated the therapeutic possibilities of this ingenious way of getting people to re-interpret their feelings. What Ross et al. did was to make explicit the claim that by getting people to attribute their negative experiences to an emotionally neutral source their capacity to cope with things that previously had aroused strong negative feelings could be improved. They suggested that attribution therapy should be used to train people to break the link between fears and objects which unnecessarily provoked them. Phobics, for example, could be treated for their fears by training them to attribute their feelings not to the phobic objects (spiders, snakes and so on), but to some neutral source like a previously-administered pill or drug. Unlike Valins's technique, which always left subjects open to conflicting information from their own internal state, any private awareness of arousal was simply grist to the mill and indeed supported the story that the pill or drug was causing the body to react. Any reaction would ideally be attributed to this pill and not to the fear-producing object. Ross et al. were careful to point out that there were limitations to the generalizability of this technique. They saw that for some anxieties and fears it would be very difficult for the therapist to arrange matters so that there would be a plausible source to which the client's anxieties might be attributed. This problem had indeed been foreseen by Nisbett and Schachter (1966) and was reiterated by Singerman et al. (1976) later. Nor would even a successful reinterpretation of the anxiety necessarily be enough to overcome a very overlearnt set of behaviours that clients had developed to avoid the stimuli that made them anxious.

Perhaps the best-known attempt to use the misattribution technique is in the treatment of insomnia. The experiment of Storms and Nisbett (1970), designed to test the technique in this clinical context, is possibly the most well-known of all misattribution studies. Just as in the experiments above, the idea was to benignly mislead people into believing that their symptoms were not caused by an internal emotional state but rather by an emotionally neutral source. The authors argued that insomniacs went to bed in a state of autonomic arousal and associated that arousal with thoughts or ideas which were emotionally toned. These associations were likely to increase emotionality and make it even harder to get to sleep. If the insomniac were able to attribute the arousal to a neutral source, however, then the emotionally toned thoughts and ideas would be less in evidence and the person should not become so emotional. Storms and Nisbett gave half their insomniac subjects a pill which, they said, would make them aroused at night, and the other half a pill which they said would calm them down. The pills were inert, so the insomniacs found sleep as elusive as it usually was. But now some of them could attribute their arousal to the effects of the pill, an emotionally neutral source. Storms and Nisbett found that the group who had been given the "arousal" pill reported falling asleep more quickly than those who had been given the other one.

The promise of the Storms and Nisbett results were that the misattribution technique, previously only used and validated in the laboratory, could be taken outside and used in the clinic. The technique was verbal, comparatively simple, cheap and apparently effective: all things which made it attractive to use. But unfortunately for the misattribution technique, further research on Storms and Nisbett's treatment with insomniacs has not been able to replicate the original findings (Kellogg and Baron, 1975; Bootzin et al., 1976). Attempts to use the technique to modify speech anxiety (Singerman et al., 1976) or smoking behaviour (Chambliss and Murray, 1979) have not proved successful either. Some critics (Bandura, 1977; Singerman et al., 1976) have written it off as a usable technique; recent reviewers Harvey and Weary (1981), however, not convinced that the underlying theory it represents is wrong, have declared the case against it not proven.

In spite of the name "misattribution therapy", the primary aim of these techniques was not to alter the client's attributions but the way in which internal states of arousal were labelled. It was this relabelling which was thought to be the effective ingredient and the manipulation of attributions was a convenient tool with which to achieve it. As in the other treatment approaches described in this section, the nature of the desired attributional change was determined by a separate theory or aetiological model. In contrast to these approaches the next section of the chapter describes a treatment orientation which is based solely on the theoretical and empirical properties of attributions themselves.

C. ATTRIBUTION CHANGE AS A THERAPEUTIC GOAL

The Exacerbation Model

In discussing the results of their treatment of insomnia by misattribution, Storms and Nisbett (1970) realized that there was an alternative explanation of their findings that was wholly consistent with an attribution theory framework:

> Sleep-onset changes may have been produced not by an alteration in the perceived intensity of emotionally toned cognitions . . . but by another consequence of the initial attribution error. Informal conversations with subjects revealed that many of them appeared to worry about the fact that they were insomniacs—about their inability to control such a basic function as sleep and about the state of insomnia as evidence of more general pathology. There is good reason to believe that the experimental manipulations would have had an effect on worries such as these. . . . The attribution error may not have resulted in a change in emotionality across the board, then, but only in a change in degree of worry about the condition of insomnia. To the extent that worry about insomnia further interferes with sleep, such changes could have produced the experimental results. (p. 326)

Storms and Nisbett went on to suggest that a number of pathological conditions might be the result of worry about symptoms leading to a further exacerbation of them. This idea was further developed by Valins and Nisbett (1972) and Storms and McCaul (1976). Valins and Nisbett reviewed a number of case studies and suggested that they revealed a common pathological process: individuals first attributed unwanted behaviour to their own dispositions or characteristics, then became anxious or depressed because of the unfavourable light in which they saw themselves, and finally suffered from a consequent exacerbation of the very symptoms that had given rise to the original attribution. In other words, attribution processes were likely to play a causal role in the aetiology of many disorders, and dispositional attributions for symptoms could be identified as potentially harmful.

Storms and McCaul (1976) proposed similarly that (a) attribution of unwanted, dysfunctional behaviour to the self would lead to an increased emotional state (which could loosely be called "anxiety"), and (b) that this anxiety might serve to increase the frequency or intensity of the dysfunctional behaviour. Storms and McCaul designed an experiment to test this out in the laboratory. Forty-four male students were asked to make two short audiotape recordings. The first was used as a baseline. Before making the second recording, the students were told that they had shown quite a few stammers and other disfluencies. One group was told this was due to the experimental situation producing nerves, and that this was quite normal. The other group was told that the stammers were a symptom of their own personal speech pattern and ability. Then they went on to make their second recording. Here a further manipulation was introduced: the students were either told that the tape would be chopped up, and part of it used anonymously by the experimenters, or they were told that it would be replayed in its entirety to an audience of psychology students and that each tape would be identified with the speaker's full name. The purpose of this condition was to elicit either low or high situational stress. In the low stress condition the authors found no differences in the performance of the students who had been induced to make the dispositional or situational attributions for disfluency. In the high stress condition, however, the self-attribution group showed a significant increase in stammering.

Storms and McCaul proposed that the exacerbation model could be applied to a wide range of disorders in which anxiety helped to produce symptoms. The model was one of the first to identify a specific class of attributions which could be linked via an aetiological theory to the onset of disorder. Not only did it identify these attributions, but it suggested that they should be the primary target of therapy. One of the few studies to have tested this hypothesis is that of Lowery *et al.* (1979). These authors compared two types of attributional treatment for insomnia with a no-treatment control condition. One of the treatments was a repetition of Storms and Nisbett's (1970) procedure, in which subjects were given a pill which they were told would lead to symptoms of arousal. The theoretical rationale was that this procedure should lead to a relabelling of any experienced arousal. In the other treatment an attempt was made to undermine any damaging self-attributions by persuading subjects that their arousal was due to a normal but rather elevated baseline level of autonomic activity. The subjects were informed that people with insomnia had higher autonomic activity levels, but did not differ from good sleepers in terms of personality, adjustment, competence or the ability to tolerate stress. False physiological recordings were produced to indicate to subjects that their basal autonomic activity was above average but within normal limits. Lowery *et al.* found that subjects receiving both treatments said they fell asleep more easily than did the controls, but only the group whose self-attributions had been manipulated reported that they also fell asleep more quickly.

There is also some less direct support for the exacerbation model from a study by Klein *et al.* (1976). These authors were testing the hypothesis, derived from the learned helplessness model of depression, that following failure on an experimental task non-depressed subjects should show deficits on a subsequent task similar to those shown by depressed subjects who had not experienced failure. In the course of their experiment Klein *et al.* found that depressed subjects too, following an experience of failure, showed a large decrement in performance on a subsequent task. In the case of the depressed subjects (although not of the non-depressed subjects) this decrement could be eliminated by telling them that they had not failed because of personal incompetence (a dispositional attribution) but because of external, situational factors. Klein *et al.* concluded that their depressed subjects had a tendency to make damaging self-attributions for failure which directly interfered with subsequent performance.

The finding of Klein *et al.* that their attributional intervention was only effective with the (mildly) depressed subjects prompts a question about the generality of the exacerbation model and about the origin of dispositional attributions for symptoms. Valins and Nisbett (1972) suggest that dispositional attributions are the result of logical thought processes and are likely to occur when the individual is unable or unwilling to use social consensus to check on a shameful evaluation. To the extent that individuals believe their attitudes or behaviour are bad or shameful, they are likely to avoid discussing them and hence arrive at self-ascriptions of personal inadequacy. This argument fails to consider why people might feel their behaviour was bad or shameful in the first place. It is equally plausible that dispositional attributions tend to be made by people who are already anxious or depressed or who have a generally low opinion of themselves. There is now considerable evidence that depression, for instance, is related to a tendency to blame oneself for failure, both in specific situations (Kuiper, 1978; Rizley, 1978) and in general (Seligman *et al.*, 1979).

The exacerbation syndrome may then be more common in people who already have a general tendency to make dispositional attributions. Such a tendency to make certain sorts of attribution has been termed an "attributional style". Specific attributional styles have been found to be associated not only with depression, but also with achievement motivation (Weiner and Kukla, 1970) and with self-esteem (Ickes and Layden, 1978). In Chapter 4 Layden discusses the concept of attributional style and how to modify it.

Maintaining Behavioural Change

The exacerbation model had suggested that internal or self-attributions for symptoms were potentially harmful. The converse of this argument was that internal attributions for therapeutic improvement might be beneficial, and this was a line that had already been pursued by Davison and Valins (1969). What Davison and Valins wanted to know was whether maintenance of improvements on a regime would be any better if the improvements were attributed to the person's own powers rather than to the effects of the therapist's efforts, medication or something equally external. They set up a copy of the clinical situation as best they could in the laboratory—sacrificing the clinical atmosphere for more reliably measurable behaviour. First they exposed their subjects to a series of electric shocks, then gave them a pill which was supposed to make the shocks less painful, and finally gave them another series of shocks—but this time at only half the original intensity. The subjects thought that the reduced pain was due to the effects of the pill. The second part of the study was to reveal to half the subjects that the pill was in fact a placebo, the implication being that it was the subjects' own expectations which had made the shocks seem less painful. All the subjects were then tested for shock tolerance in the absence of any "help" from a pill. The subjects who had been told that the pill was inert were found to tolerate more painful shocks than those who were still under the impression that their improved tolerance on the second lot of shocks had been due to the external agency of the pill. What Davison and Valins concluded from this was that the attributions made by the two groups for their previous experiences were the important thing in determining their later reactions: those who thought they had already been effective in standing up to the pain tolerated it better than those who thought that their reduced pain was the result of a drug. This was, of course, a laboratory study and the question still remained whether the findings would transfer intact to the outside world where clinicians would have less control over their clients' experiences, and would have less certainty about whether clients were improving and to what they were attributing their improvement.

This point was taken up and looked at by Davison *et al.* (1973). Internal attribution might help people deal with electric shocks, but would it help them to go to sleep at night? A group of people were given a course of treatment for their insomnia—they were given a drug (active, this time, and effective) and they were also given training in how to relax. When the week of the course was over, half the people were told that the drug was not a powerful one and would not have had any significant effect in helping them sleep better. The others were told that they had been given the optimal dosage of an effective drug. So one group was encouraged to attribute their improvement internally, to their own relaxation skills, while the other was encouraged to attribute it to the external factor of the drug. Davison *et al.* found that although both groups did equally well in the first few days after the end of the treatment, as time went on it was the group which had been told that the drug was ineffective that maintained their improvement in sleeping. The people in the group who had been told that the drug had been important fared less well once it was withdrawn. Again, the inference one can draw is that the attributions of personal effectiveness were the important things that differentiated the two groups and probably determined how they coped with their insomnia after the treatment had been terminated. Chambliss and Murray

(1979) used a similar technique to achieve a reduction in smoking, although in their study only subjects internal in their locus of control seemed to benefit. In both these studies the post-treatment check on how the groups were doing was rather soon after the end of the treatment, so perhaps it is not wise to claim too much for the effects of the attributions; but results from another study (Coletti and Kopel, 1979) suggest that even after a period of 12 months the effect of the attributions made for the success of the treatment phase is still discernible. The role of attributions in maintaining improvements in training and therapy is a topic that is attracting much attention from clinicians, and others, who see a relationship between the concept of internal attributions and other therapeutic concepts like self-efficacy, self-regard and so on. In Chapter 5 Sonne and Janoff discuss the interrelationship of these concepts, present more evidence for their importance, and use a particular training regime to show the issues involved in attributions and improvement-maintenance.

Cognitive Models of Motivation

The treatment strategies designed to maintain behavioural change were based on the assumption that it would be beneficial to increase clients' sense of personal effectiveness in dealing with their symptoms or problems. This assumption is at the core of an approach to psychological treatment which is becoming increasingly popular. The approach is essentially a motivational one and one of its best-known exponents is Bandura (1977). Among the tenets of this kind of motivational theory is the idea that symptoms may arise quite frequently and can be coped with more or less effectively; the job of the therapist is not necessarily to eliminate symptoms but to increase clients' effectiveness in dealing with symptoms themselves. To achieve this at least two things are necessary. Clients must want to reduce their symptoms and they must believe that they themselves are capable of doing so. Most clients, although not all, do want to reduce their symptoms; once this goal has been established, and it is apparently not in conflict with any other goals the client may have, the therapist's task is to persuade the client that he or she can indeed cope effectively.

Bandura (1977) suggests that clients' expectations of personal effectiveness, or self-efficacy, determine whether coping behaviour will be initiated, how much effort will be expended, and how long it will be sustained in the face of obstacles and aversive experiences. Teaching clients new skills and ways of coping is of course important, but equally important is to instil in them the belief in their own effectiveness, so that these new skills will not be abandoned in the face of failure. Beliefs about effectiveness can be altered in a number of ways, for instance by the information clients receive from what they accomplish, from their observations of other people, from what other people say to them, and from their own physiological states. Beliefs about effectiveness can also be altered by the making of causal attributions.

Weiner's (1979) cognitive theory of motivation has been briefly discussed by Antaki in Chapter 1. Weiner cites evidence to show that expectations about future performance are influenced by the stability or instability of attributions made for a past outcome. Attribution of a past failure to a stable cause like personal incompetence would, for instance, lead to lower expectations of future success than would attribution of the same failure to an unstable factor like lack of effort. Abramson *et al.* (1978) in their attributional reformulation of learned helplessness theory also propose a link between the stability of an attribution and expectations for future performance following failure. By contrast the internality or externality of an attribution that people make for their own performance is thought by Weiner and by Abramson *et al.* to influence their level of self-esteem. Attributing failure to an internal cause is thought to reduce self-esteem and attributing failure externally to enhance or at least protect self-esteem.

The stability dimension is, however, not the only dimension which may affect people's expectations of themselves and hence their ability to cope. Wortman and Dintzer (1978), among others, have suggested that the dimension of controllability may be equally, if not more, important.[1] If people attribute their failures to cope to controllable factors, they should be more confident of coping in future than if the causes of failure were perceived as uncontrollable. There is likely to be quite an overlap between these two dimensions in practice, but the distinction may prove to be worth making. People's mood, for instance, may be seen as an unstable and uncontrollable factor, while effort may be perceived as unstable but controllable. It seems possible that the stability and controllability dimensions may influence two different sorts of expectations, which may or may not coincide. Stability is likely to be related to the perceived probability of success or failure in future regardless of whether the most important influence on outcome is the person him/herself or some external factor. Controllability on the other hand is probably linked more specifically to expectations of personal effectiveness, or what Bandura (1977) calls "efficacy expectations". Finally there is the problem that these analyses have been based largely on the case of failure in tests or examinations, and hence other dimensions may turn out to be of significance when different situations are considered. In Chapter 7 Brewin considers in more detail the attributional dimensions which may be important when accounting for accidental injury.

The attributional theories of Weiner (1979) and Abramson *et al.* (1978) suggest that a re-evaluation will be necessary of previous work based solely on Heider's distinction between internal and external attributions. Storms and McCaul (1976) proposed that the attribution of unwanted, dysfunctional behaviours to the self would produce an exacerbation cycle of anxiety leading to more dysfunctional behaviour. What they had in mind was a dispositional attribution, an attribution to personal characteristics which we can now see to have been not only internal but most probably stable and uncontrollable as well. It is a matter for future research to decide the relative importance of internal, stable and uncontrollable attributions in producing the exacerbation cycle. It seems likely that the exacerbation cycle described may have contained three or more separate elements, low self-esteem, low expectations of improvement, and low expectations of personal effectiveness, and it is not clear whether all these elements would be equally important.

A similar analysis might be applied to the work emphasizing the importance of internal attributions in maintaining behaviour change (e.g. Davison and Valins, 1969; Davison *et al.*, 1973). It is possible that the attributions in question were beneficial because they referred to controllable causes rather than simply internal causes. Obviously there are a number of dimensions with which to characterize attributions. Once again it is an empirical matter to determine which dimension is most closely linked to therapeutic outcome.

Some Issues in Attribution-based Therapy

It is clear that recent attributional theories of motivation have generated a number of testable propositions about the relationship of certain types of causal attribution to various aspects of therapeutic change. Certain groups of people have also been identified as holding attributions which are likely to be maladaptive in many situations. These include people who are depressed (Seligman *et al.*, 1979) or have low self-esteem (Ickes and Layden, 1978), children who give up easily in the face of failure (Dweck and Reppucci, 1973), and hyperactive or impulsive children (Chaney and Bugental, Chapter 12 in this volume). Although the research reviewed in this chapter provides evidence that attributions are related to change in a general way, only now has it become possible to specify in more detail which attributions the therapist should seek to alter and in which direction. To maximize the possibility of lasting behaviour change, for instance, a primary aim of therapy might be to persuade clients that the cause of their problems was, at least potentially, controllable by them. This should increase clients' expectations of their personal effectiveness and hence their efforts to cope with the situation. There are, however, two important questions that are raised by this analysis.

The first question concerns the truth or falsity of any new attributions that are offered. Is the therapist replacing the client's erroneous attributions with more accurate ones? Totman points out in Chapter 3 that in this analysis the truth or falsity of the attributions is actually irrelevant. If the client believes in an attribution then its consequences are predicted by theory regardless of its veracity. The only constraint lies in the ability of the therapist to "sell" the new attribution. This also means that the analysis can be applied cross-culturally to define the properties of attributions generated by different belief systems. A tribesman may, for instance, ascribe his symptoms to witchcraft practised by a jealous brother-in-law. The attributional analyst, if asked to predict the likely course of the symptoms would be led by theory to enquire whether witchcraft represented a stable or unstable, controllable or uncontrollable cause. In many cultures there are of course prescribed procedures to be followed in order to counter witchcraft. The efficacy of the witch doctor or medicine man may lie in an ability to attribute symptoms convincingly to causes which are potentially controllable by the use of ritual or other action. It can be argued that the efficacy of the psychotherapist resides in something very similar.

The second question follows on naturally from the first. What is the relationship of an attributional analysis to other models of psychological disorder? As has already been suggested, attributional analyses are agnostic as regards the truth or falsity of aetiological theories, be they couched in psychoanalytic, behavioural, or other terms. Maladaptive attributions may be arrived at in many different ways, through processes which can never be satisfactorily determined on the basis of a retrospective account. Aetiological theories are potentially of great value, however, in that they provide alternative ways for clients to explain their symptoms, and it may be argued that the clinical success of such a theory may rest on the plausibility and acceptability to clients of the causal analysis it offers. Theories may not produce clinical change because they are true, but because they are sufficiently convincing to facilitate attributional change. To the extent that they help to change attributions along the relevant dimensions, they can be predicted to produce various therapeutic effects.

This line of argument incidentally provides an important rationale for "eclectic" psychotherapy. If therapeutic efficacy resides not in a specific theory or technique but in their ability to change attributions, then there is every justification for being able to employ a wide range of techniques. The therapist's job then becomes one of finding the approach which makes the best sense to the client and enables him or her most readily to make the desired reattribution. Sometimes a psychoanalytic interpretation will be most acceptable, sometimes an analysis in behavioural terms, and so on. What is important is the therapist's ability to provide a convincing analysis. Behavioural interventions, in which clients have the opportunity to perceive themselves carrying out difficult assignments, are likely to provide particularly convincing demonstrations of the therapist's analysis. In terms of a motivational theory, however, these interventions are like purely verbal interventions in that their value is seen to lie in the cognitive reappraisal which they promote.

D. SUMMARY

Attributional change can be employed in therapy in two main ways, either as a tool to facilitate the achievement of an externally defined goal, such as the relabelling of an emotional state, or as a goal in its own right. The latter development has been made possible by recent attributional theories which have specificed relationships between certain types of attribution and variables such as self-esteem, expectations of success and failure, etc. which are important factors in therapeutic outcome. Most of the contributors to this volume are concerned with attributions in the sense of goals in their own right. Although little is known about how such attributions are arrived at, it is possible to identify certain attributional patterns as potentially maladaptive and to seek to change them in specified directions. Certain groups of people have already been recognized as tending to hold these maladaptive attributional patterns.

It is argued that this approach is an example of a cognitive theory of motivation, which regards therapeutic interventions as effective because they induce clients to reappraise their situation in certain specifiable ways. The aim is to increase clients' perceptions of their personal effectiveness in coping with their symptoms. In the pursuit of this aim clients must first be persuaded that the cause of their symptoms is something which is potentially controllable by them. It is suggested that the usefulness of the various aetiological models employed by psychotherapists lies not in their truth or falsity, but in the ease with which they help clients to reattribute their problems in the desired direction.

NOTE

1. Weiner (1979) also proposes a dimension of controllability, but does not

distinguish between control exercisable by persons themselves and control exercisable by other people. This distinction, it seems to us, may be important.

REFERENCES

Abramson, L., Seligman, M. E. P. and Teasdale, J. (1978). Learned helplessness in humans: critique and reformulation. *Journal of Abnormal Psychology* **87**, 49–74.

Antaki, C. (ed.) (1981). *The Psychology of Ordinary Explanations of Social Behaviour.* London and New York: Academic Press.

Bandura, A. (1977). Self-efficacy: toward a unifying theory of behavioural change. *Psychological Review* **84**, 191–215.

Bootzin, R. R., Herman, C. P. and Nicassio, P. (1976). The power of suggestion: another examination of misattribution and insomnia. *Journal of Personality and Social Psychology* **34**, 673–674.

Brehm, S. (1976). *The Applications of Social Psychology to Clinical Practice.* New York: Hemisphere.

Chambliss, C. and Murray, E. J. (1979). Cognitive procedures for smoking reduction: symptom versus efficacy attribution. *Cognitive Therapy and Research* **3**, 91–95.

Coletti, G. and Kopel, S. A. (1979). Maintaining behaviour change. *Journal of Consulting and Clinical Psychology* **47**, 614–617.

Davison, G. C. (1966). Differential relaxation and cognitive restructuring in therapy. *Proceedings of the American Psychological Association* 1966, 177–179.

Davison, G. C., Tsujimoto, R. N. and Glaros, A. G. (1973). Attribution and the maintenance of behaviour change in falling asleep. *Journal of Abnormal Psychology* **82**, 124–133.

Davison, G. C. and Valins, S. (1969). Maintenance of self-attributed and drug-attributed behaviour change. *Journal of Personality and Social Psychology* **11**, 25–33.

Dweck, C. S. and Reppucci, N. D. (1973). Learned helplessness and reinforcement responsibility in children. *Journal of Personality and Social Psychology* **25**, 109–116.

Eiser, J. R. (1980). *Cognitive Social Psychology.* London: McGraw Hill.

Gould, R. and Sigall, H. (1977). The effects of empathy and outcome attribution. *Journal of Experimental Social Psychology* **13**, 480–491.

Harré, R. (1981). Expressive aspects of descriptions of others. In C. Antaki (ed.). *The Psychology of Ordinary Explanations of Social Behaviour.* London and New York: Academic Press.

Harvey, J. H. and Weary, G. B. (1981). *Perspectives on Attributional Processes.* Iowa: Wm Brown.

Harvey, J. H., Weber, A. L., Yarkin, K. L. and Stewart, B. E. (in press). Attributional aspects of interpersonal conflict. In S. W. Duck (ed.). *Dissolving Personal Relationships.* London and New York: Academic Press.

Harvey, J. H., Wells, G. L. and Alvarez, M. D. (1978). Attribution in the context of conflict and separation in close relationships. In J. H. Harvey, W. J. Ickes and R. F. Kidd (eds). *New Directions in Attribution Research* (vol. 2). Hillsdale: Erlbaum.

Ickes, W. J. and Layden, M. A. (1978). Attributional Styles. In J. H. Harvey, W. J. Ickes and R. F. Kidd (eds). *New Directions in Attribution Research* (vol. 2). Hillsdale: Erlbaum.

Johnson, W. G., Ross, J. M. and Mastria, M. A. (1977). Delusional behaviour: An attributional analysis of development and modification. *Journal of Abnormal Psychology* **86**, 421–426.

Jones, E. E. and Nisbett, R. E. (1972). The actor and the observer. *In* E. E. Jones, D. E. Kanouse, H. H. Kelley, R. E. Nisbett, S. Valins and B. Weiner (eds). *Attribution: Perceiving the Causes of Behaviour*. New Jersey: General Learning Press.

Kelley, H. H. (1979). *Personal Relationships: Their Structures and Processes*. Hillsdale: Erlbaum.

Kellogg, R. and Baron, R. S. (1975). Attribution theory, insomnia and the reverse placebo effect. *Journal of Personality and Social Psychology* **32**, 231–236.

Klein, D. C., Fencil-Morse, E. and Seligman, M. E. P. (1976). Learned helplessness, depression and the attribution of failure. *Journal of Personality and Social Psychology* **33**, 508–516.

Kuiper, N. A. (1978). Depression and causal attributions for success and failure. *Journal of Personality and Social Psychology* **36**, 236–246.

Lowery, C. R., Denney, D. R. and Storms, M. D. (1979). Insomnia: a comparison of the effects of pill attributions and nonpejorative self-attributions. *Cognitive Therapy and Research* **3**, 161–164.

Manstead, A. S. R. and Wagner, H. L. (1981). Arousal, cognition and emotion: an appraisal of two-factor theory. *Current Psychological Reviews* **1**, 35–54.

Newman, H. (1981). Communication within ongoing intimate relationships: an attributional perspective. *Personality and Social Psychology Bulletin* **7**, 59–70.

Nisbett, R. E. and Schachter, S. (1966). Cognitive manipulation of pain. *Journal of Experimental Social Psychology* **2**, 227–236.

Orvis, B. R., Kelley, H. H. and Butler, D. (1976). Attributional conflict in young couples. *In* J. H. Harvey, W. J. Ickes and R. F. Kidd (eds). *New Directions in Attribution Research* (vol. 1). Hillsdale: Erlbaum.

Regan, D. R. and Totten, J. (1975). Empathy and attribution. *Journal of Personality and Social Psychology* **32**, 850–856.

Rizley, R. (1978). Depression and distortion in the attribution of causality. *Journal of Abnormal Psychology* **87**, 32–48.

Ross, L., Rodin, J. and Zimbardo, P. G. (1969). Towards an attribution therapy. *Journal of Personality and Social Psychology* **12**, 279–288.

Schachter, S. (1966). The interaction between cognitive and physiological determinants of emotional state. *In* L. Berkowitz (ed.). *Advances in Experimental Social Psychology* (vol. 3). London and New York: Academic Press.

Schachter, S. and Singer, J. E. (1962). Cognitive, social and physiological determinants of emotional state. *Psychological Review* **69**, 379–399.

Seligman, M. E. P., Abramson, L. Y., Semmel, A. and von Baeyer, C. (1979). Depressive attributional style. *Journal of Abnormal Psychology* **88**, 242–247.

Semin, G. (1980). A gloss on attribution theory. *British Journal of Social and Clinical Psychology* **19**, 291–300.

Singerman, K. G., Borkovec, T. D. and Baron, R. S. (1976). Failure of a misattribution therapy manipulation with a clinically relevant target behaviour. *Behaviour Therapy* **7**, 306–313.

Storms, M. D. (1973). Videotape and the attribution process. *Journal of Personality and Social Psychology* **27**, 165–175.

Storms, M. D. and McCaul, K. D. (1976). Attribution processes and emotional exacerbation of dysfunctional behaviour. *In* J. H. Harvey, W. J. Ickes and R. F.

Kidd (eds). *New Directions in Attribution Research* (vol. I). Hillsdale: Erlbaum.

Storms, M. D. and Nisbett, R. E. (1970). Insomnia and the attribution process. *Journal of Personality and Social Psychology* **16**, 319–328.

Tedeschi, J. T. and Reiss, M. (1981). Verbal strategies in impression management. *In* C. Antaki (ed.). *The Psychology of Ordinary Explanations of Social Behaviour.* London and New York: Academic Press.

Valins, S. (1966). Cognitive effects of false heartrate feedback. *Journal of Personality and Social Psychology* **4**, 400–408.

Valins, S. and Nisbett, R. E. (1972). Attribution processes in the development and treatment of emotional disorders. *In* E. E. Jones, D. E. Kanouse, H. H. Kelley, R. E. Nisbett, S. Valins and B. Weiner (eds). *Attribution: Perceiving the Causes of Behaviour.* New Jersey: General Learning Press.

Valins, S. and Ray, A. (1967). Effects of cognitive desensitisation on avoidance behaviour. *Journal of Personality and Social Psychology* **7**, 345–350.

Weiner, B. (1979). A theory of motivation for some classroom experiences. *Journal of Educational Psychology* **71**, 3–25.

Weiner, B. and Kukla, A. (1970). An attributional analysis of achievement motivation. *Journal of Personality and Social Psychology* **15**, 1–20.

Wortman, C. B. and Dintzer, L. (1978). Is an attributional analysis of the learned helplessness phenomenon viable? *Journal of Abnormal Psychology* **87**, 75–90.

Wright, J. and Fichten, C. (1976). Denial of responsibility, videotape feedback and attribution therapy. *Canadian Psychological Review* **17**, 2189–2230.

3
Philosophical Foundations of Attribution Therapies

Richard Totman

A. INTRODUCTION

Attribution theory is about people's conscious reflections on their own actions and the actions of other people, and the explanations which are contrived to account for these actions. Psychology has a bad track record when it comes to producing theories and ideas that are of practical value, and one of the attractions of attribution theory, as the chapters in this volume show, is that it does seem to lend itself to practical application in therapy and education. This chapter is written from the belief that the theory does indeed have a practical role to play in these and other fields of social concern, but that in order to understand, develop and consolidate this role it is essential to appreciate what kind of innovation is contained in the theory, and what the limits are to its potential. As with all new devices, it is very easy to get carried away and overestimate their significance.

The "theory" (or rather set of ideas, for there is little by way of theory in the strict sense) rests on the two basic assumptions, (1) that people make attributions, i.e. they try to explain actions, and (2) that distinctions and generalizations are possible about the kinds of explanation that are typically contrived, i.e. we can exhaustively categorize the classes of idea people entertain to explain actions. The first of these assumptions has been the subject of some contention and qualification (e.g. Langer, 1978). Nevertheless from our own everyday observations, if not from psychological research and theory, we can be reasonably confident that individuals do spend much of their time making sense of and evaluating the things other people do, as well as justifying their own actions. Casual conversation and gossip is full of direct and oblique criticism and (more rarely) endorsement of the actions of others. Clearly, it would not be correct to suggest that every action of every person is always scrutinized and explained. Most human behaviour takes place quite casually and goes by virtually unnoticed. So when are attributions made? In what circumstances do people find it necessary to account for their own actions and explain the things other people do? Festinger's Cognitive Dissonance Theory (Festinger, 1957) suggests that explanations are called for principally when an action is perceived as out of line with what is normal and expected in the circumstances (also Totman, 1973). As Langer puts it, ". . . unless forced to engage in conscious thought, one prefers the mode of interacting with one's environment in a state of relative mindlessness, at least with regard to the situation in hand" (p. 40).

People's ordinary speech also supports this conclusion. The logic of the question "Why did he do that?", or "Why did I do that?" (one or other of these is implied in all attributional analyses as the starting point of the subject's cognitive activity) entails that the need for explanation is aroused only when the individual has appraised the possibility of departure from a standard, or rule, of normality or warrantability.

The second assumption, that the explanations people offer are themselves susceptible of explanation, or at least of sorting into theoretically meaningful categories, is the corner stone of most attribution research and theory. So attribution theory is really a set of distinctions regarding the types of explanation which are typically offered to explain past actions, and a corresponding set of hypotheses about what governs which explanation is selected in which situation and what the effect of selecting one particular type of explanation will be on the person's mood, behaviour and attitudes.

B. INTERNAL V. EXTERNAL ATTRIBUTIONS

The distinction between internal and external attributions plays a central part in many attribution theory analyses and is at the heart of programmes of prevention and intervention in attributional based therapy. Because this distinction is such an important one, it is appropriate to consider it here in some detail, returning to some of the points made in the Introduction to the book and adding to these. Is it based on a sound logic? Does it make sense to contrast causes perceived as "inside" the person with causes perceived as "outside" him? Is this distinction a genuinely fundamental one or is it mixed up with others?

In fact the internal–external distinction has parallels in ordinary language, in law and in philosophy which it is essential not to neglect. The evolution and refinement of ideas in law and philosophy is a reflection of the central concerns of social man. Attribution theory is no more than a recent development in a comparatively young field. To identify its categories and distinctions as in line with historically older ones is to give it considerable support by establishing analytical precedents which have gestated over not years but centuries and which therefore cannot be dismissed as mere superficia or fashion.

Ordinary Language

I have argued elsewhere (Totman, 1973, 1980, in press) that many of the most widely discussed theses of social psychology can be deduced from the logic and form of people's ordinary language. We know, for example, that attributions and other forms of explanation are normally only sought in circumstances of unresolved anomaly. "Why" questions are demands for explanations and they do not arise in situations of ordinariness and normality. When a persistent child, puzzled by someone's behaviour, embarks on one of those endless chains of such questions the exasperated parent, in the end, often finds no alternative but to answer along the lines "Because that's the kind of thing that kind of person does". We do not really need cognitive dissonance theory, or indeed psychological research, to be able to work out in what circumstances attributions are made.

We can also, without too much difficulty, working from intuition, sort the statements made by individuals about other people's actions into the two classes, "things done to a person" and "things done by a person". The centrality of this distinction in an analysis of act/action commentaries is readily apparent because the whole rhetoric of blame and responsibility hangs on which of these is appropriate. Definitionally, one cannot blame someone for something in which he had no choice.

But what does it mean to be seen to have no choice? To be seen to have no choice is to be seen to be acting under the influence of some powerful constraint. To the extent to which such a constraining influence is visible by an observer the individual will be attributed with less choice and will be exempted from the blame and responsibility (or credit) which his action might have attracted had no such influence been identifiable. A few observations about everyday language show us that the flow of statements concerned with blame and responsibility is strictly contingent upon an initial attribution of freedom, or, more accurately, uncon-strainedness. Something very close to the internal–external distinction of attribution theory seems to be supported in everyday casual speech.

The Legal System

The dispensation of justice in litigation, as will be obvious, is also centrally concerned with the question of personal agency. Mr. A. who shoots dead a housebreaker who had a pistol placed at his wife's head will get off more lightly than Mr. B. who shoots dead a burglar without any such excuse. The basic argument is that A had less choice than B because it is accepted as normal and reasonable, even desirable, for someone to give first priority to protecting the lives of those close to him.

Court defences of crimes frequently revolve around this question of the degree of choice with which it is appropriate to attribute the defendant. If it can be established that a particular crime was a "crime of passion" or a crime committed "when the balance of the mind was temporarily disturbed", or even if some sort of link can be established between a deprived upbringing and the conduct for which the person is accused then the penalties are lighter. Again the trick is to sell to the jury the idea that the locus of control resided outside the rational, calculating and volitional processes of the individual.

Philosophy

The distinction between attributed agency and attributed passivity also underlies some of the more important issues in the philosophy of action; for example, the debate about reasons versus causes in the explanation of human social behaviour and the controversy about freely willed versus determined action. Much of this branch of philosophy is concerned with the nature of the statements which people utter, and the pervasiveness of these controversies itself reflects the existence of two distinct major classes of explanatory account.

So there is some correspondence among distinctions basic to law and philosophy and those we are brought to in considering the syntactical structure of the statements that people make reflectively to refer to acts and actions. This has to do with the attribution of moral responsibility and it seems to relate quite closely to the internal–external distinction in attribution theory. Unfortunately though, there can be no neat tying up of the attribution concept with these older ones. Concurrence among attri-butionists as to exactly what is meant by "internal–external" has been far from perfect. Different authors have emphasized different aspects of the attribution process, and this has led to a variety of different definitions. Gergen (1978) has correctly criticized social psychologists for the narrow ahistorical perspectives which they characteristically take. Attributionists are not exempt from this criticism. It is a mark against attribution theory that its basic concepts and distinctions have mostly been set up on the strength of laboratory experiments and that forms and institutions such as our legal-judiciary systems which have been at the very core of social life for millennia get hardly a passing mention. Such institutions are themselves crystallizations of the fundamental dimensions along which distinctions are most profitably made in the explanation of human acts and actions. One of the foremost among these is a dimension ranging from (attributed) freely chosen unconstrained action on the one hand; action for which the individual can be held responsible, and (attributed) forced or constrained action on the other, for which the individual cannot be blamed.

C. ATTRIBUTION THEORY AS ANTI-EMPIRICAL

The rest of this chapter will be taken up with a discussion of how this crucial distinction can come to form the basis of policies of change and intervention which have practical value for society and the individual. I shall argue that an attribution theory organized along the lines already given in basic legal and philosophical distinctions and in the logic of ordinary language has great power as a scheme from which remedial measures can be derived, but that this power is entirely a consequence of the intellectual, or conceptual, reorientation which the theory represents. Empirical concerns, with the exception of studies whose simple aim is to evaluate the success of remedial policies based on the theory, are beyond the scope of the theory. Empirical "testings" of the theory and laboratory based "refinements" of its predictions are red herrings in relation to the value of the set of ideas that has become known as attribution theory.

In the past decade the role of experimentation in social psychology has come under critical siege from several different quarters (e.g. Gergen, 1978; Harré, 1980). No longer is controlled experimentation the Olympian god it used to be. I shall suggest that in attribution theory analyses it can be dispensed with altogether without detracting in any way from the value of the theory as a practical device for bettering society and helping the individual. Because I am best acquainted with the clinical literature I shall use the social situation formed by the encounter between therapist and patient as the point of departure in this discussion, but the arguments can equally be applied to other fields such as education where an attribution theory analysis is considered relevant.

Consider a hypothetical encounter between a therapist and a patient. A distressed woman has sought help because her husband has left her. Assume that the therapist is sophisticated in attribution theory and is keen to put into practice its principles in dealing with his patients. The therapist talks at length to the woman, anxious to get her account of why her husband went away. The patient is unforthcoming so the therapist explores a number of hypothetically relevant "attributions" by running through a list of questions, the form of which might be something like the following.

(1) Do you think there was another woman?
    If so, (a) Were sexual relations between you good?
         (b) Was there good companionship between you?
         (c) Did you have lots of rows?
             If so, What about? . . . etc.
         (d) Have you yourself been friendly with another man recently?
             . . .etc.
(2) Had you been nagging him a lot?
    If so, (a) What about? . . . etc.
(3) Was there something he wanted that you couldn't give him?
(4) Do you think he has temporarily lost his head?
(5) Has he been under very heavy strain at work? . . . or financially?

These are the kind of questions a therapist might use as prospective "ways in" to a patient's problem. The aim in asking them is to classify the patient's thoughts and reflections in various preconceived ways. Suppose, after several sessions, the therapist formed the impression that the patient believed her husband to have left her because, over the years, she had become cold and distant towards him, treating him as no more than a "piece of furniture". On Seligman's Learned Helplessness model, reformulated in terms of attribution theory (Abramson *et al.*, 1978) she has made an "internal" attribution (the source of the problem is identified as herself) which is both "global" (her attitude affected a wide range of situations and individuals) and relatively "stable (her attitude was persevering). The conclusion from the reformulated Learned Helplessness model is that in such circumstances, deficits—her depression and expectation of future helplessness—will be severe and long lived.

Excluding the possibility of persuading her husband to return, the strategy of the therapist will be to "change" some aspect of this situation and there are a number of possibilities he or she can try. He or she can try to change either the estimated value of the departed husband or alternatively some component of the explanatory scheme itself. Suppose the therapist assesses which of these two strategies will work best, rejects the idea of trying to convince the woman that she is better without her husband on the grounds that his limited knowledge of the relationship may make this argument hard to sell, and goes for the second option—manipulating the attribution process itself. Suppose also, that on further consultation with his client the therapist forms the impression that a large part of her problem is her wounded self-esteem; she sees her husband's desertion as the result of a personal failure which is in turn attributed to a relatively stable characteristic of her personality—her lack of warmth. At this stage the therapist will attempt a critique of the reasoning which has brought her to this conclusion, perhaps along one or other of the following lines:

(1) It is normal for people's relationships to change in this manner over time (i.e. she is applying false criteria for success and failure).

(2) It takes two to make a relationship go off the boil (i.e. the cause is less "internal" and more "external" than she credits).

(3) The relationship with this man may have run its course, but there is always the possibility of relationships with other men (i.e. her coldness is less "global" and more "specific" than she credits).

(4) A period of separation is a good thing as it will make her more sensitive and more outgoing (i.e. her coldness is less "stable" and more "temporary" than she credits).

Two points emerge from this hypothetical example. The first, specifically relevant to psychotherapy, is that attribution theory, while perhaps a useful and even a necessary part of any analysis of the therapeutic situation, is not on its own sufficient. Success and failure, the determinants of high and low self-esteem, are by definition relative to socially derived criteria. Attributions of success and failure involve an acceptance, or internalization, of such criteria. If the criteria which the individual takes upon himself are absurdly eccentric or unrealistically rigid and demanding so that he constantly sees himself as falling short of them, then attributions of failure are, as it were, "built into the system", and it is unlikely that by adhering strictly to attribution theory principles, the therapist will be able to make a convincing case that particular instances of failure are a result of external, specific or unstable factors. To attempt to "change" an individual's attributions in such circumstances would be to strain credibility beyond reasonable limits. So an essential consideration in counselling must be the reasonability and normality of the personal standards which the individual sets himself. Very much in line with this observation are several sources of evidence linking dispositionally extreme standards of achievement and morality with susceptibility to psychiatric and also physical illness (Blatt *et al.*, 1976; Glass, 1977; Totman, 1979 and in press).[1]

So the first thing to be noted about attribution theory principles applied in therapy is that often, certainly in cases involving wounded self-esteem, they are not on their own sufficient and must be supplemented with a detailed knowledge of the normative structure of society and the "reasonability" of individual goals. Not only must the therapist be in possession of a systematically worked out conception of society, he or she must also recognize the particular social microcosms in which the patient moves and appreciate the patient's own goals and projects pertinent to these smaller scale social systems which serve to structure his life and give direction to his efforts. Success and failure only make sense in relation to fixed criteria, and although some such criteria might reasonably be regarded as socially universal, or at least widely shared, the greater proportion probably are not and often require detailed explication and definition. Much of psychotherapy then must consist in the interchange of social information; the "negotiation" of different social worlds and the confrontation between the respective rhetorics germane to these worlds (cf. Harré, 1980). The attributionist's labelling of what is said by a patient cannot properly take place until this two way negotiative interchange is well advanced.

Attribution Theory as Relativistic

The second point to come from this illustration is a more complex one, and is that the value of attribution theory as a therapeutic device derives primarily from its philosophical underpinnings. What a therapist does when he or she is trying to put into practice attribution theory principles in the treatment of distressed individuals is to listen to a person's explanations of his misfortune, make a theoretical link between these and the person's symptoms, and attempt to intervene by changing some component of this explanatory account (an "attribution"), thereby altering the course of the cognitive stream which, it is hypothesized, culminates in the maladaptive reaction. It is the essentially "neutral" or arbitrary nature of this intervention, and its foundations in a highly relativistic conception of moral man, which, I want to argue, is the hallmark of the attribution analysis.

Consider the example quoted by Valins and Nisbett (1972) of a 25-year-old unmarried black who presents for therapy deeply worried because he believes himself to be a homosexual.

> His attribution of homosexuality was based on several observations. Sexual intercourse was unsatisfactory, he often found himself looking at the crotch area of other men, and he believed that his penis was abnormally small. This latter belief seemed to be the major source of his difficulties. . . . Therapy was initiated by explaining the laws of optics—to wit, viewed from above

objects in the same plane as the line of vision appear shorter. The client was advised to view himself in a mirror and this procedure helped convince him that his penis, though not of superhuman proportions, was of "normal" size. The therapist also explained that the client's glances towards the crotch area of other men were a natural consequence of his belief that his own penis was small. The client was thus persuaded that his behaviour was an indication of self-evaluation and not homosexuality. It was "normal" for him to be curious about the size of other men's penises. Finally his unsatisfactory sexual experiences were explained as not being a result of inadequate heterosexual interest but a "normal" consequence of anxiety about possible inadequate performance. (Valins and Nisbett, 1972, pp. 138–139)

Reading between the lines in this case history the impression we get is of the clever perpetration of a "white lie". The plan for a cure depended upon replacing one belief by another. But the *authenticity* of beliefs does not really enter into consideration at all, indeed it cannot without upsetting the very character of the attribution theory analysis. For in order to be able to embark upon a programme of intervention, whether in therapy or education, the psychologist must regard the subject's or patient's beliefs as *in principle* manipulable, and to this end it is necessary for him to disregard the relative truth value of the attributions his clients make or can be induced to make. In my earlier example, he must substitute some reason for the woman's husband leaving home other than her frigidity. In Valins and Nisbett's example, gazing at other men's crotches was presented to the patient as a perfectly normal and reasonable activity. In both cases a "sales job" is being done to persuade the client to accept one more or less arbitrarily contrived explanation rather than another. The substituted explanation is "arbitrary" in the sense that the sole criterion determining which explanation is preferable so far as the therapist is concerned is its potential consequences in changing the course of the cognitive stream and thereby ultimately alleviating the pathological symptoms. Consideration of the truth or falsity of particular beliefs is characteristically and axiomatically excluded from the analysis.

To read this argument as a critique of attribution theory on ethical grounds would be to misunderstand what is intended here. The point is that the value of attribution theory in practice comes from an assumption on which the theory is built concerning how the human mind works in dealing with social phenomena. On old models of human action, the picture, by and large, was of one authentic reason why an action was performed and various other conceivable reasons, all of which are false. Gradually, and especially through work connected with cognitive dissonance theory and the forced compliance paradigm, this conception has given way to the idea that the same action can be given quite different but equally legitimate meanings. It can be accounted for in alternative but equally authentic ways.

In the forced compliance situation, dissonance is deliberately introduced by the experimental set-up being subtly structured so that a person believes he is performing an activity (usually undergoing some unanticipated privation) not under pressure but of his own free will. The role of the experimenter is to inject free choice into the situation as cleverly as he can, and because the subject believes he is acting freely and that there are no pressures or constraints on him, radically different psychological and behavioural consequences can follow from his participation than if he sees himself as constrained (see, for example, Zimbardo, 1969; Totman, 1979).

Implicit in the design of these experiments was a quite new conception of action, based on the assumption that it is inappropriate to represent free choice as an absolute, non-negotiable quality. It is more usefully seen as an individual perception which varies systematically over different conditions, and which can be manipulated. For dissonance to be effectively aroused, the subject must see himself as acting out of free choice, but it is equally necessary that the experimenter, on the other hand, regards the subject's action as emanating from the carefully camouflaged social pressures of the situation which he has deliberately contrived. The point is that, for the purpose of analysis, these two accounts can be treated as compatible. The experimenter's causing the subject to behave in a particular way does not invalidate the subject's own account. The free choice the subject is experiencing is not an illusion. It is the corner stone of the theory of his action which he himself constructs, and his "theory" is to be treated as equally valid as the experimenter's. The two positions are not mutually exclusive but are alternatives in the new "meta" level of analysis in which the focus has shifted from action itself to people's perceptions and explanations of action. By the same token, the manipulation in dissonance experiments was not to be seen as violating ethical standards. It is this notion of the veridical equivalence of people's accounts of actions which lies at the very heart of attribution theory and which constitutes its innovatory spark. By augmenting the analysis one level, from the explanation of behaviour and actions to the explanation of people's explanations, the axiomatric status of the enquiry is fundamentally changed. Moreover, it is changed in such a way that ethical considerations founded on old ideas of non-equivalence of stated reasons are disqualified. It is not that they are callously and inhumanly brushed aside. They are simply irrelevant. Through what is essentially an intellectual move it becomes possible to start talking about "changing" the explanations a person offers. The achievement of attribution theory is therefore much more an achievement of a philosophical kind—a "thought experiment" than one of laboratory-based empiricism.

On the face of it, there is a snag with this argument. What about those instances where a rendered account is so obviously weak against an alternative account that we are forced to reject it as patently unconvincing? The attribution theory literature is thick with reports of subjects' "misattributions" of phenomena. In Storms and Nisbett's (1970) well known study, insomniacs were led to attribute the symptoms of their insomnia (fast heart, racing thoughts, sweating, etc.) to the side effects of a pill that they had been given as a drug, but which was in fact only a placebo. Storms and Nisbett successfully predicted that because these individuals were furnished with an "external" means of explaining their insomniac symptoms they would experience less emotionality and would fall asleep faster than controls who were also given the same pills but who were told that these would produce side effects unrelated to insomnia.

From the experimenter's perspective at least it appears unambiguous: subjects are being fed a false explanation of their symptoms. We can say that the explanation is false because we know that the symptoms existed before the pill was administered and that they will probably persist again after it has been taken away; there is no necessary link between pill and symptoms. But such reasoning follows logical or scientific guidelines which are not necessarily applied so rigorously and so consistently by non-scientists. Indeed, one can safely assume that in Storms and Nisbett's experiment subjects did not work things out along these strictly rational lines. If they had, the prediction would not have been confirmed because subjects would not have accepted the experimenter's story so uncritically. So in a sense, within the terms of reference of the unscientific mode of analysis applied by the subjects in this experiment, the belief that the pill caused insomniac symptoms is perfectly authentic. It is authentic simply on the grounds that the experimenter has passed information to the subject and the subject trusts the experimenter to tell him the truth. These criteria which the subject uses to judge the validity of his own attributions are, relative to his own social scheme of things—his own "world view"—sufficient.

Manipulating attribution in therapy thus depends upon exploitation of the discrepancies between two dissimilarly constituted private social schemata; two alternative social standpoints. When a therapist first meets a patient he does his best to understand his client by spending as much time in conversation with him as necessary. But however skilled he may be at communicating, however good at understanding the other person's position and however comprehensive the picture of his social world he is able to build up, he remains socially distanced from the patient by virtue of his different repertoire of prescriptive social rules; his different values, standards, attitudes, ambitions, projects, goals and styles, some of the

most salient of which, of course, are a function of his professional role at
that time. It is precisely in this difference between people in their respective social grammars that the potentiality for change (in this case
treatment) lies.

All that is necessary to support this argument is to consider the wide
differences which exist in individual definitions of abstract value-laden
terms such as "truth", "honesty" and "kindness". Jehovah's Witnesses
will offer very different definitions and exemplary instances of these
qualities than Freudians; bricklayers than thieves, etc. "Truth" means
widely different things in different cultural and subcultural contexts. Still
smaller subdivisions of society; close friends, cliques, conspiracies and
other reference groups, will nurture finer distinctions. While the structure of their respective social/moral systems may be the same, the
"content" is not. In all the examples quoted in this chapter—Valins and
Nisbett's self-attributed homosexual, Storms and Nisbett's insomniacs
and my own illustration of the cold-hearted wife—attribution-based
theory works because the patients (or subjects) invoke criteria to judge
the acceptability of what is told to them (the attribution theory
"manipulation") that are different from the criteria which go to make up
the professional equipment of the therapist or experimenter. The latter's
overriding regulative principle, is, roughly speaking, pragmatism or
utilitarianism while the former's is trust. The ascendancy of trust over
and above other things is appropriate to a seeker of help and advice; the
ascendancy of pragmatism, to a giver of it. The viability of the whole
carefully structured subject–experimenter, patient–therapist scenario
depends upon the mutual preservation of these quite distinct and
different role–rule orientations for the duration of the experiment or the
course of treatment. The ritual trappings that accompany the interaction;
the set, scenery and props of the clinic and the laboratory help both sides
to sustain this social division which is so essential to the outcome.

The therapist must therefore operate on two different levels. First, as
a co-member, with the patient, of the same culture, he must possess, if
not at first hand, an exceptional knowledge of the constitution of society
and its more esoteric ramifications. Secondly, as a professional, he must
remain socially distanced from the patient in terms of the kinds of
explanation he entertains, and the regulative criteria—the standards—
against which his theories are measured. These are the things which
define his position as therapist. Very roughly, his pragmatism, or
utilitarianism, must be set against the patient's receptivity and trust.
Without this contrast, the potential for attribution theory based intervention cannot exist. The scope for such a contrast itself inheres in the
institutionalization in our culture of the "patient–therapist" relation.

The sharpest and possibly the most interesting instance of the type of encounter which is dependent on the preservation of two alternative explanatory systems concerns the situation which arises when therapy itself revolves around getting the patient to produce self-initiated voluntary actions. A very large proportion of contemporary techniques in psychotherapy place emphasis on the remedial consequences which follow from self-initiated behaviours, being concerned with ways of getting a patient to emit voluntary or "assertive" responses. Seligman's learned helplessness model of depression itself identifies as a cause of depressive episodes a "helplessness cognitive set"—a generalized belief on the part of the patient that his responses are ineffective in procuring rewards. Therapeutic programmes are attempts to change this set, including manipulations to encourage attributions of agency (internal attributions) on the part of the patient (Abramson *et al.*, 1978).

The idea employed in cognitive behaviour therapy, that the key to "cognitive restructuring" is behaviour, and that change in a person's mental schemata can best be effected through the contrivance of new behavioural forms, is not altogether a new one. It was foreshadowed and exploited (although described in a different jargon) in cognitive dissonance theory, in the forced compliance paradigm and also, perhaps most directly of all, in Bem's self perception theory (Bem, 1972), and the related idea that attitudes can take their cue from behaviour. All these formulations are different workings out of a very similar embryonic idea; that the potentiality for cognitive change is dependent on the establishment and miantenance of a disparity between the social criteria of subject and experimenter (or patient and therapist), the source of which is their different metaphysical commitments. This difference crystallizes in the different attributional pre-sets which are at the root of the therapeutic process.

Neither, I suspect, is the idea of "assertion-training" and its watershed of techniques for producing voluntarily initiated "responses" in therapy especially new. It has become almost a cliché among the various differently styled schools of therapy, including psychiatric counselling, that early in the therapeutic series the therapist emphasizes to his patient the importance which attaches to the patient's playing an active role in the proceedings (. . . "the real initiative must come from you" . . . "you've already taken the most important step by coming to me" . . . "all I can do is steer you in the right direction, it's you who must do the real work" . . . etc.).

Such time-worn injunctions as these help to set the stage in respect of the patient's prospective attributions for the duration of the treatment sessions. They are directives or ultimata to the patient to prepare himself to make "internal" attributions about the actions he will carry out at the behest of the therapist. The latter, however, if he is to be effective in producing the desired behaviours in the patient, which to be potent as a therapist he must do, must remain committed to attributing the subject's actions to "external" causes, predominantly himself. It is this perpetuation of a discrepancy in attributional commitments which opens the way for results from psychotherapy encounters whose aim is to change the cognitive resources of the individual so that he is better equipped to meet the demands of his social environment. The patient necessarily sees himself as acting freely while simultaneously the therapist sees the patient's actions as the consequences of his manipulations and recommendations. The necessary cognitive restructuring is thereafter accomplished through the kinds of psychological mechanism described in the theories of Festinger and Bem (see also Totman, 1979), which are critically dependent, for their activation, on attributions of internality on the part of the actor. In Bem's theory these are summed up in the statement, "attitudes follow behaviour". In the context of our discussion, this might be expanded to "adaptive mental schemata are built up from (internally attributed) contextually appropriate acts". As I have tried to show, neither the patient's nor the therapist's account should be taken as the authoritative one. From the "meta-system" in terms of which it is appropriate to analyse the interaction both accounts are equally valid, and they are perfectly compatible (see Totman, 1980, for an expansion of this particular point).

On this analysis then, attribution-based therapy depends crucially on the coexistence of discrepant attributional sets,[2] and attribution theory itself rests on a meta-logic of compatibility of these alternative positions. There is no future in talking about "attributional errors" and "misattributions". To do so is to accept a half-baked version of attribution theory and to clip the wings of what is a significant element in a new genre of thinking about social behaviour which leaves the narrow laboratory based empiricism which has dominated the subject for so long far behind. It is a "pure" theory with considerable potential for application to social problems. Paradoxically it may turn out that the greater the break with classic empiricism, the more powerful a psychological theory is as a device for tackling social problems on a practical level.

NOTES

1. Abramson et al. (1978), in their reformulation of the learned helplessness model, recognize the possibility that there are two different species of

depression, only one of which is characterized by low self-esteem. Interestingly, excessively high standards and morality appear to be associated with the depression in which self-esteem deficits are prepotent.
2. How far the same can be said of other forms of psychotherapy, especially psychiatric counselling, is an interesting and provocative question.

REFERENCES

Abramson, L. Y., Seligman, M. E. P. and Teasdale, J. D. (1978). Learned helplessness in humans: critique and reformulation. *Journal of Abnormal Psychology* **87**, 49–74.
Bem, D. J. (1972). Self-perception theory. In L. Berkowitz (ed.), *Advances in experimental social psychology* (vol. 6), pp. 1–62. London and New York: Academic Press.
Blatt, S. J., D'Afflitti, J. P. and Quinlan, D. M. (1976). Experiences of depression in normal young adults. *Journal of Abnormal Psychology* **85**, 383–389.
Festinger, L. (1957). *A Theory of Cognitive Dissonance*. Evanston, Illinois: Row Peterson.
Gergen, K. (1978). Toward generative theory. *Journal of Personality and Social Psychology* **36**, 1344–1360.
Glass, D. C. (1977). *Behaviour Pattern, Stress and Coronary Disease*. New York: McGraw-Hill.
Harré, R. (1980). *Social Being: a Theory for Social Psychology*. Oxford: Blackwell.
Langer, E. J. (1978). Rethinking the role of thought in social interaction. In J. H. Harvey, W. Ickes and R. F. Kidd (eds), *New Directions in Attribution Research* (vol. 2), pp. 35–58. New Jersey: Erlbaum.
Storms, M. D. and Nisbett, R. E. (1970). Insomnia and the attribution process. *Journal of Personality and Social Psychology* **16**, 319–328.
Totman, R. G. (1973). An approach to cognitive dissonance theory in terms of ordinary language. *Journal for the Theory of Social Behaviour* **3**, 215–238.
Totman, R. G. (1979). *Social Causes of Illness*. London: Souvenir Press (also New York: Pantheon).
Totman, R. G. (1980). The incompleteness of ethogenics. *European Journal of Social Psychology* **10**, 17–41.
Totman, R. G. (in press). Psychosomatic theories. In J. R. Eiser (ed.), *Social Psychology and Behavioural Medicine*. London: Wiley.
Valins, S. and Nisbett, R. E. (1972). Attribution processes in the development and treatment of emotional disorders. In E. E. Jones, D. E. Kanouse, H. H. Kelley, R. E. Nisbett, S. Valins and B. Weiner (eds), *Attribution: Perceiving the Causes of Behaviour*, pp. 137–149. New Jersey: General Learning Press.
Zimbardo, P. G. (1969). *The Cognitive Control of Motivation*. Illinois: Scott, Foresman.

II
Psychotherapeutic Applications

4
Attributional Style Therapy

Mary Anne Layden

Everyone has met one or more individuals who constantly seem to be saying "I'm sorry." They apologize for everything; for things they did not do as well as for things they did do. They feel vaguely responsible for every disaster in your life to which they are even remotely connected. As for their own lives, they feel a sense of personal failure for every misfortune, large or small, crisis to *faux pas*.

They apologize for having called you while you were napping. They are sorry they hit the tennis ball in such a way as to make you miss it. If a clerk gives them too little change, they blame themselves for not watching more carefully. These events may be of minor importance, but the process extends to life's critical areas in the same fashion. When they do not receive a job for which they applied, the fault is quickly directed inward. They feel sure the interviewer saw them as incompetent or that their personality flaws stood out. The interview is then dissected, piece by piece, to find evidence to support their contention. It would never occur to them that the job was not right for them and that their talents would be better employed elsewhere. Nor would the information that there were 100 applicants and that many qualified individuals were turned away have any impact on their judgment of the cause of this "failure." They not only believe that they have failed but also that this experience means they are a failure. They have jumped to their typical conclusion about why things have happened.

A. ATTRIBUTIONAL STYLE

The pattern of explaining behavior outlined in the above example reflects an attributional style; that is, a habitual manner of answering questions about causality. The persons I have just described internalize failure. Negative outcomes are consistently seen as being caused by something from within the person: lack of skills, negative personality traits, lack of effort, and so forth. Frequently the complementary pattern of attributions appears when the outcome is positive. Success is viewed as being caused by external factors: help from others, good luck, an easy task, and so forth.

Certainly, externalization of success and internalization of failure is not the only attributional style, nor is it necessarily the most typical. A number of studies have indicated that, very much unlike the apologizer, the general trend among persons is to take credit for successful outcomes but not to feel equally responsible for failures (Forsyth and Schlenker, 1977; Sicoly and Ross, 1977; Snyder et al., 1976). We have all encountered these persons as well. If they fail an exam, the excuses are legion, e.g. unfair grading, tricky questions, poor teaching. Let them receive an A on an exam and suddenly the teacher and the exam had nothing to do with it; ability alone is causal. This pattern of attributions is quite common. Even uninvolved observers make stronger internal attributions for an actor's success than for an actor's failure (Frieze and Weiner, 1971; Weiner and Kukla, 1970).

Some have described this tendency to internalize success and externalize failure as an attributional bias (Miller and Ross, 1975); others have called it egotism (Snyder et al., 1976). It is true that in many cases it must be considered a biased response. If individuals are competing in a contest, the winners may consider that the major cause of their success was skill (an internal attribution for success) and the losers may consider the major cause of their not being successful was the good luck of the opponents (an external attribution for failure). In general, both cannot be entirely correct. The major cause for winning in this situation is either a skilled performance or a lucky shot. Although labeling this process "egotism" might be seen as pejorative, there is some basis for it. The attributional process is certainly enhancing. We would all like to believe that our successes are our own but that our failures are not. To believe so raises or maintains a positive perception of ourselves.

Several hypotheses have been offered to explain this attributional response. An information processing point of view maintains that we respond to success and failure like any other event. Generally, people make internal attributions for expected outcomes ("I meant this to happen; therefore, I must have caused it") and external attributions for unexpected outcomes ("I meant something else to happen; consequently, some unexpected external force must have intervened"). This process is then extended to success ("I expect to succeed and, therefore, internalize success") and to failure ("I do not expect to fail, so I externalize failure"; Miller and Ross, 1975). Another explanation is a motivational one. Individuals are motivated toward cognitions that enhance and maintain their positive self-image (Snyder *et al.*, 1978). Clearly, the assumption that we bring about our successes but are not responsible for our failures serves to protect our self-esteem.

Both the information processing and motivation explanations assume that internalizing success and externalizing failure is the general attributional style because it is the average response of the subjects tested. To assume so necessarily implies, however, that all individuals involved expect success and/or have a positive self-concept that they wish to maintain. But the apologizers we described at the beginning of this chapter neither have this particular attributional style nor do they seem to have a great deal of self-esteem to protect. Apologizers do not expect success; they expect failure, and since this is what they expect this is what may be internalized.

B. SELF-ESTEEM AND ATTRIBUTIONAL STYLE

The research on attributional bias does not take into account self-esteem, which may be a mediator for attributional style. High and low self-esteem subjects do not share the same attributional assumptions. An early study hinted at such differences even though the results were not described by the authors in attributional terms. Solley and Stagner (1956) recorded the spontaneous remarks of high and low self-esteem subjects. They reported that high self-esteem subjects, when confronted with insoluble anagrams (words with the letters scrambled), made remarks indicating that they were externalizing the cause of the failure (e.g. "Is this a word? Is this English?"). However, low self-esteem subjects, when confronted with the same experience, indicated that they were internalizing the cause of the failure (e.g. "I must be stupid.")

Research has also directly examined the question of self-esteem differences in attributional style (Layden, 1976). A questionnaire was developed to assess an individual's general attributional style across a wide range of everyday events. The Attributional Style Questionnaire (ASQ) involves choosing the cause of a hypothetical situation that has either a positive or a negative outcome in areas such as intellectual competence, inter-personal relationships, moral situations, and moods. Each situation is followed by four possible causes: internal stable, internal unstable, external stable, and external unstable. An example from the scale is "You meet someone on the bus who seems to like you" which is followed by these four causes: "you are the kind of person whom people like easily" (internal stable), "you acted in a way to make this person like you" (internal unstable), "this is the kind of person who likes most people" (external stable), "this person is in a friendly mood right now" (external unstable). Results of this study indicated that high self-esteem individuals responded to positive outcomes by picking internal causes and negative outcomes by picking external causes. This pattern resembles that described earlier in the paper as the typical attributional bias. Low self-esteem subjects, however, responded very differently. When they evaluated the same situations, they were less likely to pick internal causes for positive outcomes and were more likely to select internal causes for negative outcomes than were high self-esteem subjects.

These cognitive differences also lead to behavioral differences. Layden (1976) gave insoluble anagrams to subjects who differed in self-esteem and in their attributional style for negative outcomes. Subjects were either high or low in self-esteem and typically internalized or externalized failure on the ASQ. These subjects first solved a "warm-up" series of moderately difficult anagrams; their performance on this set was used as a baseline. Then they worked on a new series that began with insoluble items (80% of these anagrams contained no words). At the end of this series the anagrams again became solvable and moderately difficult. Individuals whose typical style was to feel personally responsible for failure showed a decrease in speed and accuracy after experiencing the insoluble items which they believed they were failing. Subjects who normally did not accept responsibility for failure did not show decrements in either speed or accuracy after this failure experience.

It may be that feeling you are failing and believing that it is your fault disrupts how well you can perform. You may give up trying or become upset, anxious or frustrated, any of which would interfere with continued performance. Whatever is the cause, this interruption occurs regardless of whether the failure is actually your fault or not. On the other hand, if you habitually decide that failures are not due to internal factors, that belief alone will protect your self-esteem and sustain your level of performance in the face of apparent failure.

In summary, there are several attributional styles or ways in which individuals typically handle success and failure information. How they process this information may affect future successes and failures. For low self-esteem individuals failure leads to self-blame resulting in reduced performance and continued failure, thereby confirming the initial beliefs. High self-esteem individuals protect themselves from the devastating effects of failure by externalizing it and thus maintaining their level of performance, which allows at least the possibility of future success. If success is not forthcoming, the sting of failure is still removed by attributing the cause outward.

C. SUCCESS, FAILURE AND SELF-ESTEEM

High and low self-esteem individuals show differences in behaviors other than attributions for success and failure. The differences in attributional style are part of a larger fabric of responses. A number of studies have found performance decrements for low self-esteem subjects after a failure experience (Cruz Perez, 1973), a lack of persistence after failure (Shrauger and Sorman, 1977), and generalization of these decrements to new unrelated tasks (Shrauger and Rosenberg, 1970). In the same studies subjects with high self-esteem displayed enhanced performance and more persistence than low self-esteem subjects. The same pattern emerges for expectancies for the future. Low self-esteem subjects more often than high self-esteem subjects failed to raise their expectancies after success. High self-esteem subjects more often than low-esteem subjects failed to lower their expectancies after failure (Ryckman and Rodda, 1972).

The pattern that is revealed in these studies is one in which information that is consistent with the prevailing self-image is attended to and has an impact on behavior. Inconsistent information is ignored or, at least, is ineffective in causing changes. High self-esteem subjects appear to respond only to success, and low self-esteem subjects appear to respond only to failure.

There may be any number of processes underlying such outcomes. One possibility is that most people do not believe information that is inconsistent with their self-image. Stroebe et al. (1977) asked subjects to read positive and negative evaluations of themselves written by a confederate. The subjects were told that some evaluators were being sincere while others wrote in a manner directed by the experimenter. Subjects indicated whether the evaluations they received appeared to be sincere or not. High self-esteem subjects felt the positive evaluations were more sincere; low self-esteem subjects rated the negative evaluations as more sincere. By discounting the validity of the information, subjects avoided the complex task of having to make sense of conflicting information and of finding a way of incorporating it into their existing self-image.

There are, however, other methods of explaining away inconsistent information. A study by Shrauger and Terbovic (1976) points to two of them. Subjects were asked to work at a concept-formation task. A week later some of the subjects evaluated their own videotaped performance, and other subjects evaluated the performance of another person. Those who evaluated another subject actually saw a confederate perform behaviors that matched response by response the moves made by the subject a week earlier. Thus, all subjects were evaluating their own performances, but only half of the subjects were aware of it. Results indicated that low self-esteem subjects rated the performance more negatively when they thought it was their own than when they believed it belonged to another. This evaluation bias was not observed in high self-esteem subjects. High self-esteem individuals were also more satisfied with their performances and were more confident of their responses than low self-esteem subjects.

The Shrauger and Terbovic (1976) study also points to a second method of dealing with inconsistency. Subjects were asked what percentage of others would outperform them, i.e. how well did they imagine others had performed? Even though low and high self-esteem subjects showed identical levels of actual performance, the low self-esteem individuals overestimated the percentage of others who had done better than they whereas high self-esteem individuals underestimated the percentage who had actually outperformed them. In summary, the Shrauger and Terbovic (1976) study presents two methods of protecting one's self-image from inconsistency: through evaluation of one's own performance and through one's estimate of others' performance. Individuals often see the world in the way they already believe it to be, making it difficult for new information or new images of the self to establish vigorous roots.

Let us now return to attribution as another of these processes that maintain the success–failure *status quo*. Low self-esteem individuals may see themselves as unsuccessful and lacking in ability, but impoverished ability is only one type of attribution that could be made. What happens to the performance of persons who are permitted another explanation? Maracek and Mettee (1972) gave all of their subjects a success experience on a task that was described as either involving skill or luck. Then subjects performed the task again. Interestingly, some low self-esteem subjects avoided continued success only when the task had been described as involving skill. Low self-esteem subjects who thought they succeeded on a luck task and high self-esteem subjects in both the skill and luck conditions showed no performance decrements. Having ability may be inconsistent with the self-image of the low self-esteem subjects but being lucky is not.

Overall, the processes examined here indicate that low self-esteem individuals have a negative self-image and a number of strategies that maintain this self-image. They dismiss contradictory information by ignoring it, by re-evaluating it, by re-attributing it or by changing their behavior to be consistent with it.

This pattern of reactions to success and failure has important ramifications for therapy. Clearly, any intervention that hopes to change self-esteem should focus on shifting the individual's attributional style. A typical intervention strategy would be to increase the actual success experience of low self-esteem individuals. This technique would most likely be fruitless given the attributional style of those with low self-esteem. As argued above, they have too many protections against internalizing success to allow an increase in frequency of success to effectively change their self-image. Rather, therapy must involve a change in attributional style which will allow future success to be recognized and incorporated into the self-image. Indeed, these individuals may already be experiencing many successes that they are simply not perceiving. Recall that the studies reviewed above have not found any differences in actual skills between high and low self-esteem individuals; the only differences have been in their perceptions of those skills.

Before I turn to a description of how a change in perception may be accomplished, I would like to broaden the scope of this discussion by indicating that low self-esteem subjects are not alone. Individuals who are depressed are in many ways similar to the low self-esteem persons just described (see Peterson, Chapter 6).

Depressives show a remarkable similarity to low self-esteem individuals in self-evaluation, self-blame, attributional style, attributions for actual performance, effects of attributions on continued performance, estimation of level of performance and responses to success and failure (see, for instance, Beck, 1967; Abramson et al., 1978; Seligman et al., 1979; Kuiper, 1978; Rizley, 1978; Loeb et al., 1971; Golin et al., 1977). According to Beck negative thoughts engender the negative mood and, according to Seligman, passivity and helplessness occur when responsibility is turned inwards. As with low self-esteem individuals, this cycle must be broken for depressives. But how does one begin to reverse the inertia of this spinning wheel?

D. ATTRIBUTION THERAPY

Attribution therapy may be one answer. Change the belief structure about the cause of an event, and you have phenomenologically changed the event.

Previous research using an attributional approach to therapy can be categorized on two dimensions: therapies producing beneficial misattributions versus beneficial veridical attributions and therapies focusing on a specific attributional issue versus a general attributional style. Four types of therapy are possible from this classification although research on only three of these types has been attempted: (1) misattributions for a specific event, (2) veridical attributions for a specific event, and (3) veridical attributions for events in general. As common sense and ethics dictate, no attempt has been made to train false assumptions as a general style.

The misattribution approach attempts to convince subjects that the emotions they are feeling are really due to some source other than the one to which they would normally attribute them. This is exemplified by the work of Storms and Nisbett (1970). Persons suffering from insomnia were given a pill and were informed that the pill would have an arousing or a sedating effect. All subjects were actually given a placebo. Storms and Nisbett predicted that those given the "arousing pill" would fall asleep faster han those given the "sedating pill." They proposed that one reason insomniacs have difficulty falling asleep stems from the emotional arousal they experience at bedtime. This arousal and inability to fall asleep is interpreted by them to be a sign of a disorder which, in turn, amplifies their arousal all the more. The availability of a pill that allegedly produces arousal allows these persons to attribute their arousal to the pill and not to their mental state. On the other hand, subjects who ingest a "sedating pill" should experience an opposite reaction. Feeling aroused despite the effect of the pill, these individuals infer that they must be very upset. Consequently, the "sedating pill" inhibits their ability to sleep relative to subjects who receive the "arousing pill." Results of the study indicated that the "arousal" group reported falling asleep more rapidly than normal, whereas the "sedated" group reported falling asleep more slowly than normal. Replication of this finding has been difficult, however (Kellogg and Baron, 1975).

Overall, misattribution as a therapeutic procedure has had both successes (Davison et al., 1973; Davison and Valins, 1968; Nisbett and Schachter, 1966; Ross et al., 1969) and failures (Borkovec et al., 1974; Gaupp et al., 1972; Singerman et al., 1976). Consequently, its usefulness as a therapeutic technique remains an open question.

Research directed at training veridical attributions to replace previous false assumptions has met with more success whether it deals with specific events or events in general. A number of case studies have reported successful treatment of psychiatric patients who had incorrectly identified the source of their problems. Johnson et al. (1977) treated a patient who was experiencing spontaneous penile erection and ejaculation which the patient had attributed to an unseen, uncontrollable vagina. The problem was alleviated when the patient accepted the more veridical cause of sexual abstinence and unnoticed leg movements that were stimulating the penis. A number of other successful case studies follow the same pattern (Davison, 1966; Skillbeck, 1974).

A different approach to veridical specific changes in attributions was developed by Dweck (1975). Using children who were identified as helpless (i.e. those who expected failure and who showed deterioration of their performance in the face of failure), Dweck structured a math task so that some children always succeeded (success only condition). Other children sometimes failed, but the experimenter noted the failure by saying, "This means you should have tried harder" (attribution retraining condition). The children received 25 training sessions following which they were retested for performance after a failure and for changes in attributions for failure. The attribution retraining group, but not the success only group, showed both improved performance after failure and changes in attributions. It is important to note that the children who had experienced only success and, therefore, had received no strategies for dealing with failure, showed no improvement.

Rhodes (1977) not only replicated Dweck (1975) but also found that the retraining generalized to tasks not used in training. Chapin and Dyck (1976) found that attribution retraining was more effective when combined with a training series in which the failure trials appeared in longer strings rather than being dispersed evenly throughout the series. Children were more persistent in the face of failure when they had received training to attribute failure to effort and when they were confronted with failure strings in which three failure trials came in a row rather than one at a time. Overall, the research has supported the notion that veridical specific attribution change can affect performance as well as cognitions.

Available data on veridical attribution change in general style are rather sparse. Two dissertations have been conducted on this topic. Rose (1978) conducted attribution retraining sessions with psychiatric outpatients. After training, patients made more stable attributions for success and more unstable attributions for failure, showed improved achievement attitudes, were more persistent on a failure task, and were rated as more improved in rehabilitation.

Avellar (1977) developed two training methods aimed at producing changes in helplessness: training directed toward attribution change through social comparison and training to see the self as the originator of behaviors which can bring about changes in the environment. Both training methods were effective in bringing about limited changes. Because the treatment only involved two sessions, significant changes could not be expected.

Available attribution therapy studies suggest that veridical attributions may be more effective as agents of change than misattributions, and, of course, that more research is needed in the area of broad changes. Let us now turn to a recent study dealing with veridical, broad attribution change aimed at self-esteem and depression. The procedures used in this study will be referred to as attributional style therapy.

E. ATTRIBUTIONAL STYLE THERAPY

Attributional style therapy grew out of earlier research on the self-esteem differences in attribution. Since high self-esteem individuals interpret their successes and failures in ways that are different from low self-esteem individuals, why not teach the lows to make attributions like the highs? For individuals who have low self-esteem, who are depressed, or who are helpless and passive, it may not be necessary to increase the level of success in their lives. Change their attributional style and successes which in the past have been denied may now be accepted. Successes which have been trivialized by attributing them to good luck or an easy task may now be attributed to a combination of ability and effort. Failures that were used as evidence of incompetence may now be attributed to external barriers or to temporary difficulties that renewed effort may overcome.

The high self-esteem pattern of attributing success internally and failure externally has many advantages relative to the opposite, low self-esteem pattern. However, I would like to be very clear that the proposed therapy is not designed to exchange one set of misattributions for another. Training an individual to make internal attributions for success does not imply learning to fabricate non-existent abilities. The therapy is designed to encourage individuals not to overlook abilities that do exist. People who consistently externalize success jump to that habitual response quickly when a success experience occurs. Having found a plausible, comfortable answer to the question "why?", they stop scanning the situation for causes. It is this lack of serious consideration of the possibility of other, perhaps more valid, causes that is the target of attributional style therapy.

In attributional style therapy, individuals are asked to scan success situations for internal causes, to focus on abilities and personality traits they normally ignore, and to make realistic estimates of the amount of effort they expend. They are also asked to examine failures and to go further than they normally would in thinking about them. Usually these low self-esteem and depressed individuals confront a failure with the immediate appraisal that they have caused it. Very little consideration is given to the external hindrances that contributed to the lack of success. During attributional style therapy, people must conscientiously examine the entire event and are not permitted merely to stop at *"mea culpa."*

Changes in attributional style are not easy for these individuals to make. Years of practice have gone into developing their current style. Mountains of evidence have been collected to support it. Early childhood training may have contained subtle messages or direct tutoring in this direction. Rewards and punishments from significant members of the child's environment may have helped to maintain it. Practice, time and hard work must be expected to overcome such a barrage. To be effective, the therapy calls for considerable attention. Positive and negative events that have occurred in the patient's life must be examined on a daily basis. When positive events are examined, internal causes are searched for and recorded in a diary. When negative events are examined, possible external causes are recorded. The diary is discussed at each meeting with the therapist. This is a simplified overview of attributional style therapy. A more detailed account with supporting research follows.

In the development of attributional style therapy, a number of basic issues arose that must be dealt with before therapy can actually begin. I found subjects in the initial testing of the therapy to be consistently placing certain blocks in the way of change. Once these blocks have been removed, change occurs more readily.

Frequently, subjects would deny their attributional style. For example, on the Attributional Style Questionnaire (ASQ) a consistent pattern of externalizing success experiences might appear, but when the experimenter would point out that pattern to the subject, the subject might deny acting or feeling that way. Responses to both hypothetical and actual success and failure events must be collected to counter attempts to deny the attributional style. By gathering a broad range of information, the subject's pattern of attributions can be identified with certainty before the experimenter discusses it with the subject. Fewer mistakes are then made which lessens the probability that the subject's denial is accurate. In addition, it is more difficult for the subject to use denial because examples of incorrect attributions for success and failure can be pointed out concretely.

A second difficulty arises when some subjects assert that their attri-butional style is accurate. Again it is helpful to have concrete attribution errors made by the subject to use as counter-examples. Thirdly, many individuals are not initially aware that it would be to their advantage to change. Often they do not realize the negative impact their attributional style has on them. A clear and precise explanation of advantages and disadvantages of changing their style hopefully solves this problem. → Finally, a few individuals will object to the type of change requested, believing that others will view them as conceited or egocentric. It may be necessary to discuss the difference between the way individuals present their successes and failures to others and how they see themselves. A change in attributional style need imply neither an increase in overt self-congratulation nor an encouragement of felt superiority over others. Self-esteem implies realizing the value of the self with no need to lie to oneself about one's successes or failures. High self-esteem does not require blaring one's trumpet in public, assuming a competitive spirit, or rubbing others' noses in one's success. Respect is the word toward oneself and toward others.

Let us now turn to the details of attributional style therapy: specifically how are attributions changed and how are the problems just discussed handled? Keep in mind that what is described here is a research project. More controls are needed for research than would be required in therapy.

A large sample of college students were tested for their levels of self-esteem, depression and attributional style. Those who fell in the lower third on the self-esteem measure and those who fell in the upper third on the depression measure were considered eligible for the therapy sessions. Contacted by phone, a description of the program was given to the students including a brief discussion of the importance of accurate attributions. Subjects were then scheduled for an interview.

The interview began with a discussion of why making accurate attributions is important. This is one of the examples provided to the students: "If you do well in a college course and you are considering making that topic your major, it is critical to know if doing well was due to some ability on your part or to some quality of the teacher (e.g. an 'easy grader'). Accuracy is vital because important decisions will be made."

Having convinced subjects of the importance of their attributions, the next step was to demonstrate the kinds of attributions they made. They had already completed the attributional style questionnaire described earlier in this chapter. In addition, I felt a broader spectrum of information was needed to be most convincing. A valuable aid would be their responses to success and failure situations as they happened. Therefore, a number of tasks were developed that use both intellectual and social skills (e.g. judgment of emotions in photographs, digit-symbol substitution tasks). These tasks were not employed to measure the subjects' actual skills at the tasks but rather to see how they would respond to success and failure at them. The tasks were programmed so that subjects could succeed on half and fail on the rest. Attribution questions followed each task, allowing subjects an opportunity to state their beliefs about why they had succeeded or failed on that task.

At this point the experimenter had attributional information from both the questionnaire and from the tasks just performed. A broad range of information makes the attributional style of the subject more apparent. Because of the necessity of research control, the amount of informational feedback was standardized for all subjects. The investigator provided subjects with one of three kinds of feedback: (1) information about the subjects' attributional patterns of both positive and negative events (i.e. they internalize failure and externalize success), (2) information about their attributional pattern for positive events only (i.e. they externalize success) or (3) information about their attributional pattern for negative events only (i.e. they internalize failure). The experimenter discussed with each subject examples of these types of attributions taken from the subject's attributional style questionnaire and task responses.

The experimenter's task was made much easier and his argument more convincing when individuals were able to see a pattern of attributions in their actual responses. The data from the tasks they performed were particularly persuasive. For example, in one task the experimenter controlled the time allowed for the subjects to work so that it was impossible for subjects to complete the task. When asked about their performance, subjects usually rated their lack of ability as the cause of their failure. Of course, this was clearly an attributional error. To be accurate, the individual should have externalized the failure; no one could have completed the task in the brief time available. Here was an example of incorrectly accepting responsibility for a failure. Explanation of the task convinced most subjects of its difficulty and the appropriateness of an external attribution for failure. This kind of information combined with the pattern revealed in the attributional style questionnaire helped to convince subjects of their particular attributional style and, at the same time, demonstrated that the style was not always accurate.

At this point the investigator presented the therapy task. Subjects were informed that they must keep a diary of daily successes and failures. Subjects were to examine thoroughly each event, looking to see if there were internal causes for the successes and external causes for the failures that might have been overlooked or discounted on superficial inspection. They were to practice what they did not normally do. In essence, they were to think like high self-esteem individuals and non-depressives. They were not to make up causes but to look closely for real, possible causes they normally missed.

The kind of events subjects were instructed to record were dependent on the type of attributional feedback they received from the experimenter. Subjects who received feedback about their attributional style for both positive and negative events recorded both successes and their internal causes and failures and their external causes. Subjects who received feedback about their attributional style for only positive events recorded positive events and their internal causes. For the sake of control, these subjects also recorded negative events. Because no problem had been indicated to subjects in the area of negative events and no new attributional style was being trained, subjects in this group could record any causes that seemed plausible for the negative events. Finally, subjects who received feedback about their attributional style for only negative events recorded negative events and their external causes. They also recorded positive events and any causes they thought appropriate. Thus, depending on treatment group, subjects practised making attributions that either totally or partially resembled those made by high self-esteem and nondepressed individuals.

The responses individuals had to information about their attributional style and to the task they were to do was often dramatic. Some persons cried with relief. One said to me that she had never been told that it was acceptable to like herself, to think she brought about successes. Some quoted parents or other authority sources to the effect that one should always feel responsible for all failures encountered to gain humility. Others were glad to be "ordered" to do the task that they would have liked to do but felt uncomfortable giving themselves permission to do. Some resisted, arguing that these "new" causes would not be the "real" ones. The therapist must reassure these persons that they need only record veridical information. Despite initial misgivings from a few subjects, all were able not only to find events to write about but also to discover appropriate causes.

Subjects kept the diaries for a week at a time. During the research program, subjects mailed their diaries to the experimenter each week. They saw the experimenter only during the initial and final sessions. Time needed to develop this new cognitive habit varied with each individual. Within the four to five week study, many subjects had changed their perspective; some may have needed more time.

A final testing session reassessed self-esteem, depression and attributional style. A measure was also taken of persistence at a failure task. Test results indicated a significant increase on two different measures of self-esteem for all three experimental groups. No increase was found for a control group of subjects who were tested in the initial and final sessions but who did not participate in the program.

Changes in attributional style were also measured. Again the control group showed no significant change in attributional style for success or failure events. The three experimental groups did show changes, however, in the areas on which they had focused. The group that focused on finding internal causes for success showed a greater frequency of internal attributions for success. No change was observed in attributions for failure. The group that focused on external attributions for failure displayed fewer internal attributions for failure but no change in attributions for success. The group that focused on both success and failure events showed a significant decrease in internal responses for failure events, and showed an increase in internal responses for success events that approached significance.

Results with the depression measures were somewhat nebulous. Only the group that focused on internalizing success showed a significant decrease in level of depression even though all groups, including the control group, decreased somewhat. Another finding shed some light on this result. Subjects completed two measures of depression: the Dempsey 30 was given at both the initial and final sessions; the Beck Depression Inventory was administered only at the final session. Correlations between these measures of depression and attributional style yielded significant effects. The correlation of changes in the Dempsey 30 with changes in attributional style was -0.59. As attributional style improved, the level of depression decreased. The correlation between the Beck inventory and attributional style was -0.40. These results indicate that depression decreased for those individuals who changed their attributional style. The difficulty, then, appears to be in getting the attributional style to change. If change does occur, it has the predicted impact on depression.

Overall, the results indicated that the subjects receiving attributional style therapy changed their attributional style and showed an increase in self-esteem. For those depressed subjects who changed their style, depression also decreased, even though not all depressed subjects altered their style.

F. FINAL COMMENTS

What has been described here is essentially a research program. Some changes are most likely necessary to span the gap between experimentation and therapy. One difference between research and therapy concerns the collection of information about the patient's attributional style. As with research, in therapy the attributional style questionnaire (ASQ) is a good place to start, and tasks involving success and failure administered by the therapist should also be valuable. In addition, it would be helpful if the patients discussed actual past events, important successes and failures in their lives and to what they attributed them. The patients' perceptions of their social and intellectual successes and failures would add depth to the picture of their attributional style. It might also be revealing to know the attributional style of their parents.

Another change that may be made is in the programmed nature of the feedback about attributional style. The therapist may consider the nature of the case in deciding how much attributional information to give to the patient. Perhaps only success or only failure events appear to be problematic or critical. Perhaps the therapist may decide to focus on one type of situation before tackling the other. The therapist may begin with the most disturbed area causing the greatest distress to the patient. Alternatively, a less serious area, in which change may be accomplished easily, may be chosen to ensure the process begins on a successful note.

Of course, unlike research, in therapy the diary should be thoroughly discussed with the therapist and the causes for events explored. In situations where the patient seems unable to generate a realistic cause or can only find causes fitting their habitual style, suggestions of possible causes or questioning of the patients' evidence may be useful.

Some situations, however, cannot honestly be attributed in the therapeutic direction, and such instances must be acknowledged and confronted. Sometimes individuals do cause themselves to fail; this is true for everyone. These events may demand an examination of new behavioral strategies. More adaptive responses may help avoid future failures; thus, behavioral change must be incorporated into the therapy when necessary. Attributional style therapy could easily make use of training in study skills, assertiveness, goal setting and social skills for those who would benefit. The therapist should be certain that the problem is really behavioral and not merely one of perception before new behaviors are trained. Without changes in the patients' notions of causality, the therapist may find that the patients attribute the success of any new behaviors to the therapist and not to themselves.

Attributional style therapy has been aimed at broad changes. Some specific problem areas, however, may warrant changes in more specific attributions. For example, people with low self-esteem may experience considerable anxiety when they are taking exams. During the exam they may be disrupting their performance by thinking negative attributional thoughts, anticipating failure and assuming they lack intelligence. The therapist may want to focus on training a more positive attitude about causality, in addition to training in relaxation and study skills. Focusing on a specific issue may be necessary to accomplish specific behavioral changes. The research described in this chapter suggests that broad attributional changes will cause broad cognitive changes in the attitude toward the self but specific attributional change is necessary for specific behavioral problems. A combination of both approaches would probably be most useful.

A broad range of problems other than low self-esteem and depression may have attributional style as an important component. Battered wives and battered children frequently tolerate rather than try to change their situations. Often they feel they deserve the physical abuse they receive. Rape victims sometimes express guilt or believe they encourage their attackers. Therapists working with non-assertive individuals, or with students who are underachievers or who have test anxiety, should pay particular attention to their patients' attributional styles.

In fact, in any type of therapy, attributional issues must be considered. Any change a patient makes must be attributed internally for the change to be really effective (see Sonne and Janoff, Chapter 5). If patients realize that they are causing their improvement and that it is stable, the improvement will generalize to non-therapeutic situations. Patients treated with drugs are in danger of attributing their improvement to the drugs. As a result, it becomes difficult to maintain the change once the drugs are discontinued (see Reading, Chapter 9). The same may be true for drug-induced relaxation used in systematic desensitization, for patients with very directive therapists or for patients who are institutionalized and attribute their behavior to the hospital environment.

In conclusion, I would like to speculate about an issue that I believe will be critical for the future of attribution therapy. It concerns the kind of attributions emphasized for failure situations. Because high self-esteem persons externalize failure, in the present research I have chosen to train individuals with low self-esteem to increase the salience of external causes for failure. External attributions lessen the feeling of responsibility for failure and the self-blame that failure engenders.

Clearly, there is, however, another possible approach that might be beneficial; that is, to decrease the stability of the perceived causes for failure. Making an internal cause unstable promotes a sense of control. For example, if I failed because I did not try hard enough (internal unstable), I have the possibility of bringing about success in the future through greater effort. Thus, making the cause unstable may be valuable for individuals who anticipate important future events with hopelessness. On the other hand, making an external attribution may often take away this sense of future control of the failure event.

Attributing failure to both external causes (the present study) and unstable internal causes (Dweck, 1975) has been effective in bringing about change. Determining which of the two methods is the most efficacious may depend on whether the individual is attributing the cause of an ongoing event that can be expected to be encountered again or a past event that is discrete and complete. It is probably not beneficial to tell someone who is guilt-ridden over, say, the death of a child, "You did not try hard enough." There will be no future opportunity to change this outcome.

The preceding example illustrates an issue that therapists and researchers must contend with: the question of what kind of attributions should be trained with whom and when. The issues discussed here are just a few that indicate the breadth of clinical questions touched by an attributional approach to human behavior. The answers to these questions will be invaluable to more than just the "apologizers" of the world.

REFERENCES

Abramson, L., Seligman, M. and Teasdale, J. (1978). Learned helplessness in humans: critique and reformulation. *Journal of Abnormal Psychology* **87**, 49–74.

Avellar, J. (1977). The effectiveness of origin-pawn training and attribution therapy in changing helpless attitudes. Unpublished doctoral dissertation.

Beck, A. T. (1967). *Depression: Clinical, Experimental and Theoretical Aspects.* New York: Hoeber.

Borkovec, T., Wall, R. and Stone, N. (1974). False physiological feedback and the maintenance of speech anxiety. *Journal of Abnormal Psychology* **83**, 164–168.

Chapin, M. and Dyck, D. (1976). Persistence in children's reading behavior as a function of N length and attribution retraining. *Journal of Abnormal Psychology* **85**, 511–515.

Cruz Perez, R. (1973). The effects of experimentally induced failure, self-esteem and sex on cognitive differentiation. *Journal of Abnormal Psychology* **81**, 74–79.

Davison, G. (1966). Differential relaxation and cognitive restructuring with paranoid schizophrenic or paranoid state. Proceedings of the American Psychological Association, 74th convention.

Davison, G. and Valins, S. (1968). On self produced and drug produced relaxation. *Behavior Research and Therapy* **6**, 401–402.

Davison, G., Tsujimoto, R. and Glaros, A. (1973). Attribution and the maintenance of behavior change in falling asleep. *Journal of Abnormal Psychology* **82**, 124–133.

Dweck, C. (1975). The role of expectations and attributions in the alleviation of learned helplessness. *Journal of Personality and Social Psychology* **31**, 674–685.

Forsyth, D. and Schlenker, B. (1977). Attributing the causes of group performance: effects of performance quality, task importance and future testing. *Journal of Personality* **45**, 220–236.

Frieze, I. and Weiner, B. (1971). Cue utilization and attributional judgments for success and failure. *Journal of Personality* **39**, 591–606.

Gaupp, L., Stern, R. and Galbraith, G. (1972). False heart-rate feedback and reciprocal inhibition by aversion relief in the treatment of snake avoidance behavior. *Behavior Therapy* **3**, 7–20.

Golin, S., Harlman, S., Klatt, E., Mung, K. and Wolfgang, G. (1977). Effects of self-esteem manipulation on arousal and reactions to sad models in depressed and nondepressed college students. *Journal of Abnormal Psychology* **86**, 435–439.

Johnson, W., Ross, J. and Mastria, M. (1977). Delusional behavior: an attributional analysis of development and modification. *Journal of Abnormal Psychology* **86**, 421–426.

Kellogg, R. and Baron, S. (1975). Attribution theory, insomnia and the reverse placebo effect: a reversal of Storms and Nisbett's findings. *Journal of Personality and Social Psychology* **32**, 231–236.

Kuiper, N. (1978). Depression and causal attributions for success and failure. *Journal of Personality and Social Psychology* **36**, 236–246.

Layden, M. A. (1976). Self-esteem and sex differences in attributional style and their effect upon performance. Unpublished Master's Thesis.

Loeb, A., Beck, A. and Diggory, J. (1971). Differential effects of success and failure on depressed and nondepressed patients. *Journal of Nervous and Mental Disease* **152**, 106–114.

Maracek, J. and Mettee, D. (1972). Avoidance of continued success as a function of self-esteem, level of esteem certainty and responsibility for success. *Journal of Personality and Social Psychology* **22**, 98–107.

Miller, D. and Ross, M. (1975). Self serving biases in the attribution of causality: fact or fiction? *Psychological Bulletin* **82**, 213–225.

Nisbett, R. and Schachter, S. (1966). Cognitive manipulation of pain. *Journal of Experimental Social Psychology* **2**, 227–236.

Rhodes, W. (1977). Generalization of attribution retraining. Unpublished doctoral dissertation.

Rizley, R. (1978). Depression and distortion in the attribution of causality. *Journal of Abnormal Psychology* **87**, 49–74.

Ross, G. (1978). Attribution retraining of the psychiatrically disabled. Unpublished dictoral dissertation.

Ross, L., Rodin, J. and Zimbardo, P. (1969). Toward an attribution therapy: the reduction of fear through induced cognitive-emotional misattribution. *Journal of Personality and Social Psychology* **12**, 279–288.

Ryckman, R. and Rodda, W. (1972). Confidence maintenance and performance as a function of chronic self-esteem and initial task experience. *Psychological Record* **22**, 241–247.

Seligman, M., Abramson, L., Semmel, A. and von Baeyer, C. (1979). Depressive attributional style. *Journal of Abnormal Psychology* **88**, 242–247.

Shrauger, J. and Rosenberg, S. (1970). Self-esteem and the effects of success and failure feedback on performance. *Journal of Personality* **38**, 404–417.

Shrauger, J. and Sorman, P. (1977). Self-evaluations, initial success and failure and improvement as determinants of persistence. *Journal of Consulting and Clinical Psychology* **45**, 784–795.

Shrauger, J. and Terbovic, M. (1976). Self-evaluation and assessments of performance by self and others. *Journal of Consulting and Clinical Psychology* **44**, 564–572.

Sicoly, F. and Ross, M. (1977). Facilitation of ego-biased attributions by means of self-serving observer feedback. *Journal of Personality and Social Psychology* **35**, 734–741.

Singerman, K., Borkovec, T. and Baron, R. (1976). Failure of a "misattribution therapy" manipulation with a clinically relevant target behavior. *Behavior Therapy* **7**, 306–313.

Skillbeck, W. (1974). Attributional changes and crisis intervention. *Psychotherapy: Theory, Research and Practice* **11**, 371–375.

Snyder, M., Stephan, W. and Rosenfield, D. (1976). Egotism and attribution. *Journal of Personality and Social Psychology* **33**, 435–441.

Snyder, M., Stephan, W. and Rosenfield, D. (1978). Attributional egotism. *In* J. Harvey, W. Ickes and R. Kidd (eds), *New Directions in Attributional Research* (vol. 2), Hillsdale, New Jersey: Erlbaum.

Solley, C. and Stagner, R. (1956). Effects of magnitude of temporal barriers, type of goal and perception of self. *Journal of Experimental Psychology* **51**, 62–70.

Storms, M. and Nisbett, R. (1970). Insomnia and the attribution process. *Journal of Personality and Social Psychology* **16**, 319–328.

Stroebe, W., Eagly, A. and Stroebe, M. (1977). Friendly or just polite? The effect of self-esteem on attributions. *European Journal of Social Psychology* **7**, 265–274.

Weiner, B. and Kukla, A. (1970). An attributional analysis of achievement motivation. *Journal of Personality and Social Psychology* **5**, 1–20.

5
Attributions and the Maintenance
of Behavior Change

Janet L. Sonne and Dean S. Janoff

A. INTRODUCTION

There is a well-known children's folk story entitled "The Little Engine That Could." The story tells of a little locomotive engine faced with a tremendous task—that of climbing a steep mountain with heavy cargo. The little engine apparently observed other, much larger engines refuse to attempt the mountain run. The little engine did finally try, and huffed and puffed, and repeated to itself: "I *think* I can, I *think* I can." And it did! The story may be interpreted by the psychologically-minded as providing the moral that one's positive thoughts, or cognitions, about one's capabilities to complete a difficult task are important variables in successful goal-oriented behavior. This book focuses on one specific realm of man's cognitive processes—*attributions*. The reader is referred at this point to the introductory chapter for a general definition and discussion of attributional processes and their effects on behavior.

The aim of this chapter is to examine the significance of attributional processes for the therapist interested in helping clients change their behavior. More specifically, the clinician currently faces a dilemma concerning the *lack of maintenance* of behavior change so efficiently and effectively brought about by the development of behavioral control techniques. Factors such as the lack of alteration of the reinforcement structure of the individual's daily social environment and the neglect of attention to discriminative stimuli that serve as cues for undesirable responses were pinpointed as reasons for the absence of durable change (e.g. Bandura, 1969). However, correction of these apparent deficiencies in behavior therapy programmes implied extensive and unrealistic control by the therapist over an individual's total social milieu.

With the evolution of the mediational (cognitive–behavioral) models of behavior in clinical psychology and the contributions of attribution research in social psychology, clinicians and clinical researchers began to entertain "the possibility that the manner in which clients and patients explain to themselves the reasons they have enjoyed therapeutic improvement may be . . . an . . . important factor in the maintenance of behavior change" (Davison *et al.*, 1973). In other words, the attributions that the client makes concerning the causes of successful behavior change may, indeed, play a crucial role in future behavior. More specifically, it was hypothesized that self-attributions for successful behavior change would lead to positive self-inferences about the individual's dispositional factors (e.g. capabilities) which would generalize beyond the treatment milieu. Environmental attributions, on the other hand, would essentially be relevant only to the setting and time during which the specific environmental conditions were present and, thus, not generalizable (Kopel and Arkowitz, 1975). Therefore, practitioners and researchers alike expected that self-attributions for therapeutic behavior change would lead to greater maintenance than environmental attributions.

B. EMPIRICAL TESTS OF THE ATTRIBUTIONAL-MAINTENANCE
HYPOTHESIS

The clinical treatment of obesity provides a specific testing ground for the attributional-maintenance hypothesis. Obesity has become an increasingly common and serious problem in the United States and parts of Western Europe. It is estimated, for example, that as much as one-third of the population of the United States may be obese and 10% morbidly obese (at least 100 pounds overweight or body weight twice what it should be). The death rate for the morbidly obese is reported to be 11 times as high as that of individuals of the same age and sex who are not obese (Danowski, 1980). Most clinical reports of the use of behavioral control techniques in effecting significant weight reduction present encouraging results though some researchers have been clearly less optimistic (e.g. Stunkard, 1959). Unfortunately, the degree to which weight loss is maintained once the client leaves the systematic therapeutic environment is questionable at best (cf. Stunkard and Mahoney, 1976; Stunkard and Penick, 1979). Researchers concerned with obesity turned their attention to the client's self-attributions for therapeutic behavior change (i.e. weight loss or changes in eating patterns) to attempt to encourage greater maintenance of behavioral gains. Two recent studies investigating the possible role of client attributions about the causes of weight loss in the maintenance process merit discussion.

Jeffrey (1974) investigated the differential effect of self-control and environmental-control behavioral procedures on the maintenance of weight loss and appropriate eating habits. The self-control program incorporated a self-attribution set that emphasized the *subject's* responsibility for weight management and self-reinforcement for behavior change. The environmental-control therapy included an environmental attribution set that stressed the *therapist's* role in promoting weight loss and therapist reinforcement. The interventions were equally effective in producing reduction in weight over a seven-week period. However, the self-control treatment proved more effective than the environmental-control therapy in promoting a six-week maintenance of weight loss. Further, measurement determining the direction of the experimental subjects' locus of control (Rotter, 1966) showed an increase in internal orientation for the self-control group compared with no change for the environmental-control group. Jeffrey concluded that an increased self-attribution set accompanied prolonged maintenance for the self-control treatment group.

A second study (Sonne and Janoff, 1979) attempted to focus more specifically on the nature of client causal attributions about weight loss and the influence such attributions have on the maintenance of behavior change. The research replicated, in part, Jeffrey's original design and procedure. However, two additional measurements were included. First, three questions were completed by the subjects at the initial treatment meeting and at the last meeting seven weeks later. The three questions were designed to elicit the subject's sense of the *cause* of weight loss and specifically asked for her perception of *responsibility* for, *control* over, and *contribution* towards weight loss. (It is important to note here that the relationships among the concepts "responsibility," "control," "contribution," and "cause" are not yet fully understood. The reader is referred again to the introductory chapter for a discussion of this issue.) The three questions administered at the initial meeting asked the subject to compare her expectation of the influence of the weight control program versus the subject's own influence over any weight loss achieved in the next seven weeks. The questions were based on a 9-point scale, with 1 designating the greatest self-attribution (e.g. "My weight loss will be all my responsibility") and 9 marking the greatest environmental attributions (e.g. "My weight loss will be all the responsibility of the program").

The three questions administered at the last meeting were concerned not with the subject's expectancy but with her perception of self versus environmental influence on the actual weight loss achieved. The second addition was the use of another follow-up weight measurement five weeks after the first follow-up (eleven weeks after the end of the treatment program).

As predicted, the self-control and the environmental-control treatments proved equally effective in promoting weight loss during the treatment period, replicating Jeffrey's (1974) findings. The self-control treatment proved superior in promoting maintenance of weight loss over the first six weeks of follow-up, and even more dramatically over eleven weeks. Contrary to prediction, no significant relationships were revealed between weight status (continued loss, maintenance, or gain) at the *first follow-up* point and subjects' post-treatment perceptions of responsibility, control or contribution. However, significant predictive relationships were evident between weight status at the eleven-week follow-up and the three post-treatment weight-loss-specific questions. The more the individual perceived that her weight loss during the formal treatment program was her own responsibility, was under her own control, and was the result of her own contributions, the more she tended to continue to lose weight during the eleven-week follow-up period. Interestingly, the subjects' actual weight loss during the treatment was not significantly predictive of weight status at the first or second follow-up measurement.

A multiple regression analysis using the perceptions of control and contribution reported at the end of the treatment program (the two measures reaching significance at $P < 0.05$ in the previous single regression analyses) revealed that these two predictor variables together accounted for 22% of the variance of weight status eleven weeks later.

Some further findings of this study are of interest. First, although the two treatment groups did not differ initially in expectations of responsibility for, control over, and contribution towards weight loss, a significant difference was found at post-treatment on all three measures. The self-control treatment group consistently showed greater self-attribution than the environmental-control group. Within-group analyses revealed that this post-treatment difference was due to the significantly increased sense of control and contribution in the self-control group in contrast to the significantly decreased sense of responsibility and contribution in the environmental-control group.

The results of the two studies just reviewed carry specific implications for the clinical treatment of obesity and the maintenance of therapeutic gains. First, the actual amount of weight lost during the treatment program was not predictive of maintenance success or failure. This finding speaks somewhat against a common sense proposition that the individual who experiences some weight loss success will naturally continue during the maintenance period to experience more. Unfortunately, it does not appear to be that simple and it does speak to the importance of the clinician's consideration of the promotion of more than absolute weight change. As Bandura (1978) suggests, the effect of outcome on future behavior depends on how the outcome is cognitively processed by the individual. The second implication is that behavioral weight loss programs which emphasize self-influence over weight loss result in greater long-term maintenance of therapeutic success. It appears that the clinician seeking better maintenance of the behavior change must enhance the client's self-attribution and minimize environmental attribution for the therapeutic success. Like the Little Engine, then, the client must be able to experience "I *think I* can," with the emphasis on "I." The third implication is that the client's pretreatment perception of "self-responsibility," "self-control," and "self-contribution" may be increased or decreased, given specific treatment conditions. It is thus the clinician's task to arrange such "behavioral conditions" in the therapeutic milieu.

C. THE PROMOTION OF SELF-ATTRIBUTIONS IN THE CLINICAL MILIEU

The arrangement of appropriate therapeutic conditions necessary to promote the client's self-attributions for successful behavior change encompasses two subordinate tasks: (1) the enhancement of the client's view of her/himself as an entity or actor in the world, and (2) the enhancement of the client's sense of freedom to behave without overt environmental pressures (Brehm, 1976; Kopel and Arkowitz, 1975). Each subordinate task will be discussed separately to present specific suggestions for the clinician.

Enhancement of the Client's Sense of Self as Object

Perhaps the most obvious way that an individual may enhance his or her sense of self as an entity or actor in the world is through full self-observation. It is argued that when the client becomes the observer of his or her own actions, the self becomes figural and dispositional or self-attributions predominate. Self-observation may be incorporated into behavioral weight control therapies in several specific ways. First, the client may be provided with a means to self-monitor the occurrence of prescribed eating habits (e.g. measuring food portions) and the nonoccurrence of inappropriate habits (e.g. eating while preparing a meal). Stuart (1967, 1970) has also prescribed the client's monitoring of weight four times daily, in the morning and following each meal, in order to familiarize him/her with the immediate effects of eating on weight. Self-monitoring of appropriate daily exercise routines may also be important. Appropriate and inappropriate eating habits may be defined and the technique of self-monitoring of the habits and weight explained and then practised within the therapeutic setting. These techniques are extended to the client's home environment to increase the generalization effects.

A second self-observation technique which may be of value in promoting internal attributions involves the use of videotape. The technique, using the client as his or her own model, combines the principles and operations of both standard modeling and self-observational strategies. It differs considerably, however, from the self-observation procedures discussed above. In the self-as-a-model intervention, clients observe only those instances of their behavior in which they are performing in the way desired (Hosford and de Visser, 1974). Instances of inappropriate behavior (e.g. having snacks or falling prey to a second helping during a meal) are deleted from the modeling tape. In the case of a weight-loss program, material for the self-as-a-model tapes may come from role-plays conducted in the therapy session or the videotaping of therapist-coached sequences of appropriate mealtime behavior in the client's home. After clients view themselves consistently performing in the desired manner, they practice appropriate responses prior to trying them out in real-life situations. The causal attributions experienced by clients seeing themselves behaving appropriately would strengthen their ability to transfer and maintain their behavior in subsequent situations.

Some social psychological research indicates that the information a client uses in forming attributions tends to have more effect if it comes from multiple sources (cf. Brehm, 1976). Thus it may be most advantageous to include several self-observation techniques in the behavioral intervention. Further, the therapist may consistently provide the client with consensus support regarding the client's dispositional characteristics (e.g. self-discipline, capabilities, etc.) necessary to perform appropriate eating behaviors.

Enhancement of the Client's Sense of Behavioral Freedom

The findings of several social psychological and clinical studies indicates that explicit external or environmental response-reinforcement contingencies, particularly when perceived as influence attempts, tend to undermine the individual's sense of self-initiation and responsibility for behavior (Bowers, 1975; Deci, 1971, 1972; Lepper *et al.*, 1973). Therefore, in order to preserve the client's sense of self-initiation and responsibility, and presumably then to enhance maintenance, several clinical researchers have advocated that the clinician hold to the "principle of least powerful reward or punishment" (Kopel and Arkowitz, 1975) or the "idea of subtle control" (Bowers, 1975).

Environmental controls may conceivably exist in the form of the therapist him or herself and/or in the form of material contingent reinforcements. The behavioral therapist concerned with the maintenance of therapeutic gains must consider specific ways in which his/her own role in the treatment can be made subtle or non-figural. And, as a corollary, the therapist must allow the client to be as active and self-directed as possible. It is true that most, if not all, clients require some treatment structure and instruction initially from the therapist. Indeed, the therapist who ignores the client's expectations of such therapeutic guidance may find his or her treatment attrition greatly increased. However, the therapist may allow an increasingly more primary role to the client as the treatment progresses.

First, for example, the overweight client may be actively involved in the initial assessment of inappropriate eating behaviors and patterns, presumably with prescribed self-monitoring. Second, the client may be specifically involved in his/her treatment by using self-control behavioral procedures. The procedures may include the use of self-instructional nutrition, eating behavior, and exercise manuals, self-standard setting of weekly weight goals, self-monitoring of daily eating and exercise behaviors, self-evaluation of daily progress, and self-reinforcement. Kopel and Arkowitz (1975) have further suggested that weight management clients be ultimately responsible for the planning of his/her maintenance program, including further weight loss goals to be achieved and appropriate eating and exercise behaviors to be monitored and reinforced. And third, the actual presence of the therapist in the therapy sessions, which undoubtedly brings some client perceptions of pressure for the client to "perform" successfully, should be reduced when appropriate for each client. For instance, the overweight client involved in weekly sessions for several weeks may begin to see the therapist once every two weeks or every month, meanwhile continuing self-control treatment procedures.

A note should be added here about the use of material, response-contingent reinforcement. Clearly, in the interest of the client's perceptions of freedom from environmental pressure and/or incentives to behave, self-administered reinforcements for weight loss and/or appropriate eating habits are recommended over therapist-administered reinforcements. Many research weight loss programs have found self-reinforcement procedures, such as monetary or activity rewards, effective in promoting both initial weight loss and maintenance (Mahoney, 1974). Eventually, however, any material reinforcements should be faded from the treatment regimen. Although the material self-reinforcement contingency may be formulated and monitored by the client, it most probably remains a source of externalized pressure for the individual. Instead, the client may be encouraged to begin to develop covert self-evaluation, instruction, and reinforcement, thereby increasing his/her sense of personal initiation, assessment, and control of behavior. Dunkel and Glaros (1978) found that training the client to make covert self-instructions to resist boredom, hunger, and overeating was the most effective treatment component in their weight loss program. Brunn and Hedberg (1974) have described a covert self-reinforcement procedure in which the client first imagines resisting temptation to eat and then visualizes an individually defined non-food reinforcer. Clearly, too, the actual performance of temptation resistance or appropriate exercise activity may be covertly reinforced. The covert reinforcers may be material images (non-food) or may be social (e.g. praise). Covert self-punishment techniques may be included as well. The use of videotapes of the client's eating and exercise behavior may prove valuable in the training and practice of covert self-evaluation and reinforcement.

D. A CASE STUDY

The following case study is presented to demonstrate how the therapist may enhance the self-attributional process through a behavior change program for losing weight. The treatment program was developed in a private clinical setting by the second author and is described here in outline form for brevity. As the reader will see, the treatment components outlined have all been shown previously in empirical studies to be effective in promoting and maintaining behavioral changes in weight and eating habits. The case study cited (Ellen will be the name used) is a specific example highlighting the importance of attributions about behavior, and as such is not meant to be an exemplar of weight-loss treatment programs *per se*.

The components of the treatment programe are as follows:

Self-Monitoring. Using a special eating-habits diary, clients record daily food patterns in three categories: food quality (high- versus low-calorie), food quantity and situational eating. Therapeutic emphasis is placed on improved eating habits rather than on simple weight loss.

Nutrition. Clients are instructed in the basics of food metabolism, calorific values and the importance of a sound balanced diet in permanent weight control. Short-lived restrictive diets are strongly discouraged. No food categories are prohibited, and food intake records are kept to evaluate the nutritional value of each client's diet.

Exercise. Clients are involved in discussions on how moderate levels of physical exercise increase the initial rate of weight loss, improve cardiovascular functioning and actually reduce hunger. The therapist stresses the fact that adequate activity also helps to maintain weight loss permanently. Clients are encouraged to develop individualized programs for increasing energy expenditure. Non-strenuous, entertaining forms of exercise are suggested (e.g. hiking, dancing, long walks, window shopping).

Eating Cues. Clients are urged to discuss the ways in which food-related cues contribute to their maladaptive eating patterns. Five specific strategies are suggested: separating eating from all other activities, making high-calorie foods unavailable, altering the size and appearance of food portions, eating slowly and disposing of foods that would previously have been eaten "to avoid waste."

Relaxation Training. Many clients argue that food intake serves as an anxiety reducer, antidepressant or a method for dealing with anger. Therefore, relaxation training is provided for interested clients to equip them with non-fattening alternative responses to such situations.

Family Support. All clients are urged to establish formal support systems that will both facilitate initial progress and enhance maintenance of behavioral gains once they terminate their formal treatment program. Family members are encouraged to attend sessions and to participate in sharing a more healthy lifestyle. Often, specific prompting and reinforcing responses are rehearsed between spouses in order to promote a reciprocal reinforcement system in the home.

Self-Reward. Clients are trained in the development and execution of self-reward contracts, which specify behavioral goals, explicit time intervals and chosen personal rewards or privileges. The ability to follow through on self-reward contracts may serve as an indication of the degree to which the client attributes successful weight-loss to him- or herself rather than environmental factors (e.g. "I really did deserve that pair of new shoes because it was really hard for me to avoid having snacks this past week, but I did it!").

Internal Cognitions. Perfectionist performance standards and maladaptive self-statements often play a major role in weight-loss failures. Extensive efforts are directed toward improving internalized statements that clients make about their behavior by monitoring, evaluating and altering negative self-verbalizations.

Ellen was a 32-year-old hairdresser who had been seeing her family doctor for help in losing weight. After four months of dieting and treatment with mild appetite depressants, Ellen had lost only three pounds. After admitting she often forgot to take her medication and how "impossible" it was to stay on such a diet, Ellen's doctor decided to refer her for behavior therapy.

Before treatment Ellen weighed 176·5 pounds at a height of 66 inches. At her initial session, Ellen claimed her primary reason for wanting to lose weight was her "boyfriend's constant complaints about her flabby figure." After exploring Ellen's attitudes about weight loss and current eating habits, she was instructed in the techniques of self-monitoring and was asked to keep close records of her daily weight and an eating-habits diary over the next two weeks. Ellen, like many individuals trying to exert more control over eating, indicated that her lack of success was believed to be mainly beyond her control (e.g. "people put irresistible pressure on me to eat fattening foods", "anxiety from work causes me to binge on weekends.")

In the ensuing 12 weeks, Ellen was instructed in the techniques of monitoring the nutritional value of her self-imposed diet, how to develop a realistic exercise regimen, detailed record-keeping of stimulus cues that prompted maladaptive eating patterns, and training in relaxation. Discussions in the therapy sessions focused on the techniques Ellen wanted to practice each week. Careful attention was placed on how Ellen made decisions and to what she attributed the consequences of her efforts. The therapist promoted a shift in the control of discussions over to Ellen during the course of treatment. Gradually she became responsible for suggesting weight-control techniques and methods for resolving potential problem areas. It was suggested to Ellen that taking control of determining the content of the therapy sessions was directly analogous to controlling the life events surrounding Ellen at home and at work. Framed as a challenge, Ellen responded with the same "professional enthusiasm" engendered by her career.

Ellen's actual weight loss was fairly consistent over the treatment program. She lost 15 pounds over a 12 week period. During that time, noticeable differences occurred in the extent of perceived control and credit Ellen gave herself for changed eating habits and increased physical activity. At one point, Ellen told her therapist that she still did not really enjoy exercising. However, by including her boyfriend in her daily routine, she reasoned that she was able to improve their relationship by spending time together "helping one another to be more healthy." The therapist was quick to applaud Ellen's "insight" into how exercise could be a key to increasing her boyfriend's support of her weight-loss efforts.

At the end of 12 weeks, however, Ellen reached her first plateau. The following three weeks were characterized by slight increases, then losses in weight. At the end of 15 weeks, Ellen's total weight loss dropped to fourteen pounds. As might be expected, inability to continue losing weight in spite of her consistent efforts caused Ellen to feel discouraged once again. Ellen missed her next appointment. Upon calling to re-schedule, the therapist asked Ellen to bring her boyfriend along to the next session.

The following week the therapist asked Ellen and her boyfriend to discuss with each other all the ways each could benefit from Ellen's continued weight-loss (the therapist served as consultant to the dis-cussion). A list of potential benefits from the discussion highlighted Ellen's increased personal control of her eating habits and the strengthening of their relationship by working together on achieving a healthier lifestyle. The therapist asked them to develop an action plan for achieving their goals during the following week. At the next session, the therapist reviewed their action plan, emphasized to each their personal responsibilities, and scheduled Ellen for a follow-up session four weeks later. (The boyfriend was not asked to come back since the therapist felt treatment success was dependent on Ellen taking a leading role in the behavior change process.)

Ellen did break through the plateau by losing eight pounds over the following four weeks. In addition, Ellen said she helped her boyfriend develop his own personalized program and he lost seven pounds over the same period. At this point formal treatment was concluded but Ellen was instructed to keep an informal diary on the consequences of her attempts to maintain control over her eating habits.

Ellen was seen once more, three months later. She weighed in at 144 pounds, down an additional ten pounds since formal termination. Recently married (to the original boyfriend), Ellen indicated she was still working to lose weight and was extremely satisfied with her progress so far.

E. A CHALLENGE FOR CLINICIANS

A variety of techniques designed to enhance the client's self-attribution for successful behavior change have been described above in the case of Ellen. Implementing the techniques of self-monitoring and tracking of the nutritional value of her diet were the first attempts to involve Ellen in the behavior change process. Promoting client responsibility for the choice of which techniques to practice at home (e.g. increasing physical exercise, monitoring stimulus cues that trigger inappropriate eating habits) provided the therapist with the opportunity to attribute all therapeutic successes to Ellen. Self-analysis of Ellen's decision making style and the attributions associated with the consequences of those decisions, were manoeuvres by the therapist to promote an internal locus-of-control for Ellen's behavior. In addition, placing responsibility on Ellen for establishing a formal support system (including her boyfriend in her efforts) was also a method to ensure the maintenance of her weight-loss. While it is impossible to conclude that the efforts of the therapist to promote internal attributions were responsible for Ellen's success, they were certainly a central part of the treatment procedures.

Since the case study described above was an individual example, it should be noted that treatment procedures vary greatly with the constraints and assets of the therapeutic environment as well as the creativity of the implementer and personal characteristics of the client. For example, Rozensky and Bellack (1976) found that subjects rated as high in self-reinforcement ability lost more weight in a self-controlled contingency treatment than in an experimenter-controlled condition. Subjects rated as low self-reinforcers lost comparable weight with either contingency condition. Gold (1977) also found significant individual variation in response to a self-control treatment. He proposed that factors such as motivation and cognitive sets may contribute to the observed variability.

The clinician must further recognize that the maintenance of therapeutic gains is not wholly determined by the self-versus-environmental attributions made by the client. Indeed, in the Sonne and Janoff (1979) research cited above, the measured attributions accounted for only 22% of the variance of the subjects' weight loss maintenance. Bandura (1978) proposes that an individual's self-observation of behavior (in this case, weight loss behavior) produces reactions about the self (such as self-satisfaction, self-dissatisfaction) through a judgmental process. That process, in turn, influences future regulation of behavior. According to Bandura, the judgmental function includes several sub-processes. First, the individual may judge a given performance as satisfying or dissatisfying according to specific *personal standards*. A client who expects a weight loss of 10 pounds in 10 weeks has set a personal standard. Weight loss of 5 pounds or of 15 pounds may be judged accordingly. Second, the client may be expected to make *referential comparisons*—comparisons of a specific behavioral performance with the accomplishments of others in the reference group. Third, the client's self-reaction to final weight loss varies according to the degree to which the weight loss is *valued* or is important to the client. And fourth, Bandura suggests that self-reactions vary according to the individual's perception of the *determinants* of the behavior—the performance *attribution*.

Bandura's (1978) model provides three cognitive processes—personal standards, referential comparison standards, and valuation of the performance, in addition to the attributional process, which may prove to be significant factors in the problem of therapeutic behavior change maintenance. The challenge to clinical researchers is clear. The researcher must investigate and report the role of individual client differences and of additional cognitive factors in the maintenance of clinical improvement. The challenge to the clinician is less obvious, but none the less critical. The clinician must observe and form hypotheses regarding those variables and attempt to operationalize research findings in the therapeutic milieu. The complexity of human adaptive and maladaptive behavior makes essential this "scientific" alliance between the clinician and the clinical researcher.

REFERENCES

Bandura, A. (1969). *Principles of Behavior Modification*. New York: Holt, Rinehart & Winston.

Bandura, A. (1978). The self-esteem in reciprocal determinism. *American Psychologist* **33**, 344–358.

Bowers, K. (1975). The psychology of subtle control: an attributional analysis of behavioural persistence. *Canadian Journal of Behavioural Science* **7**, 78–95.

Brehm, S. (1976). *Applications of Social Psychology to Clinical Practice*. Washington: Hemisphere Publishing Corporation.

Brunn, A. C. and Hedberg, A. G. (1974). Covert positive reinforcement as a treatment procedure for obesity. *Journal of Community Psychology* **2**, 117–119.

Danowski, T. S. (1980). Obesity. *American Family Physician Monograph*. St. Louis, Missouri: AAFP Publications.

Davison, G. C., Tsujimoto, R. and Glaros, A. (1973). Attribution and the maintenance of behavior change in falling asleep. *Journal of Abnormal Psychology* **82**, 124–133.

Deci, E. L. (1971). Effects of externally mediated rewards on intrinsic motivation. *Journal of Personality and Social Psychology* **18**, 105–115.

Deci, E. L. (1972). Intrinsic motivation, extrinsic reinforcement, and inequality. *Journal of Personality and Social Psychology* **22**, 113–120.

Dunkel, L. and Glaros, A. (1978). Comparison of self-instructional and stimulus control treatments of obesity. *Cognitive Therapy and Research* **2**, 75–78.

Gold, R. D. (1977). Analysis of a cognitively oriented self-management weight control program using an intensive case study withdrawal design. *Dissertation Abstracts International* **37**, 5603A.

Hosford, R. and de Visser, L. (1974). *Behavioral Approaches to Counseling. An Introduction*. Washington, D.C.: APGA Press.

Jeffrey, D. B. (1974). A comparison of the effects of external-control and self-control on the modification and maintenance of weight. *Journal of Abnormal Psychology* **83**, 404–410.

Kopel, S. and Arkowitz, H. (1975). The role of attribution and self-perception in behavior change: Implications for behavior therapy. *Genetic Psychology Monographs* **92**, 175–212.

Lepper, M. R., Green, D. and Nisbett, R. E. (1973). Undermining children's intrinsic interest with extrinsic reward: A test of the "overjustification" hypothesis. *Journal of Personality and Social Psychology* **28**, 129–137.

Mahoney, M. J. (1974). Self-reward and self-monitoring techniques for weight control. *Behavior Therapy* **5**, 48–57.

Rotter, J. B. (1966). Generalized expectancies for internal versus external control of reinforcement. *Psychological Monographs* **80** (1, Whole No. 609).

Rozensky, R. and Bellack, A. (1976). Individual differences in self-reinforcement style and performance in self- and therapist-controlled weight reduction programs. *Behavior Research and Therapy* **14**, 357–364.

Sonne, J. and Janoff, D. (1979). The effect of treatment attributions on the maintenance of weight reduction: A replication and extension. *Cognitive Therapy and Research* **3**, 389–397.

Stuart, R. (1967). Behavioral control of overeating. *Behavior Research and Therapy* **5**, 357–365.

Stuart, R. (1971). A three-dimensional program for the treatment of obesity. *Behavior Research and Therapy* **9**, 177–186.

Stunkard, A. J. (1959). The results of treatment for obesity. *Archives of Internal Medicine* **103**, 79–85.

Stunkard, A. J. and Mahoney, M. (1976). Behavior treatment of the eating disorders. *In* H. Leitenberg (ed.), *Handbook of Behavior Modification and Behavior Therapy*. New York: Appleton-Century-Crofts.

Stunkard, A. J. and Penick, S. B. (1979). Behavior modification in the treatment of obesity: The problem of maintaining weight loss. *Archives of General Psychiatry* **36**, 801–805.

6
Learned Helplessness and Attributional Interventions in Depression

Christopher Peterson

A. INTRODUCTION

The purpose of this chapter is to discuss some of the clinical implications of the reformulated learned helplessness model (Abramson *et al.*, 1978). Because these implications have already been discussed in general terms (Seligman, 1980), the focus here will be on specific attributional interventions suggested by the model. I believe these interventions are problematic to the degree that they rely on attribution theory's "man as scientist" metaphor. I plan to discuss some shortcomings of interventions based strictly on this metaphor and to relate these to other cognitive treatments of depression.

B. THE LEARNED HELPLESSNESS MODEL

The phenomenon of learned helplessness was first described systematically by animal learning theorists at the University of Pennsylvania (Overmier and Seligman, 1967; Seligman and Maier, 1967). These researchers discovered that when dogs were immobilized and given inescapable electric shocks, they showed a marked impairment 24 hours later in learning a response which would terminate shock. This impairment was characterized by (a) a failure to initiate escape responses (motivational deficit); (b) an inability to profit from an occasionally

97

successful escape response (cognitive or associative deficit); and (c) a passive acceptance of the shock (emotional deficit).

To describe the phenomenon, and to explain it, these researchers labelled it learned helplessness. It was proposed that the animals learned during exposure to the inescapable shocks that their responses and outcomes (i.e. shocks) were independent of each other—that nothing they did mattered. This learning was represented as an expectation of helplessness which was generalized into new situations, where learning was objectively possible, to produce the observed deficits.

Shortly after learned helplessness was described in animals, researchers attempted to demonstrate the same phenomenon with human subjects. Several of the early attempts to replicate learned helplessness with people were unsuccessful, and others were methodologically flawed (Wortman and Brehm, 1975), but eventually a number of clear demonstrations were reported in the research literature (e.g. Hiroto and Seligman, 1975). Following on the heels of these demonstrations were a large number of papers *applying* learned helplessness to a variety of human ills. The best known application of learned helplessness to a complex failure of adaptation has been Seligman's (1974, 1975) use of helplessness as a laboratory model of depression. He has argued that the parallels between the causes, symptoms, amd ameliorations of learned helplessness and depression are strikingly similar, and has supported his argument with a series of studies demonstrating these similarities (see Abramson et al., 1978, for a review of these studies).

The learned helplessness theory indicated several therapeutic approaches to depression. First, early mastery training should "immunize" an individual against the debilitating effects of uncontrollable events. Presumably, immunization results from the engendering of the expectation that outcomes are contingent on responses; this expectation interferes with the learning that responses and outcomes are noncontingent during exposure to uncontrollable events. Second, exposure to contingencies should break up helplessness and depression. In the animal domain, exposure was accomplished by literally dragging the animal to-and-fro across a shuttle box until the animal perceived that such movement was associated with shock termination and began to respond on its own (Seligman et al., 1968). In the human domain, exposure to contingencies could be accomplished less literally, via instructions about their nature.

After the early successful demonstrations of the phenomenon with people, several lines of research were undertaken which questioned the validity of the theory as an account of what was going on in the human laboratory. A number of anomalies *vis-à-vis* the theory accumulated in the research literature (for summaries of these, see Abramson *et al.*, 1978; Miller and Norman, 1979; Roth, 1980; Wortman and Brehm, 1975). Among the suggested anomalies were:

(1) The motivational deficit in human helplessness studies was not always present. Although "helpless" subjects did not quickly learn objectively possible responses, it was not because they failed to initiate responses.

(2) Sometimes, experience with uncontrollable events resulted not in an impairment on the test, but a facilitation.

(3) The helplessness produced in human studies seemed rather circumscribed, often not generalizing beyond the specific setting in which the pretreatment occurred. In contrast, helplessness theory predicted a global generalization of the belief "I am helpless."

(4) When subjects were instructed about how other subjects had done on the pretreatment task, these instructions affected subsequent performance. According to helplessness theory, such instructions should have been inert.

(5) A belief in response-outcome independence was not necessary to produce helplessness following experience with uncontrollable events (Peterson, 1978). Indeed some authors argued that in many helplessness paradigms, the learning of response-outcome independence was unlikely (e.g. Peterson, 1980b).

(6) A variety of competing explanations for human helplessness effects were proposed (e.g. Douglas and Anisman, 1975; Frankel and Snyder, 1978; Peterson, 1978), and to some degree supported with data.

In short, the simple explanation of the observed helplessness effects (e.g. uncontrollable events → expectation of response-outcome independence → interference with objectively possible learning) seemed not to do justice to the complexity of human helplessness. Most critics of helplessness theory as applied to people suggested that a more sophisticated account was necessary. And most critics were of the opinion that an attributional account of helplessness, one that considered the causal interpretations of the uncontrollable events, would satisfy the need (e.g. Wortman and Brehm, 1975).

In the light of the research anomalies, Seligman and his co-workers (Abramson *et al.*, 1978) indeed proposed an attributional reformulation of the learned helplessness theory, particularly as it applied to depression. Similar reformulations were also sketched by other theorists (e.g. Miller and Norman, 1979; Peterson, 1976; Roth, 1980), but in the present chapter, the reformulation refers to the theory as recast by the Pennsylvania research group.

Reformulation

According to the reformulation, experience with negative uncontrollable events and the expectation of future non-contingency are not sufficient to result in pervasive helplessness and depression. What determines the nature and extent of the deficits following experience with uncontrollable events are causal attributions made by the person. If the person attributes the cause of the uncontrollable events to internal factors (as opposed to external), to stable factors (as opposed to unstable), and to global factors (as opposed to specific), then generalized helplessness and depression will occur, and self-esteem will decrease. In the absence of such attributions, the ensuing helplessness and depression are expected to be circumscribed in time and space, and not to involve loss of self-esteem. Adding attributions to the helplessness model makes it a better account of depression but takes it a long way from the animal laboratory; worthlessness is not the same as helplessness and probably has no animal equivalent. Thus, the reformulation may not build on the original helplessness model so much as replace it.

The reformulation embodies the "man as scientist" metaphor (Peterson and Seligman, 1980) which has been popular in attribution theories (e.g. Kelley, 1973). It assumes, as do many contemporary attributional accounts, that people arrive at their attributions "logically" and that they act in accord with them "logically," even though the consequences of such actions may be harmful. Despite the maladaptiveness of helplessness and depression, they are *understandable* granted the premises that uncontrollable negative events are the result of something about the person and that they are apt to recur over time and across a variety of situations. The reader is asked to keep this metaphor in mind while I discuss its therapeutic implications.

This view of depression is an interesting one for several reasons. First, it makes depression a behavior of which everyone is "capable," since the mechanisms responsible for it are mundane ones—contingency learning, attributional processes, expectations, and generalization. Other accounts of depression, particularly psychoanalytic theories (Mendelson, 1974) and biochemical theories (e.g. Baldessarini, 1975; Schildkraut, 1965), propose special mechanisms for depression, mechanisms not present in "everyday" people. Thus, the learned helplessness theory is novel in that it assumes that mild depression and severe depression fall along a continuum (cf. Depue and Monroe, 1978), that children can be depressed (cf. Lefkowitz and Burton, 1978), and that depression can be modelled in the laboratory (cf. Costello, 1978).

Second, the learned helplessness reformulation does not see depressives "motivated" to maintain their symptoms; there is no payoff, either instrumentally (Ullman and Krasner, 1975) or dynamically (Rado, 1928). Depression results from certain beliefs and certain experiences, not from certain needs or certain reinforcers. This is not to say that depressive symptoms cannot be relieved by attention to needs and reinforcers (see general therapeutic implications below), only that motivational factors are not of *primary* importance in the development and maintenance of depression.

Third, the reformulation places depression fully in the way of the recent boom in attribution research and theory, of which this volume is only one example. A great deal of attention has been paid to the psychology of attributions, and all of this research may be applied to the therapy of depression, now that the reformulation has opened the door for these applications.

Seligman's research group has recently undertaken a number of studies of the reformulation (see reviews by Miller and Seligman, 1979, and Peterson and Seligman, 1980). Most of these studies have been concerned with "attributional style" as a risk factor for depression. Many people explain events in a habitual fashion (Seligman *et al.*, 1979). Some people impose a "depressive" framework on events, attributing bad happenings to internal, stable, and global causes, and good happenings to external, unstable, and specific causes. Several studies have shown that this depressive attributional style, measured by the Attributional Style Questionnaire (Seligman *et al.*, 1979), does in fact characterize depressives (Peterson and Seligman, 1980).

The reformulation's account of depression is a psychologically plausible one, claiming that depression results from a certain "cognitive" style with which a person makes sense of bad events. On a general level, there are therefore two ways in which the would-be therapist can intervene to prevent or relieve depressive symptoms. First, the therapist can prevent, modify, or undo the bad events which are processed through the insidious attributional style. Second, the therapist can modify attributional style or specific attributions, so that the depressing effects of bad events are thwarted.

Thus, the tension between environmental and intrapsychic interventions does not exist for the clinical applications of the reformulation. The problem of depression is not placed just in the world, nor just in the point of view of the individual, but rather in the interaction of the person and the environment. This is not to say that under special circumstances, environmental events cannot swamp the individual. Indeed, certain experiences, such as natural disasters or concentration camp internments, are apt to be so traumatic that none escape unaffected, regardless of the attributional styles they habitually employ (Dor-Shav, 1978). Neither is this to say that certain people cannot become helpless and depressed in a virtual vacuum, interpreting whatever befalls them in such a way as to result in feelings of loss and worthlessness. It is expected, though, that in most cases, depression is best understood by attending to the person-in-the-world.

General Therapeutic Implications of the Reformulation

Seligman (1980) has deduced four general therapeutic strategies from the reformulation. These will be described briefly, and then some more concrete interventions will be sketched, along with potential difficulties in implementing and justifying them theoretically.

The first strategy discussed by Seligman (1980) involves *environmental enrichment*. Since one premise of the reformulated helplessness model is that the individual expects negative outcomes to be likely in the future, an obvious way of changing these expectations (thereby preventing and/or breaking up helplessness and depression) is to change the nature of the environment in which the individual lives. If good outcomes in such domains as health, employment, friends, and family are more likely, depression should be thwarted.

Theorists as early as Freud (1917) have observed that depressed people indeed lead depressing lives. While to some degree, the depressive may encourage bad events, these events may also be the result of life in an impoverished world (Lloyd, 1980; Paykel, 1974). Thus, environmental enrichment is an important therapeutic strategy. However, Seligman (1980) has warned that environmental intervention can work at cross-purposes with "personal control training" (the next strategy to be discussed), if the person is made to feel helpless by the action of well-meaning but "uncontrollable" social agencies (Wortman et al., 1976). A useful adjunct to the strategy of environmental enrichment might be citizen participation in any social agency empowered to enrich the world (see Langer and Rodin, 1976, and Schulz, 1976, for dramatic instances of how control over an enriched setting can greatly benefit the well-being, physical and psychological, of the aged).

The second strategy discussed by Seligman (1980) is *personal control training*. This strategy proposes that an effective therapy for depression would be one in which the individual changes expectations about events from uncontrollability to controllability. Personal control training is somewhat similar to "attribution retraining," although it is directed at expectations rather than attributions. Many currently popular "behavioral" therapies in effect embody the tactic of personal control training, through assertiveness training, social skills training, graded task assignment, and so on. Interestingly, successful implementation of this second strategy will facilitate the first strategy, since the nature of the individual's objective situation will change for the better as more benefits become available through new skills.

A third strategy of combatting depression is *resignation training* (Seligman, 1980). Many of the bad events which trigger depression are inevitable, and sometimes depressive expectations are accurate (cf. Alloy and Abramson, 1979). Rather than providing the depressive with rose-colored glasses, a tactic not apt to be effective anyway (Coates and Wortman, 1980), the therapist can instead provide different norms, challenge assumptions which make the bad outcomes seem worse than they could seem, and help the person find alternative desirable out-comes.

The fourth strategy sketched by Seligman (1980) is probably of the most interest to the readers of this volume: *attribution retraining*. Both the specific attributions made by depressives, as well as their habitual attributional style, may be attacked by the therapist, whose goal is to channel them from internal, stable, and global causes for bad events to the converse (and vice versa for attributions and attributional style regarding good events). Such redirection may occur either with a talking therapy, or with *in vivo* experience which challenges the attributions typically made.

In the conclusion of his discussion of general therapeutic strategies deduced from the reformulation, Seligman (1980) argued that cognitive behavior modification (Mahoney, 1974) and cognitive therapy (Beck *et al.*, 1979) can be subsumed under the strategies he deduced. These approaches, like those based on the reformulation, assume that "abnormal" behavior is best understood by taking into account the thoughts and beliefs of individuals, and that therapy should attempt to change cognitions. Thus, much of what follows in this chapter, though directed at the implications of the reformulation, may also be extended to other cognitive approaches to therapy.

Changing Attributions

This section is concerned with some concrete aspects of the fourth therapeutic strategy described above: *attribution retraining*. My argument here will be that though attribution retraining may prove to be a good way of preventing and ameliorating depression, it cannot occur in the simple manner suggested by most contemporary accounts of attribution theory. The problem resides in the already mentioned "man as scientist" metaphor underlying attribution theories. Such a metaphor should probably be recast as "man as textbook scientist," and then discarded altogether, since even flesh-and-blood scientists are not well described by the stereotype (Mahoney, 1977).

It is not hard to understand why the "scientist" metaphor has been popular. There is considerable utility in viewing people—whether scientists, depressives, or baseball players—as scientific, if by that is meant that they actively seek to represent their understanding of the world in abstract terms, that experience is relevant to this understanding, and that changes in "theories" are possible and profound in their consequences. However, to the degree that such a "scientific" view caricatures people as "logical information processors," such a view is incapable of accounting for: (a) the tenacity to which people hold to their "scientific" theories, even in the face of contrary evidence (Mahoney, 1977; Ross, 1977); (b) the importance of affective relationships (i.e. transference) and context in the socialization and resocialization of these beliefs (Berger and Luckmann, 1966); and (c) the "web of belief" (Quine and Ullian, 1970) in which people's theories metaphorically reside, intertwined and interdependent.

First, let me explain the simple interventions based on the textbook metaphor. The starkest statement of this metaphor is in Kelley's (1973) covariation principles. According to Kelley (1973), people attribute events to those potential causes with which they covary over time and place. At a certain level, this is uncontestable, since these principles merely restate a common *definition* of cause. But at another level, the covariation principles claim that people are normative information processors, that their causal attributions are veridical summaries of the way the world really is.

The therapeutic implications of Kelley's attribution theory are straightforward: change the causal structure of the world. The person, as a veridical covariation analyst, will detect this change, modify the relevant attributions, and to the degree that such modification is away from the depressive attributional style, become less helpless and depressed. Thus, environmental enrichment automatically results in attribution retraining, and attribution retraining presumably mitigates depression. The behavioral theories of depression (i.e. depression results from low levels of positive reinforcements; e.g. Lewinsohn, 1974) dictate a similar strategy, although not because of its effect on attributions: provide the depressive with an environment in which rewards are stably and globally contingent on an individual's responses.

Kelley (1973) suggested that attributions also result from the use of "causal schemata"—*a priori* beliefs about the relationships between causes and effects (Ajzen, 1977). Thus, in the absence of repeated experiences with events, which would make possible a covariation analysis of which causes are operative, people draw on beliefs they already have about why the given event occurred. The intervention suggested here is to provide the person with a different belief, one which does not have maladaptive consequences.

Most discussions of attribution therapy seem to imply that alternative attributions can be imparted quite simply: "You should realize that the source of these problems is not you, but others; that they won't last for ever, but that they will go away at the end of the month; and that they don't have general effects, but only highly specific ones." The problem with such simple interventions is that there is no evidence that they can induce the person to change any but the most trivial beliefs. Indeed, there is good reason to expect that these interventions would usually fail if nothing else were done in therapy to assist their operation.

One of the most important problems in justifying interventions based on the covariation principles is that people are often quite poor at abstracting contingencies (e.g. Langer, 1977; Nisbett and Ross, 1980; Slovic and Lichtenstein, 1971). Research in support of the covariation analysis theory has presented people with highly abstracted *summaries* of contingency information and then shown that these summaries can be used to draw the predicted conclusions about operative causes (Frieze and Weiner, 1971; McArthur, 1972). But when subjects are asked to abstract for themselves the covariation between causes and effects, they do poorly (Cordray and Shaw, 1978), sometimes appearing not to make use of covariation information at all (Peterson, 1980a).

This failure of subjects to abstract covariation among events has been explained in terms of motivational biases (Peterson, 1980a), incorrect assumptions about the events (Peterson, 1980b), illusions (Alloy and Abramson, 1979), information-processing deficiencies (Slovic and Lichtenstein, 1971), and so on. But the point here is that people are poor at it, a finding documented in a number of paradigms (e.g. Golding and Rorer, 1972; Levine, 1971; Smedslund, 1963). If this is the case, a therapy which merely changes the causal texture of the actual world is not apt to alter the attributions of depressives, who are unlikely to notice the changes.

This pessimistic conclusion is the same reached by some critics of the misattribution technique (e.g. Davison and Wilson, 1973; Lick and Bootzin, 1975); the technique is useful for alleviating mild anxieties and fears induced in the laboratory, but has little effect on phobias and anxieties severe enough to cause the person to seek professional help. If a person is afraid of dogs, it is usually not possible to suggest to him that he is mistaken, that his real fear is of something else. The person knows that he is afraid of dogs, and that is that. Similarly, a depressive knows that he is the source of his problems and those in the world. Suggestions that he is wrong are apt to be assimilated to his depressed way of viewing things, as evidence that others are more intelligent, that he cannot think straight, and so on.

A second problem with using simple attributional interventions to treat depression comes from the literature recently reviewed by Ross (1977; Nisbett and Ross, 1980) showing that attributions are often not changed in light of contrary evidence. The typical experiment shows contrary evidence to be ignored or rationalized. When people do change their attributions, they do so much more slowly than the evidence would "normatively" dictate (cf. conservatism of Bayesian judgment; Slovic and Lichtenstein, 1971).

A third reason to suspect that simple interventions consistent with the "man as textbook scientist" metaphor would be ineffective with depressives takes as its point of departure the current controversy about whether "causal" attributions really constitute causal statements like those in scientific theories. Buss (1978) has recently argued that "causal" attributions usually do not refer to temporally prior entities, e.g. billiard balls. Instead, he observed, many attributions are justifications of the event in question, a reference to an end goal or value with which the event is congruent. For instance, when a depressive says that her date rejected her because she is "a boring conversationalist," she is not suggesting that boringness is an event that preceded the rejection. Rather, Buss (1978) would argue, she is using boringness to conceptualize the rejection— "boringness" explains without causing (Harré and Secord, 1972). Antaki and Fielding (1981) pursued this point further, observing that attributions are not always causal but sometimes descriptive, and that descriptions may stand as explanations in their own right.

If this is generally the case for attributions, or at least for depressives' attributions, it might make sense to regard depressive attributional style as evidencing a confusion about standards (Sabini and Silver, 1980) rather than a confusion about causes (Peterson, 1979). Thus, scientific evidence is apt to be quite irrelevant in dissuading depressives from their habitual attributions (cf. Mischel, 1964), since standards *make sense* of evidence, not summarize it. To the degree that attributional interventions merely supply "data" to depressives, they are apt to be unsuccessful.

In short, I am not contesting the proposal of the reformulation that insidious attributional style is a characteristic of depression. Neither am I contesting the *general* recommendation that changes in depressive attributional style are a good goal for therapy. What I am suggesting is that successful therapeutic intervention is not likely to occur simply by exposing depressed people to new information or alternative interpretations. Anyone who has tried to "reason" with a depressive is aware of the inertia of depressive beliefs.

I have implicated attribution theory's "man as scientist" metaphor as responsible for a false impression of how simply opinions may be changed. Although science may be described as in constant flux, the hypotheses of individual scientists usually are not, and neither are the hypotheses of depressives—be they causal, evaluative, or descriptive.

C. WEAVING NEW STRANDS INTO THE WEB OF BELIEF

144. The child learns to believe a host of things. I.e. it learns to act according to those beliefs. Bit by bit there forms a system of what is believed, and in that system some things stand unshakeably fast and some are more or less liable to shift. What stands fast does so, not because it is intrinsically obvious or convincing; it is rather held fast by what lies around it. (L. Wittgenstein, 1972)

I have made three arguments against simple attributional interventions in depression: (a) people are poor at contingency analysis; (b) attributions are not always responsive to contrary evidence; and (c) attributions are not always causes in the scientific sense of temporally prior entities. These criticisms center on the charge that attribution theory's account of the formation and change of attributional beliefs is much too simple. Attribution theory seems to conceive attributions as isolated "facts," able to be corrected directly and independently of other beliefs, like a mistaken phone number. A better description of attributions, one compatible with the research described above, depicts them as interrelated with other beliefs, as structured—a point sometimes made about the theories of science (e.g. Dandeker and Scott, 1979) as well as the theories of the individual (e.g. Scott et al., 1979).

Attribution theory cannot approach beliefs as if they were removable like psychological tumors. The whole of a person's belief system, and the way in which beliefs are used, must be addressed in attribution therapy. Such therapy can capitalize on the interconnectedness of beliefs, though, and attempt not to remove insidious attributions but to change them by adding other beliefs which cast them in a different light. Consider, for example, an individual with the depressive attributional style who becomes a Christian. Bad events may still be interpreted as the result of internal, stable, and global causes (i.e. sinfulness), but the different context (i.e. God's forgiveness) provided by the new religious beliefs is apt to blunt considerably the depressing effects of such attributions. Blessed are the internal, stable, and global, for they shall inherit the earth.

What, though, is needed to alter a worldview? First, there must be a good reason for the person to entertain the new belief. Further, the new belief must be sufficiently important to change other beliefs, but it should not directly contradict them, or else it would never be accepted. Finally, there must be ways in which the new belief can be used, thus binding it closely to the rest of what guides action. I will argue in the remainder of this section that Beck's cognitive therapy for depression (Beck *et al.*, 1979) precisely satisfies these conditions for changing a belief system, and hence, that its success can be easily understood in terms of them.

Cognitive therapy for depression is an explicit application of a theory similar to the helplessness reformulation, holding that depressive symptoms are produced by thoughts of helplessness and hopelessness (Beck, 1967, 1976). The therapy is described as "collaborative empiricism," because the therapist assists the patient in discerning these cognitions (automatic thoughts) and the theories giving rise to them (maladaptive assumptions). In cognitive therapy, the reasonableness of automatic thoughts is measured against experiential evidence, and changes away from depressive thoughts presumably result from challenges by evidence. Much of cognitive therapy thus entails designing and conducting "experiments." For instance, the person who believes that she is a boring conversationalist might not have fully tested this premise, instead using it as a reason not to interact with others. She and the therapist might decide that she should talk to ten people during the next week and observe their reactions to her. Predictions are made beforehand and either falsified or corroborated by the interactions. If she proves to be boring (by whatever criterion was agreed upon), then social skills training is in order; if she proves not to be boring, then the premise is called into question.

At this level of description, cognitive therapy for depression seems to involve simple attributional interventions (cf. Seligman, 1980). I have already argued that such strategies are not likely to be successful, so how can the success of cognitive therapy (Rush *et al.*, 1977) be explained? Scrutiny of the therapy manual (Beck *et al.*, 1979) reveals the answer: cognitive therapy is not simply a series of attributional interventions. Additionally stressed in the manual are (a) the importance of the therapist–patient relationship; (b) the role of underlying assumptions in giving rise to manifest attributions; and (c) the inadvisability of criticizing or contradicting the beliefs of the depressive.

106. Suppose some adult had told a child that he had been on the moon. The child tells me the story, and I say it was only a joke. . . . If now the child

insists, saying perhaps there is a way of getting there which I don't know, etc. what reply could I make to him? . . . But a child will not ordinarily stick to such a belief and will soon be convinced by what we tell him seriously. (L. Wittgenstein, 1972)

In achieving a good therapist–patient rapport, cognitive therapy creates the affective relationship necessary for resocialization (Berger and Luckmann, 1966). Once the patient is *listening* to what the therapist is saying, cognitive therapy can provide a belief not likely to have been entertained by the patient prior to therapy: thoughts cause emotions. Considerable exemplification of this belief is undertaken, and patients are urged to "see" its pervasive operation in themselves. According to Beck (1976, p. 238), "A person experiencing a mild disturbance in his feelings or behaviors may not be aware of the automatic thoughts—even though they are accessible to consciousness. . . By concentrating on the thoughts, however, he can easily recognize them."

Beck (1976, p. 239) referred to unaware conscious thoughts as a "philosophical problem," which he attempted to resolve, but I think the important point is that it is largely an unresolvable problem, like the Zen *koan*. For precisely this reason, the fundamental assumption of cognitive therapy, that "thoughts cause emotions," is not something that the patient can challenge, and the therapist is well on his or her way to becoming viewed as someone who should be listened to seriously about other matters (Haley, 1963). Further, once the premise that "thoughts cause emotions" is accepted, the depressive's previous attempts to understand the depression are recast as the *source* of the problem. Cognitive therapy thus provides a new belief likely to alter greatly other beliefs.

> 5. Whether a proposition can turn out false after all depends on what I make count as determinants for that proposition. (L. Wittgenstein, 1972)

In cognitive therapy, the attributional beliefs of the depressive are not themselves challenged so much as are the "operationalizations" consistent with them. The depressive is not told simply that she is an interesting conversationalist, but instead is also encouraged to define interesting conversationalist in such a way that it would be difficult not to qualify. Operationalizations are not apt to be held so fast in the "web of belief" as are the dispositional conclusions following from them. Indeed, if the criticism leveled against personality theories for vaguely defining traits (Mischel, 1968) also applies to intuitive personality theories, such re-definition is simply definition and easily accomplished.

> 139. Not only rules, but also examples are needed for establishing a practice. (L. Wittgenstein, 1972)

A striking aspect of cognitive therapy is its concreteness. Discussions of thoughts and behaviors are always at the level of specifics. At first glance, such concreteness seems a poor strategy. Even Hercules could not solve an infinity of problems one at a time. In the course of cognitive therapy, however, attention to details does not prove problematic. Instead, as a few specific difficulties begin to be resolved, other difficulties begin to disappear as well. In altering a belief system, concrete exemplification of a few alternative beliefs is probably more effective than abstract generalization about a multitude.

Research reviewed by Nisbett and Ross (1980) further attests to the utility of such exemplification. Specific examples (e.g. "My brother-in-law has a Toyota, and it's a lemon") carry much more weight in changing opinions than do abstractions (e.g., "*Consumer Reports* find 10,000 Toyota owners to be extremely pleased with the car"), even though the scientific validity and reliability of the generalizations are far superior. Why should examples be so compelling?

Perhaps exemplification derives its weight from the fact that a belief's meaning results partly from its use, its function and manifestation in concrete actions in concrete situations. Abstract generalizations provide no clue about how to *act*; great teachers such as Socrates and Jesus instructed instead through parables (Morris, 1980). A parable provides a clue about how to change at least *one* action, and when one action is changed, so too are other actions not directly addressed by the concrete intervention. Particularly in the light of the characterization of depressives as concrete (Kovacs and Beck, 1978), therapy via parables can be expected to be more effective than therapy via abstractions. There is no logical reason why the cessation of marital problems, for instance, should render employment difficulties less aversive, but such "generalization" seems to be the case, since interpretations of ostensibly diverse problems are interconnected.

Cognitive therapy works because it weaves new strands into the web of belief in which depressive attributions are "located," thereby changing the entire fabric. The therapist, as a trusted, admired, and expert figure, provides a different ground (thoughts cause emotions) against which figures (attributions) appear differently than they have in the past. The determinants of attributions are changed, and so then are the attributions themselves. Alternative uses of beliefs are exemplified, and these instances cast a new light on the rest of what a person believes and does. Cognitive therapy changes people by resocializing them, by providing a relationship in which the system of one's beliefs can be changed.

D. CONCLUSION: ATTRIBUTION THEORY AND ATTRIBUTION THERAPY

In his recent critique of attribution theory and research, Buss (1978) chided the field for not being true to Heider's (1958) initial view of a naive psychology. The field is simultaneously too naive and not naive enough—too naive because it defines the scientist metaphor by projection, as an experimental social psychologist mainly interested in accounting for variance (Fischhoff, 1976)—not naive enough because it frequently fails to investigate the way people actually use attributions, instead employing "reliable" closed-format questionnaires (Elig and Frieze, 1979) to access attributional beliefs.

In the present chapter, I have tried to convey a similar criticism of the field as it begins to be applied to the therapy of depression. There is considerable promise to attributional interventions, since depression has been profitably reconceptualized as a cognitive phenomenon (Beck, 1967, 1976), and particularly an attributional one (Abramson *et al.*, 1978). However, the promise of interventions following from such reconceptualization will only be realized if attributions are approached with more naiveté and conceptualized with more sophistication. The learned helplessness model was reformulated in such a spirit; its clinical implications should be similarly implemented.

ACKNOWLEDGEMENTS

The ideas in this chapter have been influenced by my conversations with Bronwen Morris, John Sabini, Martin Seligman and Richard Werner. These people have done much to enrich my life, and I gratefully acknowledge their influence.

REFERENCES

Abramson, L. Y., Seligman, M. E. P. and Teasdale, J. D. (1978). Learned helplessness in humans: critique and reformulation. *Journal of Abnormal Psychology* **87**, 49–74.

Ajzen, I. (1977). Intuitive theories of events and the effects of baserate information on prediction. *Journal of Personality and Social Psychology* **35**, 303–314.

Alloy, L. B. and Abramson, L. Y. (1979). Judgment of contingency in depressed and nondepressed students: sadder but wiser? *Journal of Experimental Psychology: General* **108**, 441–485.

Antaki, C. and Fielding, G. (1981). Research on ordinary explanations. *In* C. Antaki (ed.) *The Psychology of Ordinary Explanations of Social Behaviour*. London and New York: Academic Press.

Baldessarini, R. J. (1975). The basis for amine hypotheses in affective disorders. *Archives of General Psychiatry* **32**, 1087–1092.

Beck, A. T. (1967). *Depression: Clinical, Experimental, and Theoretical Aspects.* New York: Hoeber.

Beck, A. T. (1976). *Cognitive Therapy and the Emotional Disorders.* New York: International Universities Press.

Beck, A. T., Rush, A. J., Shaw, B. F. and Emery, G. (1979). *Cognitive Therapy of Depression.* New York: Guilford.

Berger, P. L. and Luckmann, T. (1966). *The Social Construction of Reality.* Garden City, New York: Doubleday.

Buss, A. R. (1978). Causes and reasons in attribution theory: a conceptual critique. *Journal of Personality and Social Psychology* **36**, 1311–1321.

Coates, D. and Wortman, C. B. (1980). Depression maintenance and interpersonal control. In A. Baum and J. E. Singer (eds) *Advances in Environmental Psychology* (vol. 2): *Applications of Personal Control.* Hillsdale, New Jersey: Erlbaum.

Cordray, D. S. and Shaw, J. I. (1977). An empirical test of the covariation analysis in causal attribution. *Journal of Experimental Social Psychology* **14**, 280–290.

Costello, C. G. (1978). A critical review of Seligman's laboratory experiments on learned helplessness and depression. *Journal of Abnormal Psychology* **87**, 21–31.

Dandeker, C. and Scott, J. (1979). The structure of sociological theory and knowledge. *Journal for the Theory of Social Behaviour* **9**, 303–325.

Davison, G. C. and Wilson, G. T. (1973). Processes of fear-reduction in systematic desensitization: cognitive and social reinforcement factors in humans. *Behavior Therapy* **4**, 1–21.

Depue, R. A. and Monroe, S. M. (1978). Learned helplessness in the perspective of the depressive disorders: conceptual and definitional issues. *Journal of Abnormal Psychology* **87**, 3–20.

Dor-Shav, N. K. (1978). On the long-range effects of concentration camp internment on Nazi victims. *Journal of Consulting and Clinical Psychology* **46**, 1–11.

Douglas, D. and Anisman, H. (1975). Helplessness or expectation incongruency: effects of aversive stimulation on subsequent performance. *Journal of Experimental Psychology: Human Perception and Performance* **1**, 411–417.

Elig, T. W. and Frieze, I. H. (1979). Measuring causal attributions for success and failure. *Journal of Personality and Social Psychology* **37**, 621–634.

Fischhoff, B. (1976). Attribution theory and judgment under uncertainty. In J.H. Harvey, W. J. Ickes and R. F. Kidd (eds) *New Directions in Attribution Research* (vol. 1). Hillsdale, New Jersey: Erlbaum.

Frankel, A. and Snyder, M. L. (1978). Poor performance following unsolvable problems: Learned helplessness or egotism? *Journal of Personality and Social Psychology* **36**, 1415–1423.

Freud, S. (1917). Mourning and melancholia. *Collected Works.* New York: Norton.

Frieze, I. and Weiner, B. (1971). Cue utilization and attributional judgments for success and failure. *Journal of Personality* **39**, 591–605.

Golding, S. L. and Rorer, L. G. (1972). Illusory correlation and subjective judgment. *Journal of Abnormal Psychology* **80**, 249–260.

Haley, J. (1963). *Strategies of Psychotherapy.* New York: Grune & Stratton.

Harré, R. M. and Secord, P. F. (1972). *The Explanation of Social Behaviour.* Oxford: Basil Blackwell.

Heider, F. (1958). *The Psychology of Interpersonal Relations.* New York: Wiley.

Hiroto, D. S. and Seligman, M. E. P. (1975). Generality of learned helplessness in man. *Journal of Personality and Social Psychology* **31**, 311–327.

Kelley, H. H. (1973). The processes of causal attribution. *American Psychologist* **28**, 107–128.

Kovacs, M. and Beck, A. T. (1978). Maladaptive cognitive structures in depression. *American Journal of Psychiatry* **135**, 525–533.

Langer, E. J. (1977). The psychology of chance. *Journal for the Theory of Social Behaviour* **7**, 185–207.

Langer, E. J. and Rodin, J. (1976). The effects of choice and enhanced personal responsibility for the aged: a field experiment in an institutional setting. *Journal of Personality and Social Psychology* **34**, 191–198.

Lefkowitz, M. M. and Burton, N. (1978). Childhood depression: a critique of the concept. *Psychological Bulletin* **85**, 716–726.

Levine, M. (1971). Hypothesis theory and nonlearning despite ideal S-R reinforcement contingencies. *Psychological Review* **78**, 130–140.

Lewinsohn, P. M. (1974). A behavioral approach to depression. In R. J. Friedman and M. M. Katz (eds) *The Psychology of Depression: Contemporary Theory and Research*. Washington, D.C.: Winston.

Lick, J. and Bootzin, R. (1975). Expectancy factors in the treatment of fear: Methodological and theoretical issues. *Psychological Bulletin* **82**, 917–931.

Lloyd, C. (1980). Life events and depressive disorder reviewed: I. Events as predisposing factors. II. Events as precipitating factors. *Archives of General Psychiatry* **37**, 529–548.

Mahoney, M. J. (1974). *Cognition and Behavior Modification*. Cambridge, Massachusetts: Ballinger.

Mahoney, M. J. (1977). *Scientist as Subject: The Psychological Imperative*. Cambridge: Massachusetts: Ballinger.

McArthur, L. A. (1972). The how and what of why: some determinants and consequences of causal attribution. *Journal of Personality and Social Psychology* **22**, 171–193.

Mendelson, M. (1974). *Psychoanalytic Concepts of Depression* (2nd ed.). Flushing, New York: Spectrum.

Miller, I. W. and Norman, W. H. (1979). Learned helplessness in humans: a review and attribution theory model. *Psychological Bulletin* **86**, 93–119.

Miller, S. M. and Seligman, M. E. P. (1979). *The attributional reformulation of helplessness: recent evidence*. Unpublished manuscript, University of Pennsylvania.

Mischel, T. (1964). Personal constructs, rules, and the logic of clinical activity. *Psychological Review* **71**, 180–192.

Mischel, W. (1968). *Personality and Assessment*. New York: Wiley.

Morris, B. H. (1980). *Virtue*. Unpublished senior fellowship thesis, Hamilton College.

Nisbett, R. and Ross, L. (1980). *Human Inference: Strategies and Shortcomings of Social Judgment*. Englewood Cliffs, New Jersey: Prentice-Hall.

Overmier, J. B. and Seligman, M. E. P. (1967). Effects of inescapable shock upon subsequent escape and avoidance learning. *Journal of Comparative and Physiological Psychology* **63**, 23–33.

Paykel, E. S. (1974). Recent life events and clinical depression. In E. K. E. Gunderson and R. D. Rahe (eds) *Life Stress and Illness*. Springfield, Illinois: Thomas.

Peterson, C. (1976). Learning impairment following insoluble problems: learned helplessness or altered hypothesis pool? Unpublished doctoral dissertation, University of Colorado.

Peterson, C. (1978). Learning impairment following insoluble problems: learned helplessness or altered hypothesis pool? *Journal of Experimental Social Psychology* **14**, 53–68.

Peterson, C. (1979). Uncontrollability and self-blame in depression: investigation of the paradox in a college population. *Journal of Abnormal Psychology* **88**, 620–624.

Peterson, C. (1980a). Attribution in the sports pages: an archival investigation of the covariation hypothesis. *Social Psychology Quarterly* **43**, 136–141.

Peterson, C. (1980b). Recognition of noncontingency. *Journal of Personality and Social Psychology* **38**, 727–734.

Peterson, C. and Seligman, M. E. P. (1980). *Helplessness and Attributional Style in Depression*. Unpublished manuscript, University of Pennsylvania.

Quine, W. V. and Ullian, J. S. (1970). *The Web of Belief*. New York: Random House.

Rado, S. (1928). The problem of melancholia. *International Journal of Psychoanalysis* **9**, 420–438.

Ross, L. (1977). The intuitive psychologist and his shortcomings: distortions in the attribution process. *In* L. Berkowitz (ed.) *Advances in Experimental Social Psychology* (vol. 10). London and New York: Academic Press.

Roth, S. (1980). A revised model of learned helplessness in humans. *Journal of Personality* **48**, 103–133.

Rush, A. J., Beck, A. T., Kovacs, M. and Hollon, S. (1977). Comparative efficacy of cognitive therapy and pharmacotherapy in the treatment of depressed out-patients. *Cognitive Therapy and Research* **1**, 17–37.

Sabini, J. and Silver, M. (1980). *Internal-external—Dimension or congeries?* Unpublished manuscript, University of Pennsylvania.

Schildkraut, J. J. (1965). The catecholamine hypothesis of affective disorders. *American Journal of Psychiatry* **22**, 103–117.

Schulz, R. (1976). Effects of control and predictability on the physical and psychological well-being of the institutionalized aged. *Journal of Personality and Social Psychology* **33**, 563–573.

Scott, W. A., Osgood, D. W. and Peterson, C. (1979). *Cognitive structure.* Washington, D.C.: Winston.

Seligman, M. E. P. (1974). Depression and learned helplessness. *In* R. J. Friedman and M. M. Katz (eds) *The Psychology of Depression: Contemporary Theory and Research.* Washington, D.C.: Winston.

Seligman, M. E. P. (1975). *Helplessness: On Depression, Development, and Death.* San Francisco: Freeman.

Seligman, M. E. P. (1980). *Behavioural and cognitive therapy for depression from a learned helplessness point of view.* Unpublished manuscript, University of Pennsylvania.

Seligman, M. E. P. and Maier, S. F. (1967). Failure to escape traumatic shock. *Journal of Experimental Psychology* **74**, 1–9.

Seligman, M. E. P., Abramson, L. Y., Semmel, A. and von Baeyer, C. (1979). Depressive attributional style. *Journal of Abnormal Psychology* **88**, 242–247.

Seligman, M. E. P., Maier, S. F. and Geer, J. (1968). The alleviation of learned helplessness in the dog. *Journal of Abnormal Psychology* **73**, 256–262.

Slovic, P. and Lichtenstein, S. (1971). Comparison of Bayesian and regression approaches to the study of human information processing in judgment. *Organizational Behavior and Human Performance* **6**, 649–744.

Smedslund, J. (1963). The concept of correlation in adults. *Scandinavian Journal of Psychology* **4**, 165–173.

Ullman, L. and Krasner, L. (1975). *A Psychological Approach to Abnormal Behavior* (2nd ed.). Englewood Cliffs, New Jersey: Prentice-Hall.

Wittgenstein, L. (1972). *On Certainty*. New York: Harper & Row.

Wortman, C. B. and Brehm, J. W. (1975). Response to uncontrollable outcomes: An integration of reactance theory and the learned helplessness model. *In* L. Berkowitz (ed.) *Advances in Experimental Social Psychology* (vol. 8). London and New York: Academic Press.

Wortman, C. B., Hendricks, M. and Hillis, J. W. (1976). Factors affecting participant reactions to random assignment in ameliorative social programs. *Journal of Personality and Social Psychology* **33**, 256–266.

III
Medical Applications

7
Adaptive Aspects of Self-blame in Coping with Accidental Injury

Chris Brewin

In October 1980 Larry Holmes defeated Muhammed Ali in his bid to regain the world heavyweight boxing title. How Muhammed Ali would explain this defeat immediately became an issue almost as absorbing as the result of the fight itself. Who or what would be blamed for this embarrassing failure to live up to expectations? What was unlikely was that Muhammed Ali would blame himself, and indeed the world soon learned that the defeat was due to the effects of drugs which had been used in his efforts to lose weight. This attribution appeared to serve two useful functions. First, because it was an external attribution, it was protective of self-esteem. The effect of these drugs, so the argument ran, would cause anybody taking them to become dehydrated and unable to perform effectively. The result was therefore no reflection on Ali personally. Secondly, the attribution was an unstable one and the cause something that could easily be remedied next time, the implication being that in any future contest Ali still stood a good chance of winning.

This attributional *tour de force* follows in a long tradition of justifications for failure provided daily by sportsmen, politicians and many others. Who does not weary of the football manager whose team's performance is apparently dogged by bad luck, injury and referees with poor eyesight? It appears that, among public figures at any rate, there is a marked reluctance to blame oneself for failure, a phenomenon that can be equally easily demonstrated in the laboratory (e.g. Weiner and Kukla, 1970; Miller, 1976).

A. SELF-BLAME: A HELP OR A HINDRANCE?

The fact that many people are at pains to deny being at fault leads to the conclusion that blaming oneself for failure can only have damaging consequences. On first examination, the literature would appear to bear this out. Abrams and Finesinger (1953) talked to a largely female sample of cancer patients to determine why they thought they had developed the disease, and were surprised by the number of patients who saw the illness as a form of punishment for their misdeeds. Abrams and Finesinger were of the opinion that those patients who felt guilty and blamed themselves for their misfortune were the ones who coped least well with their illness. In a study of reactions to the death of a close relative, Parkes (1965) reported on the factors which distinguished normal from pathological grief reactions. In his again largely female sample, the pathological reactions were marked by a much greater incidence of ideas of guilt and self-blame. Weisman (1976) also claimed that guilt feelings are maladaptive when they occur as a response to other people falling ill and dying. He felt that "survivor guilt" had no place in the bereavement process and should always be discouraged.

Although not all these studies report data on which to base their conclusions, they are supported by much of the literature on depression. There is a lot of evidence to suggest that depression is correlated with a tendency to blame oneself for negative outcomes (e.g. Klein *et al.*, 1976; Kuiper, 1978; Rizley, 1978; Seligman *et al.*, 1979). Beck (1976) noted that depressed patients were characterized by high levels of self-blame, self-criticism and negative self-evaluation and suggested that it was this cognitive set which was instrumental in bringing about depressed mood. Beck regarded the depressive tendency to take personal responsibility for failure as highly maladaptive and therefore as a target for clinical intervention. In support of this model, Klein *et al.* (1976) found not only that depressed students blamed themselves more than non-depressed students for failure on a cognitive task, but also that their performance on a subsequent task was more impaired. When Klein *et al.* persuaded their depressed subjects not to blame themselves for their failure, however, the behavioural deficits disappeared. Similar ideas have been put forward to account for the exacerbation of anxiety-based disorders by Storms and McCaul (1976). They describe a common syndrome in which individuals become aware of some undesirable aspect of their behaviour, such as overeating or stuttering, which they then ascribe to some part of their character. Perception of this problem or inadequacy in themselves leads to anxiety, guilt and self-deprecation, and this anxiety produces a further exacerbation of the unwanted behaviour. Like these observations by

Storms and McCaul, most discussions of attribution-based therapy have emphasized the value of not blaming oneself (e.g. Valins and Nisbett, 1972).

Self-blame has not always appeared to be maladaptive, however. Chodoff *et al.* (1964) noted that parents of a child with leukaemia often blame themselves for the child's illness, and they suggest that this belief may be more reassuring than the thought that it happened for no reason at all. Bulman and Wortman (1977) interviewed the victims of a wide range of accidents which had all resulted in spinal cord injuries and some degree of paralysis. Bulman and Wortman were interested in the relationship between successful coping and the ways in which the causes of the accident were perceived. They reported that victims who blamed other people for their accidents were rated as being poor copers by the rehabilitation staff, while blaming oneself was associated with better coping.

B. TWO ASPECTS OF SELF-BLAME: STABLE V. UNSTABLE ATTRIBUTIONS

Contrary to any conclusions which might be drawn from the reluctance of public figures to blame themselves, it appears that self-blame may sometimes possess an adaptive and sometimes a maladaptive function. Perhaps the protestations of blamelessness on the part of public figures are not matched by the attributions they make privately to themselves. The evidence suggests that there may be different aspects of self-blame which affect people's ability to cope with misfortune in different ways.

One explanation of the various effects of self-blame is given by the reformulated theory of learned helplessness (see Abramson *et al.*, 1978; and Peterson, Chapter 6). Abramson *et al.* were attempting to explain why the experience of uncontrollability or failure leads to behavioural deficits only in some people and under certain circumstances. Their explanation was that such deficits depend on the causal attribution that individuals make for their failure. If the individual attributes failure to stable unchanging causes, then deficits are likely to persist, while attributions to unstable transient causes produce fewer or no deficits. Similarly, generalization of deficits could be explained by attributions to specific and limited factors versus attributions to global factors affecting many aspects of a person's life. In the view of Abramson *et al.*, whether individuals blamed themselves or external factors might affect their self-esteem, but would not affect the magnitude of behavioural deficits: these are determined solely by attributions along the stable/unstable and global/specific dimensions. It may be inferred that self-blame should only be maladaptive when it involves factors perceived as stable and global as well, such as lack in intelligence, ability or character. Attributions to unstable and specific aspects of oneself should not however lead to behavioural deficits. Janoff-Bulman (1979) has proposed a similar model to account for the varied effects of self-blame, distinguishing between characterological and behavioural self-blame. Characterological self-blame involves blaming oneself for the sort of person one is, and this is regarded as maladaptive. It is maladaptive because, as Abramson *et al.* (1978) suggest, it involves blaming a relatively stable and global cause, but also because such a cause will be uncontrollable. Characterological self-blame therefore tends to lead to self-deprecation and feelings of hopelessness about the future.

Janoff-Bulman goes beyond Abramson *et al.*, however, in suggesting that behavioural self-blame may have a positive and adaptive function. This type of self-blame involves attributions to unstable and specific factors such as one's conduct on a particular occasion, and the significant feature of behavioural self-blame is that causes are seen as potentially modifiable or controllable. Janoff-Bulman suggests that this type of self-blame represents a positive psychological mechanism because of the implication that the individual really is in control of the situation and would be able to respond more effectively in future. There is plenty of evidence in the psychological literature for the desirability of high perceived control (e.g. Glass and Singer, 1972; Langer and Rodin, 1976).

C. SELF-BLAME AND ACCIDENTS

Attribution theory, in looking at self-blame for negative outcomes, has concentrated almost exclusively on those situations in which people attempt a task and then fail. Analyses of these failures, usually in an examination or some other educational context, has given rise to the distinction between blaming some stable aspect of oneself like one's character or ability and blaming unstable factors like effort or one's behaviour in a particular situation. There is now some direct and indirect evidence to suggest that the characterological type of self-blame is maladaptive and is linked to psychopathology, particularly depression (e.g. Janoff-Bulman, 1979).

This analysis of self-blame may not however do justice to other situations involving negative outcomes, for instance when these outcomes are accidental. Unlike examinations, which are known about in advance and can be prepared for, accidents might be expected to attract different types of attribution. There is already evidence that outcomes which violate people's expectations tend to be attributed to unstable, transient causes while expected outcomes tend to be attributed to stable causes (Ames et al., 1976; Frieze and Weiner, 1971). This suggests that accidents will usually give rise to unstable attributions such as luck or chance and that characterological self-blame will only rarely be in evidence. Indeed, the word "accident" may, in one of its meanings, imply that an event was due to chance. In its other common meaning, "accident" simply refers to any unforeseen contingency. It is quite possible that much of the acrimony which surrounds attempts to assign blame for accidents arises from this ambiguity in the use of the word. It is not difficult to picture the misunderstanding which might ensue if one party was attempting to provide an alternative causal attribution for an unforeseen event while the other party assumed that chance was by definition the causal factor in such events. Nevertheless, there are a number of transient causal factors other than luck or chance to which accidents might also be attributed.

As mentioned earlier, Bulman and Wortman (1977) reported that in a largely male sample with spinal injuries there was a relationship between blaming oneself for the outcome of an accident and successful coping. They also found that perceiving the accident to be avoidable was correlated with poor coping, a result which appears paradoxical in the light of the self-blame finding. Presumably, people who tended to blame themselves would also tend to believe that they could have avoided the accident, and both beliefs should therefore be related to good coping. The implication is that the questions Bulman and Wortman asked about the amount victims blamed themselves and about the avoidability of the accident represented two quite separate dimensions of the victims' perceived responsibility for their accident. Apparently, these two dimensions each had their own implication for the victims' ability to cope.

What were these two dimensions? There is no indication that they represented stable and unstable factors, or that any characterological self-blame was involved. Bulman and Wortman suggested that the most successful copers were those who were taking part in some freely chosen activity, whose behaviour was in no way out-of-the-ordinary, and who saw the accident as following logically and inevitably from their actions. This description calls to mind the distinction that has been made by several authors between causal responsibility and culpability (e.g. Shaver, 1975; Schroeder and Linder, 1976; Harvey and Rule, 1978). Causal responsibility refers to the extent to which an individual's actions have resulted in a particular outcome while culpability represents a moral evaluation of the deservingness of blame for an outcome. To illustrate this distinction, consider the case of a driver whose vehicle collides with another car which has pulled out in front. If the other car has pulled out unexpectedly and without warning, the first driver is likely to feel that the accident could perhaps have been avoided by driving more slowly or by showing better anticipation, but that his or her behaviour was quite reasonable under the circumstances. In other words, the driver is likely to feel some degree of causal responsibility, but not to feel particularly culpable. If on the other hand the first driver had been day-dreaming instead of concentrating on the road and had failed to notice that the other car had signalled its intention to pull out in good time, the driver is likely to feel not only causally responsible, but culpable as well. These examples can be contrasted with the case of a driver whose car is stationary at traffic lights when another vehicle drives into the back of it. In these circumstances the driver is unlikely to feel either causally responsible or culpable, but may well feel highly indignant!

Applying these ideas to Bulman and Wortman's data, it seems plausible that their question about self-blame was eliciting judgements of causal responsibility. Those who felt causally responsible for the accident coped better, perhaps because they perceived a logical relation between their actions and what happened to them, preserving their belief in their ability to exercise control in their lives. Victims who perceived that they could have avoided the accident may on the other hand have felt culpable and angry with themselves, tending to cope less well because they perceived themselves as having been the author of an unnecessary misfortune. Feelings of culpability may be particularly difficult to deal with when, as for these accident victims, the consequences are permanent and severe.

The distinction between causal responsibility and culpability is superficially similar to Janoff-Bulman's (1979) distinction between behavioural and characterological self-blame, but there are important differences. The distinction between causal responsibility and culpability is concerned with two varieties of behavioural self-blame, or in other words with two aspects of the relationship between some particular behaviour and the events which followed. In this scheme the fact that someone was grossly negligent or culpable on one occasion does not imply anything about a general tendency to be negligent. This is important because in the majority of cases steps can be taken to ensure that similar accidents do not occur again. Dangerous working practices can often be amended to reduce risk, and accident victims may often react to their misfortune by saying "Well, I'll know never to do *that* again." The fact that similar accidents often can be effectively eliminated in future, if the appropriate measures are taken, is another reason why accidents should rarely attract attributions to stable factors. In principle most causal factors should, in the light of the accident, be modifiable to prevent further mishap. Nevertheless, there may be certain circumstances in which attributions to stable factors are appropriate. The closest equivalent to characterological self-blame would appear to be "accident-proneness". This concept has sometimes been used in occupational psychology to explain why a small proportion of the work force accounts for a relatively large proportion of the accidents. Research has suggested, however, that the idea of individuals who are permanently accident-prone is a myth; what does seem to happen is that individuals may go through a period in their lives, often when there are domestic or financial stressors, when they become temporarily more accident-prone (Schulzinger, 1954). Accident proneness may also be used as an explanation by victims themselves, usually to account for minor, everyday mishaps. It seems unlikely that it would be a common explanation for more serious accidents, though, since these occur comparatively rarely. A succession of serious accidents might however make such an attribution more likely.

The other situation in which more stable factors might be invoked is where there are obvious environmental hazards which constitute a permanent threat to people in general. The situation may sometimes arise at work, for instance, where there are pressures on management and work force which maintain unacceptably high levels of risk. Employees on piecework may find that they cannot earn enough unless they take short-cuts and accept a certain level of risk. Alternatively, adherence to safety procedures might cause an employee to be seriously out of step with his colleagues on a production line. On the management side there may be considerable difficulties in replacing or adapting a dangerous machine or working practice without disrupting production, and certain changes might demand a large capital investment. Circumstances undoubtedly arise in which industrial accident victims return to work and find that a procedure responsible for their accident and known to be dangerous has not been altered. In these cases stable attributions would be appropriate.

The study of attributions for accidents requires a different framework from that which has been developed for looking at failures in tests and examinations, a framework which takes into account that to label an event as an accident may itself be a kind of attribution. The label "accident" (in its sense of an event due to chance) may be applied to an event in order to avoid attaching blame to oneself or to others. In the same way, the assignment of causal responsibility and of culpability will not simply reflect characteristics of the situation, but will involve people's desire to avoid or to accept blame. These desires may simply represent different sorts of coping strategy, but Bulman and Wortman's (1977) data suggest that these strategies will not all be equally effective.

D. A STUDY OF INDUSTRIAL ACCIDENTS

A study was designed to investigate further the relationship between attributions for accidents and subsequent coping, and to determine whether accident victims themselves recognize and use the theoretical distinction between causal responsibility and culpability. The main hypothesis was that effective coping should be positively correlated with feelings of causal responsibility, but negatively correlated with feelings of culpability.

Male victims of minor industrial accidents were selected for study for the practical reason that they were in plentiful supply. They were an interesting group for a number of reasons. First, the victims of minor industrial accidents generally have to return to the situation in which they were injured and to continue working there as normal. In this respect they differ from the victims of more serious accidents, who have primarily to cope with their disability, and from the victims of other accidents who can subsequently avoid finding themselves in similar situations. Secondly, they were generally under considerable pressures to return to work, both external financial pressures from loss of earnings and internal pressure from the boredom which arose in many cases from spending an unaccustomed amount of time at home. With these powerful external forces in evidence, and with the minor injuries requiring only a relatively short period of rehabilitation, the attributional hypotheses were being put to a stringent test.

The subjects in this study all received their injuries at their place of work rather than at home or on the way to or from work. The accidents occurred most commonly while lifting heavy objects, but a large number were the result of slipping, falling or bumping into things while walking from one place to another. Some involved vehicles or faulty machinery, but in relatively few cases was there a single clear-cut cause of the accident. The sample consisted of 70 white male manual workers employed in the Sheffield area. Any subject employed to do clerical, supervisory or managerial work was excluded from the sample, leaving a mixture of skilled, semi-skilled and unskilled manual workers from a variety of public and private industries. The occupations best represented were miners, steelworkers, fitters, drivers and machinists. The age range was 16 to 66 years, with an average age of 35 years. Subjects were approached on their arrival at an orthopaedic out-patient clinic to which they were generally referred from Casualty on the day following their accident. All the subjects had suspected bone injuries, and the vast majority were found to have sustained fractures, most frequently of fingers and toes. These injuries required an average of one month off work.

Subjects were interviewed twice, once immediately after their accident and again after they had been back at work for two weeks. At this second interview the sample size was reduced from 70 to 42. Six per cent of the original sample refused the second interview and 18% could not be contacted. The remaining 16% were lost from the study because they had returned to work immediately following the accident, in spite of their injury. This latter group was excluded from further study in order to preserve a minimum period of a month between first and second interviews. At both interviews subjects were given a number of statements about their accident with which they had to agree or disagree on a five-point scale. Six statements were designed to measure causal responsibility (Examples: "My actions contributed to causing the accident"; "My actions were unconnected with why the accident occurred"), and six were designed to measure culpability (Examples: "My actions were in my opinion proper ones under the circumstances"; "My actions were more careless than usual"). Half the items were positively and half negatively worded. Because no other measures of causal responsibility or culpability were available to check the validity of these items, factor analysis was performed to confirm that the items did indeed form two groups in accordance with the theoretical distinction.

Effectiveness of coping was measured in two ways. First, a measure was taken of how quickly the subject returned to work relative to the expected length of absence from work. For each subject, two senior orthopaedic surgeons provided estimates of how long the average man with this particular injury and doing this particular job would take to get back to work. The mean of these two estimates was then divided by the actual time taken to return to work, and this fraction constituted the measure of recovery rate. Roughly half the subjects returned sooner, and half later than expected, and the wide variation in recovery rate indicated that medical factors were not the only influence at work in this situation. The second way in which coping was measured was by asking subjects to complete the Stress and Arousal Checklist (Mackay et al., 1978) and the 12-item version of the General Health Questionnaire (Goldberg, 1972) at the time of the second interview, two weeks after their return to work. These two measures were highly intercorrelated but were relatively independent of the measure of recovery rate. The data therefore suggested that recovery after an accident contained at least two distinct components, one concerned with speed of return to work and one with self-reported feelings of health and well-being.

Factor analysis of the causal responsibility and culpability items indicated that accident victims did indeed observe this distinction when they responded to the questionnaire, both immediately after their accident and once they were back at work. The distinction was only important, however, at the time of the second interview, where the first two factors accounted for 44% of the total variance and were composed of items which clearly mirrored the theoretical distinction. At the time of the first interview the factors corresponding to causal responsibility and culpability were minor ones, accounting for little of the variance. In the subsequent analysis the scores on items uniquely characterizing the factors were therefore combined to provide a single score for causal responsibility and culpability at each of the two interviews.

As might be expected from the results of these factor analyses, it was only when causal responsibility and culpability were measured at the second interview that they correlated with the measures of effective coping. The reasons for this are discussed more fully later on, but the most likely explanation is that attributions for complex events such as accidents do change considerably over time and cannot be reliably measured as early as two or three days after the accident. At the second interview, as predicted, the more accident victims reported feeling causally responsible for their accidents, the less they reported feeling anxious and tense ($r = 0.31$, $P < 0.025$) and the more they reported feeling alert and active ($r = 0.25$, $P < 0.06$). Feeling causally responsible was not, however, correlated with symptom scores on the General Health Questionnaire or with speed of return to work.

The effects of feeling culpable were, however, quite contrary to those predicted. It was expected that feeling culpable should be maladaptive and correlate with ineffective coping. In fact culpability did not correlate at all with mood ratings or symptoms, but those subjects who reported feeling culpable had in general returned to work earlier ($r = 0.40$, $P < 0.02$). There was thus no evidence that in this sample feeling culpable was in any way maladaptive. It may be recalled that Bulman and Wortman (1977) asked their subjects whether they thought they could have avoided the accident, and in the present study subjects were similarly asked whether they could have prevented the accident occurring. This item, as expected, correlated significantly with the measure of culpability ($r = 0.42$, $P < 0.005$) and with speed of return to work ($r = 0.31$, $P < 0.025$), but not with the measure of causal responsibility ($r = 0.09$, n.s.). These results support the idea that Bulman and Wortman's questions were measuring two distinct aspects of self-blame, and correspond to the two factors described here.

One implication of the finding that causal responsibility and culpability are associated with effective coping is that there may be certain categories of accident, particularly those which leave accident victims feeling in no way causally responsible or culpable, which are likely to cause a large number of rehabilitation problems. One such category is the accident that occurs due to some unforeseeable environmental fault or failure, whether this be mechanical breakdown, structural failure, or the careless actions of a workmate, to name some examples from the present sample. On the basis of subjects' accounts of their accidents a group of 14 such cases were distinguished and compared with the rest of the samples. Subjects involved in this category of accident predictably rated themselves as less causally responsible when interviewed both at the time of the accident ($r = 0 \cdot 21$, $P < 0 \cdot 05$) and after their return to work ($r = 0 \cdot 29$, $P < 0 \cdot 05$). They also rated themselves as less culpable, although not significantly so. More importantly, subjects involved in this category of accident took longer to get back to work ($r = 0 \cdot 29$, $P < 0 \cdot 01$), and once back at work reported feeling more tense and anxious ($r = 0 \cdot 19$, $P < 0 \cdot 08$) and less alert and active ($r = 0 \cdot 23$, $P < 0 \cdot 05$).

The other category of people who were most clearly at risk were those who had several accidents over the previous two years. Compared with all other subjects this group rated themselves as more culpable, both at the time of the accident ($r = 0 \cdot 23$, $P < 0 \cdot 05$) and after return to work ($r = 0 \cdot 30$, $P < 0 \cdot 025$). In their case, however, feeling culpable was not associated with returning to work more quickly; they showed a non-significant tendency to get back to work more slowly ($r = 0 \cdot 12$, $P < 0 \cdot 17$), and when they did return were more likely to report symptoms on the General Health Questionnaire ($r = 0 \cdot 25$, $P < 0 \cdot 05$) and to say they felt tense and anxious ($r = 0 \cdot 18$, $P < 0 \cdot 09$). This confirms previous research indicating that employees involved in several accidents are likely to be in poor health (Smiley, 1955).

E. SELF-BLAME FOR ACCIDENTS AND EFFECTIVE COPING

The results of the present study and that of Bulman and Wortman (1977), even though conducted with very different populations and using different dependent measures, confirm that, among males at least, there is an association between blaming oneself for an accident and effective coping. The fact that these results are at present limited to males must be emphasized in view of the evidence that there are consistent sex differences in attributions and attributional styles (e.g. Nicholls, 1975; Dweck and Reppucci, 1973; Ickes and Layden, 1978). In addition, the present study suggests that it is blame in the sense of feeling causally responsible which is consistently important, presumably because it increases an individual's sense of personal control over the environment.

Where the two studies appear to disagree is in the significance for coping of feelings of culpability. In Bulman and Wortman's study an item which appears to be measuring culpability was associated with poor coping, while in the study of industrial accidents feelings of culpability were associated with getting back to work more quickly. This discrepancy may be due to the fact that the victims of the industrial accidents had only minor injuries and were able to deal with their feelings of anger and guilt towards themselves by taking some positive action. This course was not open to Bulman and Wortman's much more severely injured sample, who may have found it difficult, if not impossible, to assuage their feelings of culpability. The suggestion is that feelings of culpability are only maladaptive when the consequences are particularly severe or when they cannot be relieved by taking some remedial action.

It is also of interest that subjects in the industrial accident study who had had other accidents previously tended to feel more culpable and to attribute the accident more to stable patterns of behaviour on their part. This combination of attributions is very reminiscent of characterological self-blame (Janoff-Bulman, 1979) and suggests that the poor health reported by these subjects may be due in part to a different attributional mechanism. This reflects the fact that subjects' experience of accidents differs considerably and hence creates a variety of contexts in which attributions have to be made.

Care must be taken, however, in interpreting the results of these correlational studies. It is possible, for instance, that accident victims who find they are coping without difficulty are more disposed to say that they were causally responsible for their accident. This interpretation is less likely because in some cases, for instance where there was some unforeseeable environmental fault or failure, it can be shown that the subjects felt little causal responsibility two or three days after the accident, long before their return to work. In their case at least, these attributions clearly pre-dated any attempts at coping. It seems even less likely that feelings of culpability should arise as a result of returning to work early; in the absence of any plausible alternative, the most promising conclusion would seem to be that self-blame can indeed influence subsequent behaviour.

F. IMPLICATIONS FOR CLINICAL PRACTICE

A number of practical consequences follow from these findings. Perhaps the most important is that victims' understanding of why the accident occurred should be regarded as a significant element in their rehabilitation, permitting the early identification of some rehabilitation problems or failures. Although it should be emphasized that it is the individual's perception that is the important element, and that such perception may or may not coincide with a general consensus about the causes of the accident, nevertheless accidents clearly provoked by some external uncontrollable factor are likely to create more problems in subsequent adjustment.

There are a number of possible approaches in dealing with the psychological effects of accidents attributed to uncontrollable external factors. First, a therapist could attempt to encourage new attributions involving adaptive self-blame where the accident victims seemed to have overlooked the contribution their own behaviour made to the accident. This approach would probably be impossible when either this contribution was very small or when the accident victims for some other reason were anxious to deny their own causal involvement. Secondly, a therapist could help the victim to deal with feelings of anxiety and tension likely to accompany a return to work by conventional anxiety management techniques. Such feelings of tension would in most cases be mild but the author has seen a number of severe phobic and general anxiety states which developed following an industrial accident. The aim of such an approach would be to enable victims to anticipate their own likely reactions and to feel that these reactions were controllable. The victims of more serious accidents are likely to be particularly in need of this sort of treatment method or approach, which recognizes that their sense of the predictability of the environment and of their own personal effectiveness may have suffered a severe blow.

Although therapists may help accident victims to cope with their feelings of culpability and loss of effectiveness, there is much that other agents can achieve. Industrial accident victims appear to alter their pattern of self-blame as time goes on, and their attributions immediately after the accident will not necessarily be the same one month later. There was a suggestion in this study that judgements of culpability are more likely to fluctuate over time than judgements of causal responsibility. Victims' comparison of their own experience with that of colleagues and the availability of information about the accident are two factors which could explain these fluctuations.

The results of this study suggest that firms in particular could play a significant role in industrial accident rehabilitation. Most accident victims received no visits or enquiries about their welfare from employers, which was sometimes a source of considerable resentment, especially when the victim did not feel responsible for the accident. As might be expected, accident victims who were more satisfied with their job and who were less angry with their employers over the accident also tended to show better rehabilitation. There is therefore some evidence that getting back to work is related not only to perceptions about the accident, but to perceptions about the job as a whole. There is clearly a lot of scope for employers to try to improve relationships with accident victims and to be more concerned with their welfare. In particular, they should pay attention to employees who have had a number of accidents or who have been injured through no fault of their own. Quite apart from reasons of common humanity, the evidence suggests that effort spent in assuring the employee that steps have been taken to prevent the accident occurring again will be well worthwhile.

G. SUMMARY

The attribution of blame to oneself has traditionally been seen as a maladaptive response to problems and one likely to exacerbate them. Several varieties of self-blame can, however, be distinguished, some with adaptive and some with maladaptive consequences. It appears to be maladaptive to blame aspects of oneself which are perceived as stable or permanent—lack of ability or intelligence are commonly given as examples of failings usually felt to be permanent. This has also been termed characterological self-blame, in contrast to behavioural self-blame. Behavioural self-blame, the attribution of blame to one's specific acts of commission or omission, may on the other hand be adaptive because it emphasizes the contingency between what a person does and what subsequently happens.

Studies of accident victims show that other distinctions need to be made within the concept of behavioural self-blame. When considering the relationship between one's actions and the occurrence of an accident, it is possible to distinguish attributions of causal responsibility from attributions of culpability. While it appears to be adaptive to feel causally responsible for an accident, the effects of feeling culpable may vary according to circumstances. More research is needed to clarify the relationship between culpability and coping and to look at the effects of other parameters like the sex of the victim.

Studies of accident victims can illuminate new aspects of the attribution process and can attest to its importance in people's lives. Field studies are important because they indicate the limitations of studying attributions without regard to their context. In an industrial setting, for instance, the significance of the attribution process may be influenced by attitudes towards work and by how management responds to accidents. In general, however, it seems that the accident victim's perception of events has an important role to play in rehabilitation. Far from being maladaptive, it appears that the perception of self-blame can have therapeutic consequences so long as people's regard for themselves as effective agents is thereby enhanced.

REFERENCES

Abrams, R. D. and Finesinger, J. E. (1953). Guilt reactions in patients with cancer. *Cancer* **6**, 474–482.

Abramson, L. Y., Seligman, M. E. P. and Teasdale, J. D. (1978). Learned helplessness in humans: critique and reformulation. *Journal of Abnormal Psychology* **87**, 49–74.

Ames, C., Ames, R. and Felker, D. W. (1976). Informational and dispositional determinants of children's achievement attributions. *Journal of Educational Psychology* **68**, 63–69.

Beck, A. T. (1976). *Cognitive Therapy and Emotional Disorders*. New York: International Universities Press.

Bulman, R. J. and Wortman, C. B. (1977). Attributions of blame and coping in the "real world": severe accident victims react to their lot. *Journal of Personality and Social Psychology* **35**, 351–365.

Chodoff, P., Friedman, S. and Hamburg, D. (1964). Stress, defenses and coping behaviour: observation in parents of children with malignant disease. *American Journal of Psychiatry* **120**, 743–749.

Dweck, C. S. and Reppucci, N. D. (1973). Learned helplessness and reinforcement responsibility in children. *Journal of Personality and Social Psychology* **25**, 109–116.

Frieze, I. and Weiner, B. (1971). Cue utilization and attributional judgements for success and failure. *Journal of Personality* **39**, 591–606.

Glass, D. and Singer, J. (1972). *Urban Stress*. London and New York: Academic Press.

Goldberg, D. (1972). *The Detection of Psychiatric Illness by Questionnaire*. London: Oxford University Press.

Harvey, M. D. and Rule, B. G. (1978). Moral evaluations and judgements of responsibility. *Personality and Social Psychology Bulletin* **4**, 583–588.

Ickes, W. and Layden, M. A. (1978). Attributional styles. *In* J. H. Harvey, W. Ickes and R. F. Kidd (eds) *New Directions in Attribution Research* (vol. 2). Hillsdale, New Jersey: Erlbaum.

Janoff-Bulman, R. (1979). Characterological vs. behavioural self-blame: inquiries into depression and rape. *Journal of Personality and Social Psychology* **37**, 1798–1809.

Klein, D. C., Fencil-Morse, E. and Seligman, M. E. P. (1976). Learned helplessness, depression and the attribution of failure. *Journal of Personality and Social Psychology* **33**, 508–516.

Kuiper, N. A. (1978). Depression and causal attributions for success and failure. *Journal of Personality and Social Psychology* **36**, 236–246.

Langer, E. J. and Rodin, J. (1976). The effects of choice and enhanced responsibility for the aged: a field experiment in an institutional setting. *Journal of Personality and Social Psychology* **33**, 951–955.

Mackay, C., Cox, T., Burrows, G. and Lazzerini, T. (1978). An inventory for the measurement of self-reported stress and arousal. *British Journal of Social and Clinical Psychology* **17**, 283–284.

Miller, D. T. (1976). Ego involvement and attributions for success and failure. *Journal of Personality and Social Psychology* **34**, 901–906.

Nicholls, J. G. (1975). Causal attributions and other achievement-related cognitions: effects of task outcomes, attainment value and sex. *Journal of Personality and Social Psychology* **31**, 379–389.

Parkes, C. M. (1965). Bereavement and mental illness. Part I. A clinical study of the grief of bereaved psychiatric patients. *British Journal of Medical Psychology* **38**, 1–12.

Rizley, R. (1978). Depression and distortion in the attribution of causality. *Journal of Abnormal Psychology* **87**, 32–48.

Schroeder, D. A. and Linder, D. E. (1976). Effects of actors' causal role, outcome severity and knowledge of prior accidents upon attributions of responsibility. *Journal of Experimental Social Psychology* **12**, 340–356.

Schulzinger, M. S. (1954). A closer look at "accident-proneness". *National Safety News* **69**, 6.

Seligman, M. E. P., Abramson, L. Y., Semmel, A. and von Baeyer, C. (1979). Depressive attributional style. *Journal of Abnormal Psychology* **88**, 242–247.

Shaver, K. G. (1975). *An Introduction to Attribution Processes.* Cambridge, Massachusetts: Winthrop.

Smiley, J. A. (1955). A clinical study of a group of accident-prone workers. *British Journal of Industrial Medicine* **12**, 263–278.

Storms, M. D. and McCaul, K. D. (1976). Attribution processes and the emotional exacerbation of dysfunctional behaviour. *In* J. H. Harvey, W. J. Ickes and R. F. Kidd (eds) *New Directions in Attribution Research* (vol. 1). Hillsdale, New Jersey: Erlbaum.

Valins, S. and Nisbett, R. E. (1972). Attribution processes in the development and treatments of emotional disorders. *In* E. E. Jones, D. E. Kanouse, H. A. Kelley, R. E. Nisbett, S. Valins and B. Weiner (eds) *Attribution: Perceiving the Causes of Behaviour.* Morristown, New Jersey: General Learning Press.

Weiner, B. and Kukla, A. (1970). An attributional analysis of achievement motivation. *Journal of Personality and Social Psychology* **15**, 1–20.

Weisman, A. D. (1976). Coping with untimely death. *In* Moos, R. D. (ed.) *Human Adaptation.* Lexington, Massachusetts: Heath.

8
Attributional Aspects of Medicine

Fraser N. Watts

A. INTRODUCTION

There are few things about which people are more concerned to have explanations than their illnesses, though the difficulties in arriving at them are considerable. Most people's awareness of their bodily processes is limited, though some pay more attention to them than others. Even when an area of bodily discomfort or abnormal functioning has been identified, it is hard to know what illness if any it represents. It is in the nature of things that most people have limited experience of serious illness; they have had no opportunity of learning the various symptoms through first-hand experience. Even when an illness has been correctly identified, it is difficult to work out in retrospect what has caused it. It is sometimes difficult to discriminate at first between a mild condition like indigestion and a serious one such as a heart attack (Cowie, 1976), but there is a powerful inclination to arrive at some view or other as to what has caused the symptoms that are experienced. Uncertainty is unwelcome to most people, especially about something such as serious illness. The vast majority of patients will therefore reach some view or other about the nature of an illness and what has caused it.

This chapter will be concerned with these explanations of illness. In particular it will examine their significance within the framework of attribution theory, though so far there has been surprisingly little attempt to apply attribution theory to medicine (Rodin, 1978). Nevertheless, there is reason to believe it is relevant. As attribution theory would suggest, patients' emotional reactions to their illness are closely related to the attributions they hold. How patients cooperate in the treatment of their condition is also influenced by their attributions. For such reasons it is always important for clinicians to be aware of their patients' attributions. On occasions they will wish not just to be aware of them, but to try to modify them using the methods of attribution therapy (Kopel and Arkowitz, 1975) to help patients respond to their illness more constructively.

Clinicians also need to be alert to the systematic differences that may obtain between their own attributions and those of their patients. Rodin (1978) has suggested that doctors as observers may be much more likely to make attributions to stable factors, whereas patients as actors will invoke temporary factors. Thus doctors might explain a patient not taking medication in terms of his uncooperative personality, the patient in contrast might emphasize the fact that the medication made him nauseous. There is probably a similar tendency for doctors to ascribe symptoms to stable causes to a greater degree than patients.

B. LAY EXPLANATIONS OF ILLNESS

There are a variety of factors that will influence patients' explanations of their illnesses. Their intelligence, medical knowledge and exposure to illness all impose constraints. Particularly important are the explanations of illness that are the norm in a patient's social or cultural group, and the effect of the patient's habitual methods of coping with stress on his or her reactions to illness.

The impact of cultural norms is illustrated in Marby's (1964) field study of patients' explanations of their illness in rural and urban parts of Kentucky. The urban residents were more likely, for example, to explain a range of conditions including headaches, common colds and heart racing in terms of situational factors like their place of work. In contrast the rural residents invoked inheritance more commonly than their urban counterparts to explain heart racing; and germs and viruses to explain colds. There are presumably widespread cultural assumptions of this kind about the explanation of illness. Marby relates the anecdote of a patient in rural Kentucky with eye irritation who was given a medical explanation for the condition by the doctor and prescribed some ointment. As it was clear to the doctor that his patient could not comprehend his explanations he added "Some folks would call it weed poisoning", on the sound assumption that an agreed explanation of this kind would increase the chances of the prescription being followed. It was the "weed poison" explanation that the patient remembered and later said he had been given by the doctor.

The explanations people favour for illnesses will also reflect the methods they habitually use for coping with stress. Bard and Dyk (1956) noted that 47 of 100 medical patients they were studying in another connection spontaneously expressed beliefs about the cause of their illness, but that very few of these appeared to have a rational basis. Many blamed themselves or blamed some other person for their illness; the one which they blamed seemed to reflect their preferred ways of handling emotional stress and their general personality development. Patients' emotional reactions to illness will influence the range of explanations they are able to accept. Chodoff *et al.* (1964) pointed out that the parents of children with leukaemia find it difficult to accept that there is no established explanation of why their children have contracted the disease, and that they may even apparently prefer to blame themselves rather than accept this uncertainty. Voluntary self-blame of this kind may also be influenced by feelings of guilt about the child that have some quite different origin.

There has so far been insufficient attention given to methods of eliciting patients' explanations, though the problems involved are considerable. For most clinical purposes a structured interview will be the best assessment method. It is common for patients to present initially with a single and simplistic explanation of their illness (Bard and Dyk, 1956). However, it is an established problem in interviewing that patients can hold a variety of views on a particular subject, but tend to only present one of these initially. For example, adolescents have a spectrum of vocational aspirations ranging from the realistic to the unrealistic but tend to present a job choice at just one or other end of the spectrum in response to an initial interview question (Small, 1953). The interviewer exploring a patient's explanation for an illness needs to spend long enough and ask questions in sufficiently varied ways to elicit the range of explanatory ideas the patient may hold. Frequently those ideas will not be integrated into a complex model of the interaction of the relevant causal factors. Indeed many patients seem to have great difficulty in grasping interactive-causal models of illness; but they may nevertheless be able to entertain a varied series of discrete explanations. Different explanations may be entertained at different levels of awareness. Weisman (1976) has pointed out that dying patients may consciously believe that they have an illness from which they can recover but may nevertheless have some "hidden knowledge" that it is a terminal condition. Perhaps many patients can entertain at some level of awareness more explanatory factors regarding their medical condition than they care to admit fully either to themselves or others.

There is also the problem that the answers elicited from patients about their attributions may largely reflect the way questions are asked. Farr (1977) has commented critically from this point of view on Herzlick's (1973) study of the attributions of 80 naive informants about health and illness. The interviews were only loosely structured and were designed to provide informants with an opportunity to give their views on several broad themes to do with health and illness, without negotiation or criticism from the interviewer. Nevertheless the informants were guided towards particular topics and in particular were invited to give their views on both health and illness. Farr's point is that it is inherent in the biases known to govern attributions that, faced with a contrast between a good outcome (health) and a bad outcome (illness), health will be attributed internally and illness externally (e.g. to the modern urban environment). However, it cannot be assumed that, for example, people believe that with no urban stress there would be no illness. Other ways of asking questions could have elicited different answers; those that were obtained could have been predicted from the way the interview was conducted. Clinicians who are seeking to elicit patients' attributions need to be aware that the way they ask questions can influence the answers they get.

C. INTERNAL AND EXTERNAL ATTRIBUTIONS OF ILLNESS

An enduring theme in attribution therapy has been the proposition that if symptoms are attributed to a neutral, external cause they will be less disruptive and cause less distress than if attributed to a personal, internal cause (Storms and McCaul, 1976). The meaning of the terms "internal" and "external" in this context has been explained in the introductory chapter of this book and will not be discussed again here. If this proposition about the effects of internal and external attributions is correct, it suggests an approach to treatment that would be especially relevant to patients whose worry about their symptoms disables them, unnecessarily.

An early application of this approach was to the treatment of insomnia (Storms and Nisbett, 1970). Some subjects were given what was in fact a placebo pill at bedtime, which they were told would produce symptoms such as increased alertness, increased heartrate and increased body temperature (i.e. the symptoms of heightened arousal that the insomniacs usually experienced on retiring to bed). Because they were able to reattribute these symptoms to the pill, it was hypothesized that they would be less disturbed by them and get to sleep sooner. This proved to be the case. Control subjects who were given a pill which they were told was a sedative, and to which they could not therefore attribute their arousal symptoms, took longer to get off to sleep.

Liebhart (1974) has reported an analogous application of a reattribution method for a more troublesome medical problem, cardiac neurosis. These are patients who worry excessively about relatively minor cardiac problems, and who are thus disabled by them to an unnecessary extent and for an unnecessary length of time. Patients who were provided with a pill to which they could attribute their symptoms showed significantly less affective, somatic and behavioural deterioration, as compared with control subjects who were either given an irrelevant placebo or put on a waiting list.

These are two of the more medically relevant of a series of experimental treatments based on the so-called "misattribution" phenomenon. Unfortunately, the effectiveness of this attributional approach to insomnia has not been replicated (Kellogg and Baron, 1975; Bootzin et al., 1976). In addition, methodological weaknesses have left the interpretation of reattribution effects very much in doubt. As Calvert-Boyanowsky and Leventhal (1975) have pointed out, there has generally been no check on whether the patients have reattributed their symptoms in the intended way. Also, the experimental condition has generally differed from the control in that it has included the provision of a list of arousal symptoms and at least *some* plausible rationale of why they are occurring. There remains some doubt about whether there is any particular advantage in attributions to an external cause.

It is also worth noting that helpful external attributions can be adopted spontaneously and do not always need to be supplied. This is clear from Rodin's (1976) study of attribution to the menstrual cycle. Her subjects were given tasks which were presented in a stressful way designed to produce symptoms of arousal. Those subjects who generally experienced prominent menstrual symptoms and were currently at the relevant stage of the menstrual cycle attributed this experimentally induced stress to menstruation and were less impaired in their task performance as a result. The menstrual cycle may have functioned here as a reassuring, external attribution. But, more importantly, these subjects had at least *some* readily available explanation for the unusual arousal symptoms that were experienced. This is likely to be what was most important. The most significant difference is probably between the patient who is worrying over unexplained symptoms and the patient who has something specific to attribute them to. It will help if the attribution is a reassuring one. It will also help if it is correct, because correct attributions will generally be more plausible and be better confirmed by experience. Correct attributions may also lead to more appropriate self-regulatory behaviours. Where these criteria are in conflict it is a matter for clinical judgement what attribution will be most helpful for the individual patient.

Psychological and Organic Attributions

It is interesting to reconsider attributions to psychological or organic causes of symptoms in the light of the proposition that symptoms attributed to an external cause are less disabling than symptoms attributed to a personal cause. Patients who attribute somatically based symptoms to internal, psychological causes may be unnecessarily disturbed by them. Rodin (1978) has discussed some of the symptoms of obesity in this connection. The hormone-induced changes in circadian rhythms found in obesity may be misattributed by patients to emotional arousal. Equally, the hyper-reactivity to tasty foods mediated by high basal insulin levels may be misattributed to gluttony or depression. The symptoms of obesity will be unnecessarily distressing when misattributed in this way.

The reverse problem, symptoms that have a predominantly psychological basis being attributed to an organic origin, is probably much more common. Imboden's work on recovery from infectious diseases illustrates one context in which this occurs. He first carried out a study on patients who had had brucellosis in recent years, divided into (a) those in whom the condition had been acute (b) those in whom it had been chronic but who were now recovered and (c) those chronic patients who were still presenting symptoms (Imboden *et al.*, 1959). All three groups were administered a battery of psychological tests and given a psychiatric interview. The two chronic groups differed from the acute group on several scales of the MMPI, especially the depression scale. The chronic patients who still had their symptoms were also distinguished by a preoccupation with bodily symptoms, a strong conviction that they had an organic disease, coupled with an assertion of good "emotional" health and an unwillingness to discuss any personal or emotional issues. This is a pattern that has been reported in many "psychosomatic" patients and will be discussed more fully below.

What interested Imboden was the similarity between the symptoms of chronic brucellosis (fatigue, headache, myalgia, arthralgia, nervousness and depression) and symptoms of anxiety or depression, thus providing considerable scope for confusion between the two. The possibility arises that such patients were in fact experiencing psychological symptoms but misattributing them to an organic cause that no longer applied. The higher depression scores of both chronic groups on the MMPI supports this view, but the interpretation of the relationship is unclear because the personality tests were administered *after* the onset of brucellosis. Because of this possibility Imboden *et al.* (1961) subsequently carried out a study of influenza patients in which the psychological tests were administered several months before its onset. Some of the influenza patients continued to complain of various symptoms (especially tiredness and weakness) three weeks after the end of the acute infection. These patients could be predicted from the depression scale of the preadministered MMPI. The explanation Imboden *et al.* favour is that these patients had a general proneness to develop depression, did in fact do so as a response to the influenza, and then misattributed their depressive symptoms to a continuation of the influenza. Another possibility is that these patients simply had a tendency to complain of physical symptoms more readily than other patients, and so continued to complain of the mild symptoms they experienced after the infection had abated. It is consistent with this that the chronic patients also obtained higher scores on the Cornell Medical Index which was administered at the same time as the MMPI. However, such an explanation of chronicity in terms of a greater general tendency to complain of symptoms would be expected to be detectable also at the acute stage which it apparently was not.

Assuming that Imboden's misattribution theory of delayed recovery is correct, what are its clinical implications? The hope would be that if patients were able to avoid the mistaken attribution of their continuing symptoms to infection they would be less disabled by them. But rather than trying to correct the misattribution once it had arisen it would be better to prepare patients during the early infectious stage and to alert them to the changing pattern of symptoms. If these patients knew what to expect they should, like surgical patients (Cohen and Lazarus, 1979), show faster recovery.

Attributional Aspects of Hypochondriasis

Delayed recovery from an infectious disease is one example of the general illness behaviour problem of hypochondriasis which, as Pilowski (1967) has shown, has three main components, preoccupation with bodily symptoms, disease phobia (recurrent anxieties about suffering from a variety of diseases) and disease conviction (a stubborn belief that one is suffering from a serious disease, often coupled with somewhat paranoid attitudes to medical staff who do not share this view). Disease phobia and disease conviction require rather different attributional approaches.

Disease phobic patients are likely to misattribute their symptoms to one of the illnesses that they are anxious about getting. The first stage in dealing with this phenomenon clinically is to get the patient to see what is happening. Once there is agreement about this, he or she can be taught to monitor the development of these disease-phobic misattributions of physical symptoms, to recognize them for what they are, and to avoid believing them. For example, patients who had mild stomach pains to which they were hypersensitive, and who were anxious about having a heart attack, might mistakenly take the pain to be a cardiac symptom. Such patients can be taught to recognize (a) the number and variety of pains people experience, (b) that in as far as they are aware of more pains than average, this arises largely from their hypersensitivity to them (c) that the vast majority of pains do not indicate any pathology, (d) that their attribution of pains to a cardiac condition reflects their disease anxiety, and (e) that this attribution is probably false. Establishing this at a rational level will not altogether stop the mistaken attributions occurring spontaneously. The patient will also need to learn to recognize them when they occur and recollect his rational stance to help him to dismiss his hypochondriacal attribution. This is done in much the same way as an anxious patient can use coping self-talk to exclude "negative" self-talk about his inability to cope with an anxiety arousing situation (Meichenbaum, 1977).

Disease conviction presents a rather different clinical problem. This often seems to be found in the context of the pattern of emotionality that Imboden *et al.* described in their chronic brucellosis patients, an unwillingness to explain any personal or emotional issues and a defensive assertion of good emotional adjustment. It is essentially these characteristics that have been called "alexithymia" (Nemiah and Sifneos, 1970). Sifneos (1973) lists eight alexithymic characteristics: (a) the patients' tendency to describe details instead of feelings, (b) their inability to use appropriate words to describe emotions, (c) their lack of a rich fantasy life, (d) their use of action to express emotions, (e) their use of action to avoid conflicts, (f) their tendency to describe endlessly circumstances surrounding an event rather than feelings, (g) their inability to communicate, and (h) their thought content, associated more with external events rather than fantasy or emotions. The fact that patients avoid emotional issues implies, amongst other things, that their emotional states are not available to them as attributions for somatic disorders. Sifneos (1973) found that a group of patients with classical "psychosomatic" disorders referred to a psychiatric clinic were rated as having more than twice as many alexithymic characteristics as a control group of neurotic patients. This is an interesting and suggestive finding though sampling and rating biases cannot be excluded as explanatory factors. It is also being recognized that psychosomatic patients are too heterogeneous to be a useful category (Wright, 1977). Alexithymic features seem to be particularly common in disease conviction patients. Other recent work on alexithymia can be found in symposium proceedings edited by Brautigam and von Rad (1977).

The most direct attributional approach to disease conviction patients is to challenge their organic attributions, though this will not always be either feasible or helpful. An organic attribution probably represents for these patients a relatively reassuring external one and to some extent reduces the distress caused by the symptoms. It is no doubt because of the function organic attributions serve for these patients that they are reluctant to abandon them. To challenge such attributions strongly can simply set up psychological reactance, i.e. the authoritative challenge may lead to the patient taking up a more extreme view and holding it more strongly. However, there are ways of challenging patients' beliefs without doing this (Watts *et al.*, 1973). One can begin with some of the patients' minor complaints, those that they are less certain are a sign of serious disease, and work up a "hierarchy" to the more central symptoms. For each one the clinician can ask the patient to generate as many explanations for the symptoms as possible, encouraging him or her to keep an open mind about which is the correct one. Such an approach is able to reduce the conviction with which patients hold beliefs that initially have an intensity characteristic of delusions. It is a very different approach from that described earlier for anxious, preoccupied hypochondriacal patients who generally have much greater insight into the status of their health worries.

The aim in working with disease conviction should not be to move the patient from a belief in organic aetiology to belief in a psychological one. This would not only be an unrealistic aim, it would usually represent replacing one distortion of reality with another. Illnesses cannot be classified neatly into those with organic and those with psychological aetiologies. Almost always there is a complex interaction of factors. The aim should be to encourage patients to see the full range of aetiological factors that apply. Often patients will initially have a crude dichotomy of aetiologies, believing that they must either have genuine symptoms with an organic aetiology or that they have psychological symptoms that are simply "all in the mind". There is often an educational job to be done in explaining how it is possible, for example, for social stresses to interact with a biological predisposition to produce genuine symptoms.

The value of reducing disease certainty lies partly in the reduction of abnormal illness behaviour that has previously gone into trying to establish the credentials of the "illness" and to secure appropriate treatment. Sometimes this illness behaviour can be so extensive as to be seriously disabling. However, if patients are able to adopt a more subtle interactive explanation of their symptoms this will also allow scope for them to take action to manage their illness. For example, if "irritable bowel" patients come to accept that, among other relevant causal factors, they have particularly bad diarrhoea after certain stressful events, they can avoid such events and consequently avoid this exacerbation of their condition.

It is also possible to take an attributional approach to the "alexithymic" characteristics that many disease conviction patients manifest. The working assumption, as yet unproved, is that the presentation of somatic complaints in the context of relatively insubstantial organic aetiology is to some extent a consequence of an underlying difficulty in identifying and expressing subjective feelings, and that the somatic complaints are some kind of substitute expression of subjective feelings. Within an attributional framework one can train patients to identify apparently nonspecific states of arousal, relate them to the situations in which they had occurred, and help them to identify the particular subjective feelings involved. Such a therapeutic programme would be a very direct application of Schachter and Singer's (1962) attribution theory of emotion. It would permit a direct test of the hypothesis that in such patients improved awareness of subjective feelings would lead to reduced somatic complaints.

D. EXPLANATION AND COPING

The importance of a patient's explanation of his or her illness lies in its implications for the way the patient will cope with it. The misattribution studies discussed above have been concerned with the value of providing patients with a reassuring attribution that will minimize the emotional exacerbation of their symptoms. In some cases this will be the most important consideration. However, in other cases, the priority will be to help patients to adopt an attribution that will increase the likelihood of their making an optimal contribution to the treatment and management of their condition. It may thus be that different considerations will indicate different attributions as being helpful. It then becomes a matter of clinical judgement which considerations are most important in a particular case.

In general it seems that patients who accept some responsibility for their condition are more likely to believe they can contribute to their own recovery. However, it is important to be clear that any such connection is a matter of empirical contingency. There is no necessary connection between attributions of the causes of an illness and attributions of prospective treatment effects.

The assumption that accepting personal causal responsibility for an illness is associated with a constructive style of managing it has received some indirect support from studies that have used a general questionnaire measure of locus of control. This assesses whether people perceive events that happen to them as resulting from their own behaviour or as being beyond their control. There is now a considerable body of evidence relating locus of control to health behaviour (Strickland, 1978; Wallston and Wallston, 1978) which has generally found that "internals" show more constructive health behaviour. However, the weakness of this approach is that a general measure of locus of control may be a poor guide to how patients make attributions for a particular illness. Wallston *et al.* (1976) have improved matters slightly by developing a locus of control scale specifically related to health, but even then patterns of attribution may vary from one specific illness to another. There is also the problem that the locus of control scale may relate more to attributions about negative than about positive outcomes, or vice versa (Brewin and Shapiro, 1979).

There are also a number of studies that have looked at the correlates of attitudes related to attributions, such as self-blame among patients with a particular illness. At first glance the evidence on this connection appears very conflicting. Chodoff *et al.* (1964) found that guilt in the parents of children with leukaemia was correlated with good coping. In contrast, Abrams and Finesinger (1953) found that guilt in adult patients with cancer was correlated with poor coping. Bulman and Wortman (1977) found that accident victims who blamed themselves coped well, whereas those who blamed others coped badly; curiously, however, victims who believed that they could have avoided the accident coped badly. Cromwell *et al.* (1977) found that myocardial infarction patients with an internal locus of control responded best to a programme requiring a high level of participation whereas "externals" responded best to a low participation programme.

One of the reasons why these studies are difficult to compare is that we do not know exactly what relationship there is between concepts such as guilt, self-blame, personal responsibility etc., though all of them are clearly connected with internal attributions. Recently, Brewin and Shapiro (1979) have emphasized the importance of making a clear distinction between culpability and causal responsibility (see Brewin, Chapter 6). But if one thing is clear from the available evidence it is that the relationship between explanation of illness and coping is very complex.

Clearly no progress is likely to be made until finer distinctions are made between the explanations of illness that people give, and account is also taken of the kind of coping style that is optimal in a particular condition. It is one of the general weaknesses of attribution theory that it has been over-preoccupied with a crude distinction between internal and external attributions that is of doubtful validity (Semin, 1980). Lipowski (1970) has described eight common meanings of illness, a number of which have attributional implications. Illness can be seen as a sign of *weakness* with the associated feelings of shame and reparation. Alternatively it can be seen as a *punishment*, sometimes a just one in which case, Lipowski suggests, it is likely to be associated with passive resignation, and sometimes as an unjust punishment in which case the patient is likely to feel aggrieved. Sometimes it can be seen as an *enemy*, whether internal or external, that has to be fought. It might also be seen as a *challenge* demanding rationally modulated activity. Lipowski describes some other meanings of illness, as relief, strategy, irreparable loss and value, which are less obviously related to patients' attributions. If future research is to explore the implications of such a complicated spectrum of attributions, subtle assessment procedures and relatively large numbers of subjects will be needed.

It also has to be recognized that it may not be possible to generalize results from one condition to another. A sense of self-responsibility is likely to be more helpful in conditions such as hypertension or asthma where there is considerable scope for self-regulation. On the other hand, a sense of personal responsibility could lead to frustration and be a handicap with patients such as those undergoing chronic kidney dialysis, where there is high dependence on external medical technology.

Even within a single condition, as the Cromwell data on infarction patients showed, what pattern of attributions is advantageous will depend on the kind of treatment approach provided. It may, therefore, be difficult to generalize even within particular categories of patients. However, the interaction between patients' attributional styles and the type of treatment regime has even more important practical consequences. Clinicians will get best results if they are sophisticated enough to adapt their treatment programmes to the attributional styles of their patients. Patients who like to take responsibility for their own condition should be encouraged to do whatever they can to improve it, other patients who have no aptitude for this may be better at passively complying with a well-supervised treatment programme.

Management of Chronic Kidney Dialysis Patients

The best way of developing these rather general points is to consider particular groups of patients in some detail. Chronic kidney dialysis patients are an interesting case in which the problems of psychological adjustment are considerable (Abram, 1977). The dialysis programme may take up about 30 hours a week and severely disrupt normal life, but nevertheless patients will feel that they must maintain the maximum semblance of normality during the rest of the time. Patients may well come to feel resentful of their dependence on their dialysis machine and perhaps experience some unpleasant perceptual phenomena while undergoing dialysis. There will also be a variety of physical complications and symptoms that will leave them feeling far from healthy. In the end they may come to have rather ambivalent feelings about continued life sustained by dialysis, afraid of death but with little enthusiasm for living.

Of the available psychological studies an interesting series of research reports by Pritchard (1974a, b, c, 1977, 1979) is the most relevant to attribution theory. The response to illness questionnaire that Pritchard has developed is a tool that could be used in other medical conditions to study the relationships between explanations and coping. Unfortunately, the number of subjects employed by Pritchard was rather small (14 in the first study, 30 in the second) for the correlational and factor-analytic methods of data analysis that he used. However, the fact that a replication was reported (1977) is helpful. Though there is some broad similarity in the factors obtained, the loadings of individual items vary substantially. Too many factors were extracted (seven in the first study and eight in the second) for the factors to achieve invariance with such a small number of subjects.

Of the items in the questionnaire concerned with explanation of the illness only two were used by enough patients to provide useful discrimination, *not self-responsible* ("I cannot think of any reason to do with me why I should have it" and "I do not think there is any explanation on my part why it occurred") and *unjust punishment* ("It is wrong that I should have to suffer it" and "It is a punishment that I do not deserve"). It is clear from the detailed bivariate analysis reported for the first study (1974a) that seeing the illness as an unjust punishment was not associated with any kind of constructive coping response. This item had substantial negative correlations with both seeing the illness as a challenge or as something to be fought. In contrast, feeling not self-responsible was positively correlated with fighting it but negatively correlated with seeing it as a challenge. Seeing it as a challenge was associated with low levels of anger and anxiety, though this was not true for fighting it. Appreciating help was negatively correlated with seeing it as a challenge but positively with fighting. Seeing the illness as a challenge is thus a style of coping that is cooler and more independent than fighting the illness. Regarding the illness as an enemy seemed to be ambiguous and could be linked either to fighting it or seeing it as an unjust punishment.

When the factors derived from the two studies (1974b, 1977) are examined there is confirmation for this pattern. Both studies obtained a paranoid withdrawal factor on which "unjust punishment" had high loadings. Both also had an "illness as challenge" factor, though interestingly in the second study there was a particular emphasis on this being a non-attributable challenge. There were also in both studies factors concerned with hostility to the illness as an enemy, though here there were quite marked divergencies in the detailed loadings.

It is worth noting that there seem to be two alternative "tackling" stances, one relatively "internal" (accepting it as a challenge) and one relatively "external" (regarding it as something to be fought). There are no grounds at present for thinking one of these is preferable to the other. It will presumably depend on the individual patients' personality and general coping style which one he or she gravitates towards. The attributional position that a clinician might want to help patients move away from is the helpless, unjust-punishment stance. It is not a guilty sense of culpability that is the problem here, as would be indicated by a perception of the illness as a just punishment. So few patients in Pritchard's study saw their illness as a just punishment that this item was of no value in discriminating among the patients. The problem represented by the unjust punishment stance is closer to a state of learned helplessness (Seligman, 1975), acquired after a single, traumatic, and apparently inexplicable event, than it is to a sense of personal culpability.

Many of those who have studied the coping mechanisms of kidney dialysis patients qualitatively (see Abram, 1977) have commented on the tendency of these patients to avoid recognizing the extent of their handicap, and there is some evidence that this is linked with a passive approach to coping. Pritchard (1977a) found a high correlation between not thinking about the illness and not feeling self-involved. Goldstein (1976) found a correlation of 0·70 in his sample of 22 kidney dialysis patients between a questionnaire measure of denial and the locus of control scale, though interestingly these were not correlated in a control group of patients with minor medical problems. Though this stance of passive denial is understandable in the face of such a serious condition it can be unconstructive if taken too far. It is necessary therefore to consider what can be done to give patients a sense that their illness can be coped with. McKee (1977) found that when patients were given training for *home* dialysis they became more internal on the locus of control scale. Such arrangements for the structure of treatment provision may affect patients' attributions more powerfully than verbal interventions.

Management of Asthmatic and Diabetic Patients

There are other groups of medical patients who can make much more contribution to their own state of health. Asthma is a good example. Here it is very important that patients recognize the influence they can exert over their condition and be ready to attribute some of the responsibility for good management of the condition to themselves. A distinction needs to be made here between personal responsibility for the *aetiology* of the condition and for *fluctuations in severity* of the condition. The latter is more likely to be relevant to good management of the asthma and is generally accepted by patients much more readily than aetiological responsibility.

Asthmatic patients differ considerably among themselves in the factors that account for fluctuations in their condition (Purcell and Weiss, 1970). There are some in whom the main factors are allergens or infections, external factors over which they have little control. In others, behaviours such as excessive exercise, voluntary coughing or hyperventilation may contribute to asthma attacks. Most patients will have been prescribed inhalers which they will need to use appropriately, the instructions for which are often quite complicated. A patient may be asked to use one inhaler which has short-term effects, and follow this ten minutes later with another that has long-term effects. Both need to be pressed just as air is being inhaled, and in the correct position in relation to the mouth.

Patients often lapse into inappropriate behaviours because they have not fully grasped the causal connections between their behaviour and their breathing capacity. They may cough excessively when they start to get breathless, believing that this will clear their airways. Repeated experience to the contrary does not always lead to its extinction. Also patients may use inhalers which have immediate effects, but neglect to use those which have less immediate but more significant treatment effects. For some patients, repeated explanation of the effects of their inhalers seems to have little effect in the absence of a directly experienced causal connection. In such cases more sophisticated methods of health education may be needed. For example, to see long-term effects presented visually in a film may be of more help than simple verbal explanations in enabling patients to establish necessary causal links.

In at least a significant proportion of patients, emotional states will be a major contributor to broncho-constriction (e.g. Tal and Miklich, 1976). Sometimes the relevant emotions will arise from an external event. An asthmatic wife having an asthma attack after an argument with her husband who has come home drunk is one common pattern. In other cases anxiety that arises as a response to some initially quite mild breathing difficulty will play a major part in producing an attack. A variety of self-regulation methods may be appropriate to reduce emotionally-induced broncho-constriction. Sometimes a patient will be able to achieve significant results by avoiding the critical situation, as would be the case with the patient reported by Metcalf (1956) whose attacks coincided with seeing her mother. In other cases anxiety management methods will be of value, such as with the patient Sirota and Mahoney (1974) reported who was trained to relax at regularly timed intervals during the day.

There is a circular relationship between such self-regulation methods and the attributions to which they are linked. Patients will not begin to use such methods unless they can grasp their relevance and are ready to attribute changes in their asthmatic condition to their own efforts. Equally, self-attributions are substantially confirmed by the experience of successful self-regulation, and some patients will only really accept their own causal efficacy when it has been confirmed in this way. Clinicians using such self-regulation methods need to follow this gradual development of personal attributions, making sure that they are sufficiently established at a verbal level before the beginning of treatment, and if necessary training patients to recognize their self-efficacy in treatment and consciously make the appropriate self-attributions.

A variety of other psychological methods can be used in the treatment of asthma (Knapp and Wells, 1978) of which desensitization is one of the more successful (Yorkston et al., 1974). Asthma is also a medical condition in which the results of hypnosis have been relatively good (e.g. Report to the Research Committee of the British Tuberculosis Association, 1968). This suggests another clinical application for an attributional framework, which is its use in selecting patients for alternative kinds of treatment. The prediction would be that patients with a tendency to internal attributions of changes in their asthma would respond better to desensitization, whereas those with tendency to external attributions would respond better to hypnosis.

Diabetes represents another condition in which the patients have to exercise considerable self-management (Watts, 1980) and again it is important if patients are to do this successfully that they are willing to attribute some responsibility for their degree of metabolic control to themselves. Very often to achieve tight control of sugar levels it is not sufficient for patients to simply adhere to the prescribed diet and injections of insulin, though this is difficult enough for many of them. It is also necessary to monitor sugar levels and make adjustments to compensate for fluctuations due to exercise, emotional stress and other relevant factors.

Lowery and DuCette (1976) have investigated the implications of locus of control for diabetic management. Though internals clearly acquired more information about diabetes than the externals, this did not always result in better management. Three years after onset internals had slightly more problems (missed appointments, weight gain and physiological problems) than externals. Among patients who had had their diabetes for six years internals had substantially more problems. Unfortunately not much is known about the nature of the diabetic regimen. It would be predicted that internals might respond better to a programme in which they were given a lot of autonomy in the management of their condition, and could see the beneficial results of conscientious self-care. On the other hand if they were provided with a system of medical directives, over which they had little control and the usefulness of which they doubted, it is understandable that their response should be poor. This once again illustrates the importance of matching treatment programmes to how patients explain their illnesses.

E. AN ATTRIBUTIONAL FRAMEWORK FOR MEDICINE

Nearly all patients entertain some attributions about their condition, and often appear very eager to understand what they are suffering from and how it has arisen. It is a reflection of the extent to which this matters to patients that they are twice as likely to remember diagnostic information that their doctor gives them than they are to remember his treatment advice (Ley and Spelman, 1967). Further it is clear from the evidence reviewed in this chapter that they are not only preoccupied with attribution of illnesses but are very much influenced by them in their approach to the treatment and management of their condition. Patients' attributions thus constitute an ubiquitous framework within which medicine has to be practised. This being so it is important that all those engaged in the care of medical patients become sensitive to the attributions of their patients and sophisticated about how they deal with them.

This chapter has emphasized that there is no single kind of causal attribution that is desirable in every condition. It is necessary to make an appraisal of how particular patients' attributions are affecting their response to their condition. Internal attributions tend to be less reassuring than external ones and may lead to excessive levels of anxiety and exacerbation of symptoms, as with cardiac neurosis patients. On the other hand patients such as those recovering from influenza who attribute their symptoms to infection when this is no longer the case can make a slower recovery to normal functioning. Hypochondriacal patients are a noteworthy group whose incorrect illness attributions are disabling in their effects. In these various cases clinicians may wish to help patients to adopt a pattern of attributions that will result in their being as little disabled as possible by their illness.

Another criterion that clinicians need to bear in mind is whether patients' attributions will help them to play a constructive role in the management of their condition. Again, it is not possible to generalize about which attributions are best. Internal attributions are more useful in a condition like asthma where fluctuations are largely in the hands of the patient. In other conditions where there is less patients can do to help themselves, internal attributions are less valuable. Individual differences in patients' natural attributional styles also need to be taken into account and there is sometimes scope for choosing a treatment approach that will suit the patient, asking for more involvement from patients who tend towards internal attributions. However, there is a need, as work on kidney dialysis patients has made particularly clear, to get beyond a crude dichotomy into internal and external attributions. It will be recalled that an internal tackling approach and a more external "fighting an enemy" approach could both be helpful here, whereas it was seeing the condition as an "unjust punishment" that was unconstructive. There is a long way to go in the subtle exploration of the conceptual domain of illness attributions.

In developing a style of medical practice that takes full account of attributional factors, there will be a need for clinicians to have access for consultation to colleagues with expertise in the attributional approach, and there will be some patients who need to be referred as individuals for attributional therapy. However, the major need is for an effort to educate the broad range of clinicians about the attributional framework for medicine. It should certainly have an important place in the training of medical practitioners.

REFERENCES

Abram, H. S. (1977). Survival by machine: the psychological stress of chronic hemodialysis. In R. H. Moos (ed.) Coping with Physical Illness. New York: Plenum.

Abrams, R. D. and Finesinger, J. E. (1953). Guilt reactions in patients with cancer. Cancer 6, 474–482.

Bard, M. and Dyk, R. B. (1956). The psychodynamic significance of beliefs regarding the cause of serious illness. Psychoanalytic Review 43, 146–162.

Bootzin, R. R., Herman, C. P. and Nicassio, P. (1976). The power of suggestion: another examination of misattribution and insomnia. Journal of Personality and Social Psychology 34, 673–679.

Brautigam, W. and von Rad, M. (eds) (1977). Toward a theory of psychosomatic disorders. Psychotherapy and Psychosomatics 28, whole volume.

Brewin, C. R. and Shapiro, D. A. (1979). Beliefs about the self and their importance for motivation in rehabilitation. In D. J. Oborne, M. M. Gruneberg and J. R.

Eiser (eds) *Research in Psychology and Medicine* (vol. 2). London and New York: Academic Press.

Bulman, R. J. and Wortman, C. B. (1977). Attributions of blame and coping in the "Real World": severe accident victims react to their lot. *Journal of Personality and Social Psychology* **35**, 351–363.

Calvert-Boyanowsky, J. C. and Leventhal, H. (1975). The role of information in attenuating behavioural responses to stress: a reinterpretation of the misattribution phenomenon. *Journal of Personality and Social Psychology* **32**, 214–221.

Chodoff, P., Friedman, S. and Hamburg, D. (1964). Stress, defences and coping behaviour: observations in parents of children with malignant diseases. *American Journal of Psychiatry* **120**, 743–749.

Cohen, F. and Lazarus, R. S. (1979). Coping with the stresses of illness. *In* G. C. Stone, F. Cohen and N. E. Adler (eds) *Health Psychology: A Handbook*. San Francisco: Jossey-Bass.

Cowie, B. (1976). The cardiac patient's perception of his heart attack. *Social Science and Medicine* **10**, 87–96.

Cromwell, R. L., Butterfield, E. C., Brayfield, F. M. and Curry, J. J. (1977). *Acute Myocardial Infarction: Reaction and Recovery*. Saint Louis: C.V. Mosby Co.

Farr, R. M. (1977). Heider, Harré and Herzlick on health and illness: some observations on the structure of "representations collectives". *European Journal of Social Psychology* **7**, 491–504.

Goldstein, A. M. (1976). Denial and external locus of control as mechanisms of adjustment in chronic medical illness. *Essence* **1**, 5–22.

Herzlick, C. (1973). *Health and Illness: A Social-Psychological Analysis*. London and New York: Academic Press.

Imboden, J. B., Canter, A. and Cluff, L. E. (1959). Brucellosis III: psychological aspects and delayed convalescence. *Archives of Internal Medicine* **103**, 406–414.

Imboden, J. B., Canter, A. and Cluff, L. E. (1961). Convalescence from influenza. *Archives of Internal Medicine* **108**, 393–399.

Kellogg, R. and Baron, R. S. (1975). Attribution theory, insomnia, and the reverse placebo effect: a reversal of Storms and Nisbett's findings. *Journal of Personality and Social Psychology* **32**, 231–236.

Knapp, T. J. and Wells, L. A. (1978). Behaviour therapy for asthma: a review. *Behaviour Research and Therapy* **16**, 103–115.

Kopel, S. and Arkowitz, H. (1975). The role of attribution and self-perception in behaviour therapy. *Genetic Psychology Monographs* **92**, 175–212.

Ley, P. and Spelman, M. S. (1967). *Communicating with the Patient*. London: Staples Press.

Liebhart, E. H. (1974). Attribution therapy: changes in cardiac neurotic symptoms via explanations of external causes. *Zeitschrift für Klinische Psychologie* **3**, 71–94.

Lipowski, Z. J. (1970). Physical illness, the individual and the expiry process. *Psychiatry in Medicine* **1**, 91–102.

Lowery, B. J. and Ducette, J. P. (1976). Disease related learning and disease control in diabetics as a function of locus of control. *Nursing Research* **25**, 358–362.

McKee, D. C. (1977). Effects of haemodialysis and home dialysis training on kidney patients and their spouses. *Dissertation Abstracts International* **37** (8–8), 4155.

Marby, J. H. (1964). Lay concepts of etiology. *Journal of Chronic Diseases* **17**, 371–386.

Meichenbaum, D. (1977). *Cognitive Behaviour Modification*. New York: Plenum.

Metcalfe, M. (1956). Demonstration of a psychosomatic relationship. *British Journal of Medical Psychology* **29**, 63–66.

Nemiah, J. C. and Sifneos, P. E. (1970). Affect and fantasy with psychosomatic patients. *In* O. W. Hill (ed.) *Modern Trends in Psychosomatic Medicine* (vol. 2) London: Butterworth.

Pilowski, I. (1967). Dimensions of hypochondriasis. *British Journal of Psychiatry* **113**, 89–93.

Pritchard, M. (1974a). Reaction to illness in long term haemodialysis. *Journal of Psychosomatic Research* **18**, 55–67.

Pritchard, M. (1974b). Dimensions of illness behaviour in long term haemodialysis. *Journal of Psychosomatic Research* **18**, 351–356.

Pritchard, M. (1974c). Meaning of illness and patients' response to long-term haemodialysis. *Journal of Psychosomatic Research* **18**, 457–464.

Pritchard, M. (1977). Further studies of illness behaviour in long-term haemodialysis. *Journal of Psychosomatic Research* **21**, 41–48.

Pritchard, M. (1979). Measurement of illness behaviour in patients on haemodialysis and awaiting cardiac surgery. *Journal of Psychosomatic Research* **23**, 117–130.

Purcell, K. and Weiss, J. (1970). Asthma. *In* C. G. Costello (ed.) *Symptoms of Psychopathology*. New York: Wiley.

Report to the Research Committee of the British Tuberculosis Association (1968). Hypnosis for asthma: a controlled trial. *British Medical Journal* **4**, 71–76.

Rodin, J. (1976). Menstruation, reattribution and competence. *Journal of Personality and Social Psychology* **33**, 345–353.

Rodin, J. (1978). Somatopsychics and attribution. *Personality and Social Psychology Bulletin* **4**, 531–540.

Schachter, S. and Singer, J. E. (1962). Cognitive, social and physiological determinants of emotional state. *Psychological Review* **69**, 379–399.

Seligman, M. E. P. (1975). *Helplessness: on Depression, Development and Death*. San Francisco: Freeman.

Semin, G. R. (1980). A gloss on attribution theory. *British Journal of Social and Clinical Psychology* **19**, 291–300.

Sifneos, P. E. (1973). The prevalence of alexithymic characteristics in psychosomatic patients. *Psychotherapy and Psychosomatics* **22**, 255–267.

Sirota, A. D. and Mahoney, M. J. (1974). Relaxing on cue: the self-regulation of asthma. *Journal of Behaviour Therapy and Experimental Psychiatry* **5**, 65–66.

Small, L. (1953). Personality determinants of vocational choice. *Psychological Monographs* **67**, whole no. 351.

Storms, M. D. and McCaul, K. D. (1976). Attribution processes and the emotional exacerbation of dysfunctional behaviour. *In* J. H. Harvey, W. J. Ickes and R. F. Kidd (eds) *New Directions in Attribution Research* (vol. I). Hillsdale, New Jersey: Lawrence Erlbaum.

Storms, M. D. and Nisbett, R. E. (1970). Insomnia and the attribution process. *Journal of Personality and Social Psychology* **16**, 319–328.

Strickland, B. R. (1978). Internal–external expectancies and health-related behaviours. *Journal of Consulting and Clinical Psychology* **46**, 1192–1211.

Tal, A. and Miklich, D. R. (1976). Emotionally induced decreases in pulmonary flow rates in asthmatic children. *Psychosomatic Medicine* **38**, 190–200.

Wallston, B. S. and Wallston, K. A. (1978). Locus of control and health: a review of the literature. *Health Education Monograph* **6**, 107–117.

Wallston, B. S., Wallston, K. A., Kaplan, G. D. and Maides, S. A. (1976). Development and validation of the Health Locus of Control (HLC) Scale. *Journal of Consulting and Clinical Psychology* **44**, 580–585.

Watts, F. N. (1980). Behavioural aspects of the management of diabetes mellitus: education, self-care and metabolic control. *Behaviour Research and Therapy* **18**, 171–180.

Watts, F. N., Powell, G. E. and Austin, S. V. (1973). The modification of abnormal beliefs. *British Journal of Medical Psychology* **46**, 359–363.

Weisman, A. D. (1976). Coping with untimely death. *In* R. H. Moos (ed.) *Human Adaptation*. Lexington, Massachusetts: Heath.

Wright, L. (1977). Conceptualizing and defining psychosomatic disorders. *American Psychologist* **32**, 625–628.

Yorkston, N. J., McHugh, R. B., Brady, R., Serber, M. and Sergeant, H. G. S. (1974). Verbal desensitization in bronchial asthma. *Journal of Psychosomatic Research* **18**, 371–376.

9
Attribution and the Management of the Pain Patient

Anthony E. Reading

A. INTRODUCTION

The past decade has witnessed an exponential growth in the number of specialist clinics for the management of pain in the United States. Many of these are truly multidisciplinary, and there are indications that this trend will be repeated in the United Kingdom (Kaye, 1979). Pain is one of the most common presenting complaints in medical practice. In the majority of cases it will be shortlived and relieved by prompt medical intervention. In these circumstances pain serves as a warning or signal of underlying pathology, which may be obvious as in the case of injuries, or less so as with the pain of acute appendicitis. Such pain is symptomatic in that it will respond to treatment of the cause, namely repair of the injury or removal of the appendix. In other cases pain may be relatively shortlived but recurrent, as with headaches or rheumatoid arthritic pain. Both are forms of acute pain and can be distinguished from chronic pain, which is enduring and unresponsive to treatment. Although acute pain will be considered, the discussion will focus on chronic pain. As pain becomes chronic it no longer functions as a symptom reflecting underlying pathology, it may continue long after the disease state has been recognized, and it can be thought of as the disease or problem in its own right, relief from which will not easily be found. Crue (1979) has suggested that in addition to the broad distinction between acute and chronic pain, further distinctions can be drawn between chronic pain associated with a terminal illness, chronic pain with which the patient copes reasonably well, and chronic intractable benign pain syndrome in which the patient is disabled by pain in the absence of life-threatening pathology. The latter makes up a large proportion of patients seen at specialist pain clinics.

It is proposed to consider the relevance of attribution theory to the understanding and management of the pain patient. Following a discussion of the nature of psychological influences on the pain experience, laboratory research will be presented which has studied the effects of manipulating attributions on experimentally induced pain. The clinical applications of attribution theory will be discussed in terms of understanding the pain patient, detoxification, and psychological management of the pain.

B. THE PSYCHOLOGICAL BASIS OF PAIN

Psychologists are becoming increasingly involved in the clinical management of pain and have demonstrated they have a significant contribution to make at both research and treatment levels. Psychological research has extended our understanding of the nature of pain, although the reasons why pain relief remains elusive for some patients continues to be a puzzle. What is clear is the absence of a straightforward relationship between an apparently objective stimulus, in terms of the amount of injury or observable tissue damage, and the resulting level of pain. This variation in pain response has also emerged from laboratory research which has shown wide individual differences in response to standard noxious stimuli, employing threshold and tolerance measures. Dramatic illustrations of the complexity of the pain experience come from reports of rituals performed in primitive societies, where stimuli are endured in the apparent absence of pain (Kosambi, 1968)—stimuli which would have the connotations of torture in the Western World! Similarly, Beecher (1959) has contrasted the analgesic requirements of soldiers injured on the battlefield with those of patients following surgery in civilian hospitals. He reported that only one-third of the soldiers requested morphine despite sustaining extensive injuries, as compared with 80% of civilian post-operative patients, whose wounds if anything were less severe or extensive. This discrepancy could not be accounted for by virtue of the fact that the soldiers were in a shock state and so anaesthetized to pain, as they were able to feel and complain of pain resulting from medical procedures, such as a poorly performed venipuncture. Beecher postulated that the difference in drug requirements could be accounted for by considering the meaning of the situation in which the pain was experienced. For the soldiers, the pain signified escape from the battle-field and survival, and so had positive connotations against which the suffering could be offset. Whereas for the civilians who were healthy and became sick, the post-operative pain had only negative and possibly calamitous implications.

Beecher (1959) further observed that psychological state influenced the efficacy of morphine when administered. In a trial in which morphine was compared with placebo, it was found that placebo gave relief from post-operative pain in 35% of the cases studied. As morphine is only effective for 75% of patients, Beecher (1959) suggested that a significant proportion of its effect is via psychological pathways, as it was most effective when patients were also anxious. This is consistent with experimental work in which morphine has been shown to improve pain tolerance only in the presence of anxiety (Hill *et al.*, 1952). Beecher (1972) concluded that the psychological status of the individual will influence the effect of pharmacological interventions, and proposed that certain pharmacological agents are effective only in the presence of a specific mental state. As anxiety is commonly associated with pain and pain increases in the presence of anxiety (Sternbach, 1978), it appears that medication at least initially has the effect of reducing anxiety and with it the impact of the pain experience.

The preceding observations challenged existing models of pain which contended that the pain experience was linked either directly to pain receptors in the periphery or to patterned input from the periphery (Melzack, 1973). Research demonstrating the importance of psycho-logical factors, along with the way in which pain may arise in the absence of peripheral input, as in the case of phantom limb pain, highlighted the limitations of such theories (Melzack, 1973). It was with the formulation of the gate control theory of pain (Melzack and Wall, 1965) that a means of understanding the many influences of the pain experience became avail-able. This constituted a departure from traditional theories which viewed the subjective experience in direct proportion to the level of nociceptive input, as it stated that the pain experience is the outcome of competing sensory impulses of an inhibitory and facilitatory nature. This helps to explain why counterstimulation may abolish pain and has led to the use of vibrators and transcutaneous electrical stimulation as a means of achieving pain control. It appears that such stimulation is sufficient to close the gate on the pain messages transmitted by pain fibres. It also makes explicit the influence of descending impulses from the cortex in opening, as in the case of anxiety, or closing the gate on the pain experience. This theory reflects the complexity of pain as well as the importance of cerebral functioning, even though the physiological predictions and tenets have not been substantiated. It has also stimulated considerable research and provided an impetus and rationale for clinical treatments of pain patients. Methods of enervating the input from inhibitory nerve fibres have already been mentioned. It also endorses the development and application of treatments designed to activate psychological processes which will dampen the pain input, such as distraction or hypnosis.

It is clear, therefore, that pain occurring in response to an injury may be acted upon in a variety of ways according to many psychological factors. These may function in a similar fashion to a flexible lens, magnifying and reducing the amount of sensation that is felt. Amongst the descending influences are past experience, social learning histories, cultural background, personality, emotional state, the prevailing reinforcement contingencies and the cognitive appraisal that takes place (Sternbach, 1978). It is largely with the latter that this chapter will be concerned, as the appraisal and interpretation placed upon a symptom will influence its impact. This is also true for other symptoms as there is an accumulating body of evidence that individuals do not react uniformly to illness or concomitant signs (Campbell, 1975) so that presumably objective physical conditions, such as illness, health, pain and hunger, are greatly influenced by subjective perceptions (Rodin, 1978). Physical symptoms of whatever nature produce a degree of confusion, uncertainty and fear, and these emotional drive states develop a need to seek explanations. In such an emotionally charged context symptoms may be interpreted in a variety of ways according to individual value systems, needs and other idiosyncratic factors in an effort to reduce uncertainty and establish control. Such processes provide fertile ground for perceptual distortion and misinterpretation which may be beneficial or disadvantageous depending upon the context in which the symptoms occur and their true medical significance.

Pain is a strong motivational force; it prompts immediate action for seeking relief. This will inevitably involve arriving at some understanding of the cause of the pain, in the course of seeking appropriate and effective treatment or measures to abolish it. Attributions associated with causation and recovery will influence the pain experience. Their significance may be illustrated by considering the occurrence of chest pain in a middle-aged man. If the discomfort is attributed to cardiovascular disease with the prospect of imminent cardiac arrest, the pain will be magnified and assume greater proportions than if attributed to a commonplace cause, such as muscle strain sustained while mowing the lawn earlier that day. Before considering the relevance of attribution theory in clinical assessment and management, it is proposed to appraise experimental work which has manipulated beliefs and studied the response to noxious stimulation.

C. LABORATORY RESEARCH ON ATTRIBUTIONS

Attributions have been systematically manipulated in the laboratory in order to understand their influence on the way in which bodily sensations are appraised. Part of this work has been concerned with pain. As with other research on attribution and emotional states, predictions have been studied at intermediate levels of pain stimulation, for as Nisbett and Schachter (1966) have remarked: "Common sense would indicate that no amount of argument would persuade a man dodging machine gun bullets that his physiological arousal was due to anything but the exigencies of the situation." The research focus has been on the labelling of bodily sensations and addressed the question, On what basis is a particular stimulus identified as painful? This research represents an extension of studies which have shown emotional labels attached to aroused body states to be in part cognitively determined (Schachter and Singer, 1962). The parallel for pain was thought to be attempting to convince subjects that arousal contingent upon receiving electric shocks was to some extent the effect of an outside agent, such as a drug. Nisbett and Schachter (1966) hypothesized that if arousal were attributed to drug effects greater levels of pain stimulation would be endured. The experimental manipulation was designed to create conditions of high and low fear and then to induce an attribution of symptoms to the shock or to the placebo pill. As predicted, attributions were irrelevant to the high fear group, who correctly attributed their bodily sensations to the effects of receiving shocks, as this was a more plausible explanation for them. The manipulation of attributions was successful for the low fear group, so that subjects who attributed their symptoms to the drug tolerated on average four times as much shock as the controls. These results confirm that within the limits of credibility, labelling of bodily sensations is to some degree manipulable.

In addition to situational cues which may alter the impact of physiological arousal, the subject's behaviour, verbal and non-verbal, may also be a source of information which will influence judgements as to pain intensity or discomfort. Bandler et al. (1968) have suggested that individuals may use their own behaviour in response to an aversive stimulus as evidence for deciding that the stimulus is painful. In other words, the behavioural response to an aversive stimulus may partially control and shape the perception of the stimulus as uncomfortable or painful. Support comes from a study in which subjects observed themselves escaping or enduring a series of electric shocks. The hypothesis was supported by the data in that on trials where subjects escaped, ratings of discomfort were higher than on those where the shocks were endured. This suggests that observers and participants draw parallel inferences in assuming shocks which were escaped to be of higher intensity. Bandler *et al.* (1968) speculate as to the clinical relevance of this formulation. They suggest that through hypnosis or placebos patients may be encouraged to suppress an escape reaction and their perception will be based upon their observations of their response. Thus, where escape is suppressed, pain ratings would be expected to be less.

This work is helpful in offering a means of understanding clinical reactions to pain. Patients who habitually reach for the bottle of pain killers may come to perceive the intensity of the pain through their dependence on pain killers. As it is uncommon for medication to be completely effective in delivering relief from the pain, it is typical for the strength of the drugs to be gradually increased in the quest for better treatment. The attributional framework associated with this increase may be important, in that the knowledge that they require stronger and stronger drugs may confirm to patients the seriousness of their condition. It is a commonly expressed sentiment that "the pain must be bad, as I have to take so many capsules and they are the strongest ones available." However, as will be discussed later, it is evident there are many factors other than pain severity which determine pill-taking behaviour (Bond and Pilowsky, 1966). It is also possible to observe the way in which behaviour influences pain reports in clinical settings. The patient with a fear of vaginal examination may clamp her legs together as a conditioned response to touch and yet take this extreme reaction as confirmation of the painfulness of the sensations produced.

Finally, the influence of medication on the maintenance of change has been studied in the laboratory and this work has relevance to the pain patient. The focus has been on understanding the implications of attributing behaviour to internal or external causes. The most common and relevant external cause of behaviour is medication induced change. Thus, do anxious patients maintain their improvements when medication is withdrawn? Similarly, with pain patients, dependency on medication may develop and with it a downgrading of the possibility that pain relief may have been achieved through other means than by taking drugs; particularly as drugs are rarely totally effective and a part of their action derives from non-pharmacological mechanisms. Davison and Valins (1969) hypothesized that behaviour change which is attributed to internal factors will persist or be maintained to a greater degree than behaviour change which is attributed to an external agent such as a drug. In their study subjects endured electric shocks having ingested a drug. Half were then told the drug had improved their pain tolerance while the remainder were told that it was in fact a placebo. On further testing subjects who had been disabused of the notion that the drug had been of benefit, and therefore attributed their behaviour and pain tolerance to themselves, maintained these changes to a greater degree than control subjects who had attributed their tolerance to the drug which was now absent. Such work concerned with medication and the way in which effects can be mediated through cognitive appraisal has important implications for the clinical management of the pain patient and its relevance will be elaborated in greater detail in a later section on detoxification.

D. CLINICAL MANAGEMENT OF THE PAIN PATIENT

The Data Base: Understanding the Patient's Pain

The doctor–patient consultation is the setting in which the patient, desiring relief from the pain, will be required to convey the nature of the pain experience, while the physician will attempt to arrive at a diagnosis and so identify the most appropriate treatment. This communication process is fraught with pitfalls. Pain defies straightforward understanding. It is a private, subjective experience continuously influenced by a multitude of extrinsic and intrinsic stimuli (Sternbach, 1978). The absence of a common language for expressing pain and of consensus over the meaning of pain descriptors continues to limit understanding, although progress is being made on developing pain scales for this purpose (Melzack, 1975; Leavitt and Garron, 1980). Very often the clinical inteview, in the face of these difficulties, will degenerate into the scenario of the patient becoming more and more frustrated by the doctor's apparent unwillingness to understand and the doctor becoming irritated by the patient's inability to explain adequately. This first stage of the therapeutic process is an essential and important one. Some of the distorting influences will be considered.

The patients' attributions of the symptom and their construction as to the cause and significance of the pain will affect and modulate the way in which the complaint is expressed. If the pain is attributed to a serious cause, then this may lead to more vociferous attempts to seek help by a more emotional presentation. Such factors as culture, social learning and personality, along with the patient's attributional framework, will affect the patient's style of interaction and therefore their influence will need to be gauged and understood by the physician. This will enable the doctor to obtain a context or perspective within which to view and appraise the pain complaints. For example, dismissing a complaint of severe pain from a superficial injury would be a possible medical reaction. Another might be to understand the reasons for such an extreme reaction. If the patient believed injuries of this kind signified the onset of melanoma or skin cancer, then the exaggerated response becomes reasonable and careful counselling and reassurance are indicated. While understanding of this kind should be an integral part of the clinical examination, research suggests it seldom is and in fact it is more likely that doctors and patients will differ in the attributional frameworks they bring to bear on the problem.

It appears that physicians have a tendency to prefer general attributions in understanding patient behaviour and patients more specific ones (Rodin, 1978). For example, where a patient fails to comply with therapy the physician may view this failure as an indication of a non-compliant and uncooperative personality style, whereas the patient may attribute this non-compliance to situational factors, such as the medication having unacceptable side effects or the treatment being at an inconvenient time or location. Similarly, doctors tend to attribute the style of reporting to habitual factors, such as "this kind of patient is never satisfied or always grumbles", rather than attempt to understand in a more differentiated way the reasons for patient non-compliance (Blackwell, 1976).

Achieving an understanding of the patient's attributional framework will enable a more balanced and thorough assessment of the problem to be made, as inevitably when pain occurs there is a need to seek a cause and explanation. The conclusion reached will influence the perception of the pain and also the subsequent presentation. In order to appreciate the potential for distortion and communication breakdown, it is necessary to introduce the notion of psychogenic pain. This term has commonly been applied to patients for whose complaints no cause or sufficient cause can be found. It implies that psychological factors predominate. This conclusion can be reached either by default—when no physical problems are found—or where there is also a psychological problem in evidence. Psychogenic pain has been contrasted with real or physical pain. While this formulation has extended the range of approaches employed in dealing with the chronic pain patient, it is inappropriate to view this as a dichotomy. Psychological factors enter into all pain problems and so it is necessary to discard an either/or perspective and attempt to chart the influence of both psychological and physical factors in order to understand the complaint and select the most appropriate treatment methods.

Where pain is thought of as either real or imaginery many problems arise. An exaggerated display of pain resulting from attribution of cause, cultural background, social learning or some combination of factors may lead the physician to take one of two courses of action. It may result in prompt, extensive and invasive investigations, should there be a failure to recognize the emotional factors colouring the presentation. Alternatively, where there is a case history of such investigations or where the physician may be sensitive to emotional factors, it may result in the label "psychogenic" being applied and the patient discarded and sent to the psychiatry department. This may happen even when physical investigations are called for. It is most common for the first approach to be followed by the second and with it the patient develops feelings of abandonment and resentment.

Neither of these courses of action is effective medicine. The disease model principle, that assumes symptoms or illnesses are controlled by some underlying pathogenic factor or antecedent stimulus, may be inappropriate for the chronic pain patient (Fordyce, 1976). Fordyce and Steger (1979) comment on the need for the patient to authenticate the pain, particularly where the label "psychogenic" has been applied. By attempting to understand both the physical status of the patient and the way in which symptoms are being interpreted and acted upon, the clinician can arrive at a balanced view of the patient in pain. In many cases it will be unlikely that the complaints will be abolished by medical intervention alone, although this is a necessary first step. However, by understanding the patient's own construction of the pain, inroads may be made in the degree to which it is causing suffering or limiting behaviour. For example, an exaggerted presentation may result from the patient attributing symptoms to serious causes. Hyperawareness of bodily symptoms, combined with a fear of contracting disease, provides fertile ground for misattribution. Many patients, particularly where a relative contracted an apparently similar pain which was diagnosed as cancer, will be convinced their pain is a forerunner of malignancy. This fear may not emerge unless the clinician enquires as to their perceptions and understanding of the pain. Attempting to elicit such fears and discuss them, therby avoiding subscribing to the "wall of silence" conspiracy (Morris et al., 1978), will help in reducing anxiety, which by itself will exacerbate pain. Where the topic is avoided altogether, it may be construed as confirmation of the worst by the patient. In a similar vein, a patient may refrain from activities through the irrational fear that these will accelerate the disease process. Sometimes counselling will by itself lead to restoration of functioning, although in other cases more systematic interventions will be needed, as will be seen in a later section.

The process of labelling symptoms and attributing causes is an essential consideration in the understanding and management of the chronic pain patient. As pain becomes prolonged, so pain behaviours may become entrenched and problems in their own right. As pain persists the autonomic responses decrease and vegetative signs, such as sleep and appetite disturbances, irritability and somatic preoccupation appear (Reuler et al., 1980). In this case a whole range of sensations may be construed as continuing confirmation of sickness. For example, everyday experiences such as becoming tired or noticing an ache or discomfort are taken as reinforcing the notion of illness and the sick role.

As will be seen in a later section, labelling pain in a passive, helpless way may constitute a further impediment to recovery. For, as more restrictions are placed on activities, attention becomes focused on the symptoms so that fewer opportunities are available for distraction from the pain. A passive attitude, where opportunity to exercise control is denied, will reinforce the negative symptoms. Recent approaches to treatment have emphasized the modification of pain behaviour (Fordyce et al., 1973; Levundusky and Swett, 1979).

Detoxification

The patient attending pain clinics with chronic intractable benign pain syndrome will typically have been taking a number of pain medications for an extended period of time and will have seen a whole range of physicians and pain experts. Over the course of this and with the failure to obtain relief, medication requirements escalate and with them the state of psychological and physical dependency. As drugs fail to provide complete pain relief, they may be taken more frequently and increased in analgesic potency. It is not uncommon to see patients with relatively minor pelvic or menstrual pain admitting to taking more than 16 or 20 proprietary pills per day, even though they admit that the drugs have little or no effect on their pain! As will be seen, pill-taking can become an autonomous behaviour maintained by reinforcement contingencies irrespective of the pain experience. The process of taking more and more drugs is often inadvertently supported by the medical profession. Physicians may present new drugs in a way likely to raise expectations. In conjunction with the search for better tablets there will be a reluctance to give up those that have helped in the past, so that patients often ingest combinations of analgesic drugs.

It is necessary to return to work discussed previously concerned with placebo effects. This was presented in an earlier section in order to illustrate the way in which psychological factors may exert an influence on the pain experience. It is extremely likely that new drugs will provide some pain relief, at least initially, if they are associated with expectations of relief. Critical to the placebo effect is the conviction of the therapist about the drug's potency (Liberman, 1962). However, as will be seen in the clinical setting and as was demonstrated experimentally by Davison and Valins (1969), such convictions may be counter-therapeutic. As was presented earlier, Beecher (1959) reviewed 15 studies assessing the placebo effect in a large number of patients with organic pain and found that placebo brought about a decrease in pain in about 35%. He concluded that placebo was about 50% as effective as morphine. The analgesic effect appears to have similar mechanisms. With repeated use placebo analgesia diminishes, an abstinence syndrome appears when suddenly withdrawn, and placebo may partially reverse withdrawal symptoms in narcotic addicts. Placebos may work at least partially because they affect the emotional aspects of the pain experience through reducing the suffering or reaction component. The route of action may be through activation of endorphins (Levine et al., 1978), as administration of naloxone, a narcotic antagonist, causes a significantly greater increase in pain ratings in placebo responders than non-responders, and prior administration of naloxone decreases the likelihood of a positive placebo response.

From the foregoing analysis it is clear that the conditions are such that polypharmacy is likely along with the development of psychological dependency. This will frequently be accompanied by physical dependency as patients gravitate towards stronger and stronger drugs. As a result, pain patients may also display symptoms of narcotic dependence, symptoms which may be misattributed to their pain condition. Where this occurs, treatment should initially focus on detoxification. Patients may resist such an approach, believing their symptoms are confirmation of their ill health, and believing that because they feel bad as the drug effects wear off, they will feel much worse if they are withdrawn altogether. They fail to appreciate that they have created a need state, which will only be resolved by quitting the narcotic drugs. As a result, it is common for such patients to "doctor shop" in an attempt to secure a dependable supply of medication.

Attribution theory is relevant to detoxification, as it recommends that in parallel with efforts to withdraw the drug, attempts should be made to understand and restructure the cognitive framework of the patient. The experimental work presented earlier by Davison and Valins (1969) is instructive in this respect. The aim is to encourage patients to substitute internal control for the external control in the form of medication. This follows from experimental evidence which shows greater persistence in therapeutic gain when change is attributed to one's own efforts rather than to an external agent (see Sonne and Janoff, Chapter 5). The with-drawal may be gradual, in that patients may be told their medication will be progressively diluted with saline solution with the proportion of saline to active drug being gradually increased until total withdrawal is achieved. Patients are usually unaware of the exact proportion of active to inert drug, although they will have understood and accepted the general principle (Kelman, 1975). Under these ambiguous conditions and in conjunction with instructions in alternative controlling strategies, which will be considered in the next section, patiets will begin to attribute control to internal factors and less to the drug.

Psychological Methods of Pain Relief

It is well established that psychological processes exert considerable influence over the pain experience in terms of exacerbating or diminish-ing the sensations perceived. This knowledge has been used to teach patients to achieve psychological states which attenuate their perception and awareness of the sensory input or reduce the emotional impact or aversiveness of such noxious stimulation. Experimental studies have evaluated a number of approaches with varying results. These include:

(1) somatization, in terms of focusing on the sensations of the pain (Bobey and Davidson, 1970);

(2) imaginative inattention (Chaves and Barber, 1974);

(3) imaginative transformation of the pain (Neufeld, 1970);

(4) imaginative transformation of the context (Weisenberg, 1977);

(5) relaxation and deep breathing (Mulcahy and Jany, 1973).

The results have been inconsistent in the laboratory owing to a number of methodological problems concerning the instructions given, the de-mand characteristics operating and the type of stressor selected. There is the additional consideration of a ceiling effect, in that no matter how efficacious a procedure or coping strategy may be, at some point the pain will become unbearable for any subject. A more serious objection con-cerns the inability of such studies to replicate the anxiety which inevitably accompanies clinical pain, for in the laboratory the subject knows there is a time limitation (Proccaci *et al.*, 1979).

An important ingredient of such approaches is the attempt to bring about cognitive restructuring. Laboratory experiments have shown that people who believe themselves unable to relieve or avoid pain or stress suffer more than those who perceive themselves to have control available (Bowers, 1968). An important element of psychological treatment is the attempt to restore the patient's potential for control, as the traditional dependence of the chronic pain patient on the family and professional–

medical help diminishes self-help skills. For example, rather than attributing the pain to factors outside their control, patients have been trained to conceptualize it in ways which provide opportunities for control. Levundusky and Pankratz (1976) presented a case of a chronic pain patient in which the sensations were described as resembling steel bands being progressively tightened around the chest. Treatment consisted first of relaxation and instructions in imagining the bands tightly affixed to the chest and the sensations produced by this; it proceeded by imagining the bands being slowly loosened, noticing the reduction in painful sensations and appreciating the comfort accompanying the release of the bands. Similar use of imagery may be employed with back pain patients who describe their pain as like a knife being turned in the small of the back. In this case patients can be instructed to imagine the knife being slowly withdrawn and to focus on the sensations of relief which ensue.

A similar approach was adopted in the following case. A woman with unremitting facial pain attested to feeling helpless about her life owing to the fact that it was completely dominated by the pain, over which she had no control. It presented difficulties for her continuing to work, as she had no warning when incapacitating pain attacks might occur. Although she was loth to abandon work altogether as she appreciated its distracting benefits, she saw no alternative. A careful assessment indicated that tension of a psychological and bodily nature was also a problem which precipitated and exacerbated the pain. While the pain was perceived to be beyond control owing to the long history of failure, tension was accepted at the outset as potentially modifiable. Hypnotic induction of relaxation was implemented with good result. As the tension was a precipitating factor in the build-up of the pain, the relaxation offered control where it had been absent in the past. This case example is instructive in that it identifies an essential component of psychological therapy: namely, attempting to encourage the patient to take a more differentiated view of events, so that not all problems are automatically attributed to the existence of pain, over which there may be little control, and then attempting to identify other factors which may be responsive to change.

Hypnotic procedures can also be viewed within this framework, as these may be a means of inducing the belief that the sensations can be construed in a less threatening or distressing way. Rather than attempt to induce an implausible suggestion to a chronic pain patient of the kind, "Your pain is disappearing," a more permissive induction strategy may be of greater benefit. Such an approach may also reduce the likelihood of reactance occurring. For if the physician suggests the pain is diminshing and the patient is aware it is not, rapport it likely to be lost. However, if instead the therapist adopts the strategy of asking the patient to notice the sensations and wonders whether these can become part of a general feeling of comfort and relaxation (Barber, 1977), then the suffering component of the pain may be reduced.

So far, pain has largely been considered within a respondent framework. However, the state of pain is recognized through witnessing pain behaviour. This makes it possible to view pain within an operant framework in that the behaviours, whether verbal or non-verbal, can be thought of as operants influenced by consequences and amenable to modification by the manipulation of reinforcement contingencies. The basic thesis of such a viewpoint is that pain behaviours can be shaped and reinforced independently of the original physiological sensation and tissue damage. As with other manifestations of ill health, the occurrence of pain brings about radical changes in reinforcement contingencies. In some cases the reinforcement contingent upon the pain may maintain pain behaviours, such as withdrawal from activities or complaints, even when the nociceptive input has become quiescent or when such reactions are counter-therapeutic. For example, the occurrence of pain makes a person the focus of attention for his family and also the medical profession. In the event of unremitting pain, the patient may come to derive a high proportion of reinforcement through the expression of the pain, as other reinforcing activities may be suspended. Although for the majority of people continuing medical investigations would be aversive, for some these offer the opportunity for a certain celebrity status, with the motivation to continue deriving from the need to obtain relief. Such circumstances promote the tendency to attribute control to external factors, as there is an implicit belief in the knowledge and treatment potential of the medical profession. Attempts have been made to study chronic pain patients using the locus of control scales to see whether greater externality is in fact a characteristic of such patient groups. Skevington (1979) reported that undiagnosed chronic pain complainers displayed a tendency to believe in the importance of chance factors, although the hypothesis that chronic arthritic patients would display an externality profile was not confirmed. Patients attributing control to chance factors may have lost faith in the efficacy of treatment. Such attributions are reminiscent of work on helplessness and depression (Abramson et al., 1978), which may not be surprising as depression is common in pain patients (Sternbach, 1978).

Once again, an integral part of operant approaches is the demonstration of personal effectiveness and control. The pain-maintaining implications of contingent medication have already been described and deserve no further mention. Another implication is that the imposition of a regimen of rest and withdrawal may enable a patient to legitimately avoid certain odious tasks. A woman with a fear or dislike of sex with her husband may find pelvic pain an effective means of avoiding the "pain" of intercourse. Under such circumstances the powerful reinforcing contingencies may consolidate and maintain illness and pain behaviour, irrespective of the original cause and level of nociceptive input. As a result, attempts have been made to implement operant approaches to modify pain behaviour. In this context improvement derives from a decrease in specifically defined pain behaviours and an increase in "well" behaviours (Fordyce, 1976).

E. SUMMARY AND IMPLICATIONS

Considerable advances are being made in the management of the pain patient. Current models of pain emphasize the complex, multi-dimensional nature of the pain experience and the way it is subject to multiple influences. For a proportion of patients, pain does not remit following treatment and it is now clear that no single approach can offer complete relief. The patient with chronic intractable benign pain syndrome represents a serious psychosocial problem accompanied by a high prevalence of iatrogenic complications, including adverse drug reactions and ineffective surgical procedures involving an excessive use of health care resources. To date none of the most commonly employed procedures has proved to be completely satisfactory for adequate or permanent amelioration of pain. Melzack and Casey's (1968) conclusion from a review of the medical literature is still relevant today: "The surgical and pharmacological attacks on pain might well profit by redirecting thinking toward the neglected and almost forgotten contribution of motivational and cognitive processes. Pain can be treated not only by trying to cut down sensory input by anaesthetic blocks, surgical intervention and the like, but also by influencing the motivational–affective and cognitive factors as well" (p. 435).

A major and unifying theme in the psychological treatment of pain patients is its attempt to encourage the patients to explicitly or implicitly change their formulation of the pain. This involves reattributing problems and difficulties from stable, unremitting causes, in this case the pain, to transitory and modifiable events or experiences, over which there are real or perceived opportunities for control. Chronic pain patients are likely to adopt a passive–helpless orientation, which will undermine treatment efforts and impair their everyday functioning. Well behaviours tend to be discarded as the patient becomes entrenched in the sick role. As Fordyce and Steger (1979) have pointed out, the adoption of a sick, passive role will only serve to focus attention on the pain and so have further debilitating effects. It is more appropriate to educate the patient in ways of coping with the pain and leading as full a life as possible. This follows from the realization that abolition of the pain will not lead to a restoration of functioning, as protracted impairment may mean well behaviours are no longer accessible. Reattribution may be accomplished by removing the focus on the pain and attempting to work with problems over which there is perceived control.

While attribution theory has relevance for pain understanding and management, its therapeutic contribution in its own right is necessarily limited. Although experimental work involving manipulation of attributions has been shown to exert an influence over laboratory pain measures, it would be unrealistic to expect modification of attributions alone to alter pain experience, even if it were clear how this could be accomplished outside of the laboratory setting. Rather, it appears that treatment effects will be potentiated where patients attribute their gains to their own efforts or skills which are developed in the course of treatment. As has been seen, this has particular relevance for the administration of pain-relieving medication. Engendering a psychological dependence on medication to the exclusion of alternative methods of influencing or controlling pain very often has unsatisfactory consequences. As has been stated, medication will rarely abolish pain in these patients. It encourages a passive attitude where the pain is accepted as being outside of personal control and amenable to external control only. This attitude is counter-therapeutic and leads to a compounding of the problems. Medication needs to be administered in such a way that the patients' own resources are being tapped as an adjunct to medication therapy. It is necessary to move towards the position whereby it is routinely ensured that in addition to providing therapy aimed at abolishing the pain, the conditions permit patients to attribute the change to internal factors, in order that progress be maintained and gains transferred from the clinic to the patients' everyday environment.

REFERENCES

Abramson, L. Y., Seligman, M. E. P. and Teasdale, J. D. (1978). Learned helplessness in humans: critique and reformulation. *Journal of Abnormal Psychology* **87**, 849–874.

Bandler, R., Madaras, G. and Bem, D. (1968). Self observation as a source of pain perception. *Journal of Personality and Social Psychology* **9**, 205–209.

Barber, J. (1977). Rapid induction analgesia: a clinical report. *American Journal of Clinical Hypnosis* **19**, 138–147.

Beecher, H. K. (1959). *The Measurement of Subjective States*. London: Oxford University Press.

Beecher, H. K. (1972). The placebo effect as a nonspecific force surrounding disease and the treatment of disease. *In* R. Jongen, W. D. Keidel, A. Herz, C. Steichels, J. P. Payne and R. A. P. Burt (eds) *Pain: Basic Principles, Pharmacology, Therapy*. Stuttgart: George Thieme.

Blackwell, B. (1976). Treatment adherence. *British Journal of Psychiatry* **129**, 513–531.

Bobey, M. and Davidson, P. (1970). Psychological factors affecting pain tolerance. *Journal of Psychosomatic Research* **14**, 371–376.

Bond, M. R. and Pilowsky, I. (1966). Subjective assessment of pain and its relationship to the administration of analgesics in patients with advanced cancer. *Journal of Psychosomatic Research* **10**, 203–206.

Bowers, K. G. (1968). Pain, anxiety and perceived control. *Journal of Consulting and Clinical Psychology* **32**, 596–602.

Campbell, J. D. (1975). Attribution of illness: another double standard. *Journal of Health and Social Behaviour* **7**, 114–126.

Chaves, J. and Barber, T. (1974). Cognitive strategies, experimenter modeling and expectation in the attenuation of pain. *Journal of Abnormal Psychology* **83**, 356–363.

Crue, B. L. (1979). *Chronic Pain: Further Observations from the City of Hope National Medical Center*. New York: SP Medical and Scientific Books.

Davison, G. and Valins, S. (1969). Maintenance of self attributed and drug attributed behaviour change. *Journal of Personality and Social Psychology* **11**, 25–33.

Fordyce, W. S. (1976). *Behavioural Methods for Chronic Pain and Illness*. St. Louis: The C.V. Mosby Co.

Fordyce, W. S. and Steger, J. C. (1979). Behavioural management of chronic pain. *In* J. P. Brady and O. Pomerleau (eds) *Behavioural Medicine: Theory and Practice*. Baltimore, Maryland: Wilkins and Wilkins.

Fordyce, W. S., Fowler, R. S., Lehmann, J. F., Delateur, B. J., Sand, P. L. and Treischmann, R. B. (1973). Operant conditioning in the treatment of chronic pain. *Archives of Physical Medicine and Rehabilitation* **54**, 399–408.

Hill, H. E., Kornetsky, C. H., Flanary, H. G. and Wikler, A. (1952). Studies of anxiety associated with anticipation of pain. *Archives of Neurology* **67**, 612–618.

Kaye, B. D. (1979). *A pilot study of pain relief clinics and the possible role of psychologists in them*. Unpublished MSc Thesis, University of Leeds.

Kelman, H. C. (1975). Was deception justified—and was it necessary? *Journal of Abnormal Psychology* **84**, 172–174.

Kosambi, D. D. (1968). Living prehistory in India. *Scientific American* 105–114.

Leavitt, F. and Garron, C. (1980). Validity of a back pain classification scale for detecting psychological disturbance as measured by the MMPI. *Journal of Clinical Psychology* **36**, 186–189.

Levine, J. D., Gordon, N. C. and Fields, H. L. (1978). The mechanism of placebo analgesia. *Lancet* **ii**, 654–657.

Levundusky, P. and Pankratz, L. (1975). Self control techniques as an alternative to pain medication. *Journal of Abnormal Psychology* **84**, 165–168.

Levundusky, P. and Swett, C. (1979). Inpatient contracting: a behavioural treatment approach to chronic pain. *In* D. J. Oborne, M. Gruneberg and J. R. Eiser (eds) *Research Psychology and Medicine* (vol. 1). London and New York: Academic Press.

Liberman, R. (1962). An analysis of the placebo phenomenon. *Journal of Chronic Disease* **15**, 761–783.

Melzack, R. (1973). *The Puzzle of Pain*. London: Penguin Books.

Melzack, R. (1975). The McGill Pain Questionnaire: major properties and scoring methods. *Pain* **1**, 277–299.

Melzack, R. and Casey, K. (1968). Sensory, motivational and central control determinants of pain: a new conceptual model. *In* D. Kenshalo (ed.) *The Skin Senses*. Springfield, Illinois: Charles C. Thomas.

Melzack, R. and Wall, P. D. (1965). Pain mechanisms: a new theory. *Science* **150**, 971–979.

Mulcahy, R. and Janz, N. (1973). Effectiveness of raising pain perception thresholds in males and females using a psychoprophylactic childbirth technique during induced pain. *Nursing Research* **22**, 423–427.

Neufeld, R. and Davidson, P. (1971). The effects of vicarious and cognitive rehearsal on pain tolerance. *Journal of Psychosomatic Research* **15**, 329–335.

Nisbett, R. E. and Schachter, S. (1966). Cognitive manipulation of pain. *Journal of Experimental Social Psychology* **2**, 227–236.

Proccaci, P. Zoppi, M. and Maresca, M. (1979). Experimental pain in man. *Pain* **6**, 123–140.

Reuler, J. B., Girard, D. E. and Nardone, D. A. (1980). The chronic pain syndrome: Misconceptions and management. *Annals of Internal Medicine* **93**, 583–596.

Rodin, J. (1978). Somatopsychics and attribution. *Personality and Social Psychology Bulletin* **24**, 531–540.

Schachter, S. and Singer, J. (1962). Cognitive, social and physiological determinants of emotional state. *Psychological Review* **69**, 379–399.

Skevington, S. M. (1979). Pain and locus of control: a social approach. *In* D. J. Oborne, M. Gruneberg and J. R. Eiser (eds) *Research in Psychology and Medicine* (vol. 1). London and New York: Academic Press.

Sternbach, R. (1978). *The Psychology of Pain*. New York: Raven Press.

Weisenberg, M. (1977). Pain and pain control. *Psychological Bulletin* **84**, 1008–1044.

IV
Educational Applications

10
The Effects of Teachers' Behaviour on Pupils' Attributions: a Review

Daniel Bar-Tal

A. INTRODUCTION

In recent years, with the growing interest in attribution theory and with the increasing demand for a relevant and applied social psychology, the study of attribution processes has been applied to different social problems (see, for example, Frieze *et al.*, 1979, and the present volume). One attributional model which has been applied specifically to educational problems is Weiner's attributional model of achievement-related behaviour (Weiner *et al.*, 1971; Weiner, 1974).

This chapter will review Weiner's model, present its application to the analysis of pupils' and teachers' perceptions and behaviours in the classroom, discuss the antecedents of pupils' attributions and, specifically, focus on the influence of teachers on pupils' causal perception of success and failure. Finally, the paper will discuss several educational applications.

B. WEINER'S ATTRIBUTIONAL MODEL OF ACHIEVEMENT-RELATED BEHAVIOUR

Weiner presented his model as an attributional analysis of an individual's achievement-related behaviour, suggesting that individuals' causal perception of success and failure may be of major importance in understanding such behaviour. According to Weiner, causal perceptions of success and failure mediate between the antecedent conditions and achievement-related behaviour (Weiner, 1974; Weiner *et al.*, 1971).

Specifically, in the most recent formulation, Weiner (Weiner, 1977, 1979; Weiner *et al.*, 1978) has suggested that individuals use a variety of causes to explain their success or failure on achievement tasks. These causes can be classified in three dimensions. One dimension, locus of causality, differentiates the causes in terms of their internality/externality. While some causes, such as ability, effort, personality, mood or health might be considered internal, because they might be believed to originate within the person, other causes such as luck, others' interference, home conditions or task difficulty might be considered external, because they might be believed to originate outside the person. The second dimension differentiates causes in terms of their stability over time. While some causes, such as mood, effort or luck, may be considered unstable, because they may be believed to fluctuate over time, other causes, such as ability, task difficulty or home conditions may be considered as stable, since they may be believed not to change over time. The third dimension differentiates the causes in terms of their controllability. While some causes, such as effort, attention, or others' help, may be believed to be under the volitional control of the person, other causes, such as mood, luck, health or ability, may be believed not to be under the volitional control of the person.

The above described dimensions have important consequences. They are related to individuals' cognitive reactions (such as their expectations regarding future outcomes), to their affective reactions (such as self-esteem changes), and to their behavioural reactions (such as achievement-related behaviour). Weiner (1974, 1979) postulated that expectancy for future success is determined by stability of the causes. Ascription of an outcome to unstable causes produces greater shifts in expectancy of achievement to the desired outcome than does ascription to stable causes (see McMahan, 1973; Valle and Frieze, 1976; Weiner *et al.*, 1976 for empirical support). Failure at an achievement task attributed to unstable causes may result in expectations for eventual success, since unstable causes might change. Failure due to stable causes is expected to continue, since these causes are believed to remain. Similarly, if success was attributed to stable causes, continued success would be expected.

The locus of causality dimension is an important determinant of affective reactions (Weiner *et al.*, 1978). Individuals who attribute their success to internal causes experience affects of pride, competence, confidence, and satisfaction, while individuals who attribute failure to internal causes experience feelings of guilt and resignation.

Of special interest for the present paper is the link between causal perception of success or failure and achievement-related behaviour. There is a substantial amount of evidence indicating that causal perception of success and failure influences the individual's persistence, intensity and choice behaviour of achievement tasks (e.g. Butkowsky and Willows, 1980; Diener and Dweck, 1978; Dweck, 1975; Fyans and Maehr, 1979; Kukla, 1972; Weiner et al., 1972). Individuals who tend to attribute their failure to unstable-controllable causes, such as effort, tend to persist for a long time even in failure situations. This attribution of failure enables them to believe that there is a possibility of modifying the outcome in the future. Conversely, attribution of a failure to stable-uncontrollable causes does not leave the possibility of changing the outcome in the future and, therefore, there is no reason to persist. The belief in unstable-controllable causes such as effort causes the person to assume that the outcome depends on will. Therefore, these individuals perform with great intensity on achievement tasks. On the other hand, the belief in stable or uncontrollable causes, such as ability or mood, does not motivate the person to perform with intensity, since there is no belief in having control over the causes of success or failure. Finally, it was found that pupils tend to prefer to perform tasks that are compatible with their causal perception. For example, pupils who generally attribute their achievement outcome to ability are likely to choose tasks in which competence is requisite to outcome. Conversely, pupils who tend to attribute their success to luck prefer tasks which depend on chance and avoid tasks requiring competence. In view of these findings, which demonstrate the importance of causal perception for achievement behaviour, it is not surprising that Weiner's model has been applied to education for the analysis of pupils' behaviour.

C. ANTECEDENTS OF PUPILS' ATTRIBUTIONS

The first, important question is how pupils decide what causes are responsible for their success or failure. On the basis of Weiner's model (Weiner, 1974) it is suggested that two general categories of antecedents influence pupils' causal perception: their own personal dispositions and the external information available to them. The personal dispositions category consists of three subcategories: (a) personality tendencies; (b) demographic status; and (c) causal schemata. The available information consists of five subcategories: (a) own performance; (b) others' performance; (c) constraints and nature of the achievement task; (d) parents' or others' influence; and (e) teachers' influence. The list of antecedents and their effects are depicted in Fig. 1.

Antecedents

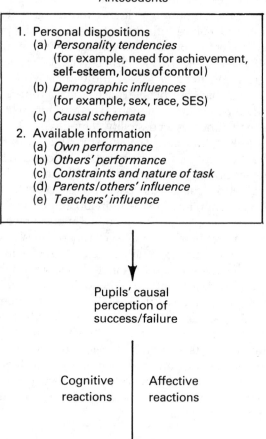

1. Personal dispositions
   (a) *Personality tendencies*
       (for example, need for achievement,
       self-esteem, locus of control)
   (b) *Demographic influences*
       (for example, sex, race, SES)
   (c) *Causal schemata*
2. Available information
   (a) *Own performance*
   (b) *Others' performance*
   (c) *Constraints and nature of task*
   (d) *Parents/others' influence*
   (e) *Teachers' influence*

Pupils' causal
perception of
success/failure

Cognitive   Affective
reactions   reactions

Pupils' achievement-
related behaviour

Fig. 1. Antecedents of causal perception mediating achievement-related behaviour.

Differences in Pupils' Personal Dispositions

Personal dispositions consist of the motivational biases of pupils to form and hold attributions that serve their needs and desires. The personal dispositions to ascribe specific patterns of causality derive from personality characteristics, demographic status and causal schemata.

Several studies contended that certain personality characteristics are related to differential attributional tendencies. Thus, for example, a series of empirical studies (e.g. Bar-Tal and Frieze, 1977; Kukla, 1972; Murray and Mednick, 1975) has demonstrated that need for achievement influences causal ascription. While persons high in achievement needs tend to attribute success to ability and effort, persons low in achievement needs do not display clear attributional preferences for success. In cases of failure, while persons high in achievement needs tend to attribute failure to lack of effort, persons low in need for achievement tend to attribute it to lack of ability. Differential attributions were also found with regard to different self-esteem tendencies (e.g. Ames and Felker, 1979; Fitch, 1970) and different locus of control dispositions (e.g. Davis and Davis, 1977; Krovetz, 1974). Regarding self-esteem the results showed that low self-esteem persons tend to take more personal responsibility for failure than do high self-esteem persons. Differences regarding locus of control indicate that internal individuals tend to use more internal causes to explain their achievement outcome, especially in the case of failure, than do external individuals.

There is evidence that demographic characteristics are associated with attributional patterns. For example, sex differences indicate that females tend to be more external and to employ more luck attributions than do males and that females, in general, rate their ability less highly than do males (e.g. Bar-Tal and Frieze, 1977; Dweck *et al.*, 1978; Murray and Mednick, 1975; Nichols, 1975). Attributional differences were also found with regard to race and socio-economic status (SES) variables. Friend and Neale (1972) found that white children considered internal causes (ability and effort) to have more influence on the outcome than external causes (luck and task difficulty), especially in failure situations. Black children, on the contrary, considered external causes to have more influence than internal ones. Raviv *et al.* (1980) found that low SES pupils tended to attribute their failure more to stable than to unstable causes, while high SES pupils tended to attribute their failure more to internal than to external causes, especially unstable ones. In this vein, Falbo (1975) found that middle-class children tended to choose effort as causal ascription more often than did lower-class children.

Causal schemata, defined as personal conceptions as to which causes produce specific effects, and formed on the basis of past experience (Kelley, 1972), also determine individuals' attributional patterns. Bar-Tal (1974), for example, identified groups of students who employ similar causal schemata in explaining their achievement outcomes. Kun and Weiner (1973) and Kun (1977) demonstrated how students use different causal schemata in achievement situations.

Differences in the Information Available to Pupils

The information on which pupils base their attributions comes from many sources. The most salient information is one's own performance. It has been shown that information regarding one's own outcome, past outcome history, or past outcome history on similar tasks may indicate to pupils why they succeeded or failed. Thus, for example, outcomes evaluated as successes tended to be ascribed to internal causes, while outcomes evaluated as failures to external ones (e.g. Bar-Tal and Frieze, 1976; Luginbuhl *et al.*, 1975). A comparison of the achievement with past outcomes indicates the stability of the causes involved. That is, on the basis of this comparison, the pupil can know whether the outcome was accidental and unusual due to unstable-uncontrollable causes, such as luck or others' help; planned, due to unstable-controllable causes, such as effort; or usual, due to stable causes such as ability.

The results show that the consistency of the achieved outcome with past results on the same task increases the attribution to stable causes, such as ability and task difficulty, while an inconsistent outcome increases attribution to unstable causes, such as effort and luck (e.g. Ames *et al.*, 1976; Frieze and Weiner, 1971; Frieze and Bar-Tal, 1980; Meyer, 1980).

Knowledge about others' performance may also be important information for attribution. When one's outcome is different from others', one can learn a great deal about oneself. The inconsistent outcome provides information about one's ability and exerted effort. Consistent outcome provides information, mainly about the difficulty of the achievement task. Frieze and Weiner (1971), Frieze and Bar-Tal (1980) and Meyer (1980) found, for example, that students tend to ascribe outcomes inconsistent with others' results mainly to internal causes (such as ability and effort), but also to luck, and consistent outcomes to external causes (mainly to task difficulty).

The nature of the task and the constraints regarding the performance can be another source of information about the causes of the outcome. On the basis of such information, pupils can decide how the nature of the task influenced their achievement outcome. Moreover, it provides insights regarding other causes, such as ability, luck, or effort. For example, Frieze and Weiner (1971) found that the amount of time a person spends on a task affects the causal ascription. When a person spends a short time at the task, failure tends to be attributed to lack of effort and success to good luck and ease of task. However, when a person spends a long time at the task, failure is ascribed to bad luck and task difficulty, while success is attributed to the presence of effort.

Pupils do not only infer causes of their successes or failures on the basis of the available information about their own performance, others' performance or the nature of the task, but are also provided directly, often explicitly, with information about the causes from significant individuals in their lives. It seems obvious that parents react to their children's achievement outcomes and either explicitly or implicitly supply causes as to why such outcomes were achieved. Empirical evidence indicates that parents ascribe causes to the successes or failures of their children (e.g. Bar-Tal and Guttmann, 1981; Beckman, 1976). In addition, it has been demonstrated that parents communicate their attributions to their children (e.g. Bar-Tal and Goldberg, 1980). It can be assumed, therefore, that parents, being important agents of socialization, influence their children's attributions. Such information can also be provided by other significant figures in the social environment of the pupil, such as other members of the family, friends, or teachers.

Of special interest for the present paper is the influence of teachers on pupils' causal perception of success or failure. Teachers have been found to have powerful influence over pupils' perceptions and attitudes regarding achievement situations (Cooper, 1979; Good and Brophy, 1974; Hargreaves, 1972). In the case of attribution, Bar-Tal and Guttmann (1981) found that pupils' causal perceptions of success or failure were more similar to that of their teachers than that of their parents. These results were interpreted as indicating that teachers have more influence on pupils' attributions than do parents. This raises the possibility that, where little can be done on such things as pupils' demographic status and personal characteristics, it might be possible to affect children's attributions by guiding and training their teachers. The remainder of the paper will explore this possibility by analysing in greater details teachers' influence on pupils' attributions.

D. AN ATTRIBUTION MODEL OF PUPILS' AND TEACHERS' BEHAVIOUR

Bar-Tal (1979) extended the Weiner model and applied it specifically to the classroom situation, where it is used to analyse the perceptions and behaviours of pupils and teachers in interaction. The model suggests that many classroom situations involve evaluation of pupils' achievements as success or failure. In these situations, both pupils and teachers tend to ascribe causes to explain the pupils' success or failure on achievement tasks (e.g. Bar-Tal and Darom, 1979; Bar-Tal *et al.*, 1980; Cooper and Burger, 1980; Darom and Bar-Tal, 1981; Frieze and Snyder, 1980). The teachers' causal perceptions, which may not correspond to those of their pupils, are important determinants of teachers' behaviour towards their pupils. The relationship between teachers' causal perception and their behaviour towards pupils can be explained through the mediating process of teachers' expectations regarding pupils' future outcomes. It is suggested that teachers decide whether the same outcome will be repeated in the future on the basis of the classification of the causes on the dimensions of stability and controllability. If the teachers believe that the success or failure of their pupils is caused by stable causes, they might expect the same outcome to be repeated, since people believe that stable causes do not change over time. If the success or failure is attributed to unstable, but controllable, causes, the teachers might believe that the pupils will experience success in the future, on the assumption that pupils want to succeed. However, if the success or failure is attributed to unstable and uncontrollable causes, the teachers cannot predict the future achievement outcome of the pupils. In turn, it is proposed that teachers' expectations regarding pupils' future achievement affect their behaviour towards the pupils. This proposal has been supported by numerous studies which have shown that teachers' differential behaviour towards pupils is determined by their expectations regarding future outcomes (see reviews by Braun, 1976; Dusek, 1975; Cooper, 1979; and Rogers in Chapter 13).

Finally, the model suggests that pupils' achievement behaviour influences teachers' causal perception of pupils' success or failure and that teachers' behaviour towards pupils determines pupils' causal perception of their success or failure. The former link is supported by evidence reviewed by West and Anderson (1976) which indicates that teachers' expectations seem to be formed on the basis of observed pupils' behaviour and not on the basis of irrelevant cues. The latter link will be extensively discussed in the final sections of this paper, before which, however, the effect of teacher's behaviour on pupils' attributions will be described.

The Effect of Teachers' Behaviour on Pupils' Attributions

In classroom situations, teachers dominate the interactions with the pupils, pupils' attention is directed towards the teachers, whose verbal and non-verbal behaviour provides much information regarding not only academic content, but also regarding events occurring in the classroom, the pupils themselves, etc. To a large extent, this information determines pupils' reactions, such as attitudes, self-perception, or causal perception of success and failure. With regard to pupils' causal perception, it seems that teachers sometimes communicate the causes directly and sometimes pupils infer them on the basis of teachers' behaviour (Blumenfeld et al., 1977). It is suggested that teachers' behaviours which influence pupils' causal perception, can be classified into five categories: (a) verbal appeals; (b) instructions; (c) reinforcements; (d) verbal feedback; and (e) direct references to causality.

Verbal Appeals

Verbal appeals are defined as teachers' addresses to pupils with reference to their behaviour (achievement or non-achievement), without relation to a specific performance outcome on an achievement test. Studies by Dweck and her associates (Dweck and Bush, 1978; Dweck et al., 1978) showed how verbal appeals and direct reference to causality influence pupils' attributions. In a study by Dweck et al. (1978), teachers' reactions towards pupils were observed and coded. The observations revealed that: (a) teachers more often approach boys than girls with negative appeals regarding non-intellectual aspects of their work; (b) teachers more often approach boys than girls with positive appeals regarding intellectual quality of their work; (c) teachers provide girls more often than boys with positive appeals regarding non-intellectual aspects of their work; (d) teachers provide girls more often than boys with negative appeals regarding intellectual quality of their work; and (e) teachers refer directly to lack of motivation of boys more often than that of girls in cases of failure. These differential reactions were found to determine differences in boys' and girls' causal perceptions of success and failure: girls place less emphasis than do boys on effort as a cause of failure and are more likely than boys to attribute failure to a lack of ability. The negative appeal of teachers towards intellectually irrelevant aspects of boys' behaviour is attributed by pupils to teachers' attitude toward them, but is not perceived as an objective evaluation of their academic ability. However, the teachers' positive appeal towards boys, which was focused mainly on intellectual performance, provides a good indicator of boys' academic ability. In addition, teachers' use of effort attribution, in the case of boys' failure, indicates to boys that their failure is due to lack of effort exertion. Girls were not taught to use effort attribution, because teachers do not tend to use this cause in making attributions for girls' failure.

Teachers' appeals increase girls' tendency to attribute failure to lack of ability. The diffuse use of positive appeals is attributed by girls to teachers' attitude towards them, and not as a reflection of their academic ability. On the other hand, a highly specific negative appeal regarding the intellectual quality of girls' work in the case of failure indicates to girls that they failed as a result of low ability.

Cooper (1977) confirmed Dweck's findings. In his study, pupils who were criticized, often for reasons external to their personal effort, were found not to perceive that effort covaried with outcome on achievement tasks.

Instructions

Instructions are teachers' explanations of a task given prior to its performance. Instructions can refer to such elements as task difficulty, constraints, skills required, and motivation required. Several studies demonstrated how instructions may affect pupils' causal perception of success and failure and their achievement behaviour. These studies compared two groups of subjects who differed in their needs for achievement. As described previously, individuals low in achievement needs do not recognize the importance of effort in performance needs in general, and specifically tend to attribute their failure to lack of ability. Conversely, individuals high in achievement needs emphasize the importance of effort for success or failure.

In an experiment carried out by Kukla (1972), one group of subjects was instructed to perform a task and was told that successful performance on it depended only on ability. Another group was instructed to perform the same task, but was told that successful performance on it depended on ability and effort as well. Both groups consisted of students high and low in achievement needs. The results of this study showed that although there was no difference in achievement performance between students with high and low needs for achievement in the situation that emphasized the importance of ability, students with a high need for achievement performed significantly better than did students with a low need for achievement when the instructions emphasized ability and effort. These results indicate that the instructions probably affected students' causal perceptions. Students with a high need for achievement, who recognized the importance of effort, tried harder to succeed when they heard that the outcome depended also on exerted effort. They believed that effort would be one of the determinants of the achievement. In contrast, for students with a low need for achievement, effort was not perceived as a determinant of successful outcome, therefore they were not influenced by the instructions that also emphasized effort. These students, receiving the information that ability would determine the outcome, did not try hard, since ability either existed or did not. Similar reactions were recorded in the case of students high in achievement needs who were instructed that the outcome of the task would depend on their ability only. In another experiment by Weiner and Sierad (1975), two groups of subjects, consisting of students high and low in achievement needs, were instructed to perform an achievement task, each under different instructions. Subjects in one group were given a placebo pill and were told that it would interfere with their performance on an achievement task, while the second group did not receive a placebo and no reference was made to possible causes of their success or failure. The results showed that, while students high in achievement needs displayed greater achievements on the task having taken the pill than they did in the no-pill condition, an opposite direction of achievement was displayed by students low in achievement needs. Thus, students low in achievement needs could use the pill as a cause for failure, and thereby reduce their anxiety caused by attributing failure to lack of ability. Therefore, they performed with great intensity on hearing the instructions in reference to possible pill interference with performance. Students high in achievement needs, who usually recognize the importance of effort attributions, accepted the instructions about the interference of the pill and shifted their usual beliefs to the placebo. In this case, students believed that the detrimental effects of the placebo could not be changed, and, therefore, did not try as hard as they normally did.

Reinforcements

Reinforcements refer to teachers' use of tangible rewards or punishments in relation to a performance on an achievement task. Ames *et al.* (1977) demonstrated that the form of reward contingencies used by the teachers in the classroom might be an important factor determining pupils' causal perception of success or failure following achievement tasks. In this study, pupils were rewarded either under competitive reward contingencies or under non-competitive reward contingencies for their performance on an achievement task. Whereas under the former reward contingency only one person (the winner) of two people could receive a reward, under the latter reward contingency both pupils could get their reward irrespective of their outcome. After the task, the pupils were asked to ascribe causes for their success or failure to ability, effort, task difficulty and luck. The results showed that under a competitive reward contingency pupils tended greatly to use luck attribution. Moreover, pupils failing under a competitive reward contingency rated their own ability lower than did those failing under a non-competitive reward contingency. Thus, competitive reward structures may lead to self-derogatory attribution. The consequence of such attribution could be negative. As Ames *et al.* noted:

> Repeated experiences of this nature could conceivably contribute to a low-achievement-motive syndrome or to "learned-helplessness". Students may begin to expect failure since a low-ability attribution is a relatively stable dispositional property, and to associate negative affect with achievement setting. The consequences of failure are obviously negative, but the impact of failure in competitive conditions seems to be rather devastating to a child's self-perceptions. (p. 7)

The competitive situation probably accentuates social comparison, and failure under this condition exposes one's own ability, thus enhancing the possibility of attributing failure to lack of ability.

Verbal Feedback

In a series of experiments Meyer *et al.*, Plaeger, and Spiller (1979) investigated the effect of verbal feedback (praise or criticism) on perceptions of ability following performance. Most (5 out of 6) of the experiments they reported were studies of subjects' perception of the abilities of other people (always hypothetical). Subjects were adults, university students, high school students and grade school pupils. The experiments showed that hearing that someone had been praised after success on an easy task, or had received only a neutral reaction after failure, led subjects to conclude that the person's ability was low. If they heard however that the person had received only a neutral reaction after success on a difficult task, or had been criticized after failing on an easy task, then subjects concluded that the person must have had a high ability. One way of explaining the findings is to suppose that subjects expected those with low ability needed to be praised comparatively extravagantly while those who really could do the work did not, and could take negative criticism. Although these findings come from paper and pencil tests they do seem plausible accounts of what people think of the meaning of praise and blame feedback. One experiment (experiment 5) provided data on how people assessed such feedback information when they heard it applied to themselves. Subjects were asked to imagine themselves in the place of a student who received positive neutral or negative feedback after failing or succeeding at an easy or difficult task. The university students in this experiment responded in a way consistent with the general finding reported above.

Direct Reference to Causality

Dweck (1975) demonstrated that direct reference to causality by teachers may influence pupils' causal perception and also their achievement behaviour. In her study, subjects identified as helpless—those who do not take personal responsibility for their outcomes and did not perceive a covariation between outcome and the effort exerted—were given an achievement task on which there were programmed failures. Following each failure, the teacher said that the pupil had failed and added, "That means that you should have tried harder" (p. 679), implying that the effort was the cause of failure. Following a training session, these pupils showed a significantly greater tendency to emphasize the role of effort in determining failure. Moreover, these subjects started to show one adaptive pattern of reaction in the face of failure—persistence.

Similar results were obtained by Chapin and Dyck (1976). They also provided their pupils with a direct reference to causality following a failure. The teacher said, "No, you didn't get that. That means you should have tried harder". (1976, p. 512) Lack of effort was explained as a cause for failure. Pupils who heard this reference began to persist in their achievement performance.

Finally, Andrews and Debus (1978) also demonstrated that direct reference to causality by teachers influenced pupils' causal perception and achievement behaviour. Subjects who did not recognize the importance of effort for achievement outcomes were given a task, following which they were asked to ascribe causes for the outcome. When they did not use effort attribution, the teacher directed them to use this cause and even explicitly stated, following failure, that pupils usually fail because they do not try hard enough. If the pupils used this cause to explain their outcome, they were reinforced. The results showed that following this training pupils increased their effort attributions and improved their achievement performance.

E. EDUCATIONAL APPLICATIONS

Three major conclusions can be derived from the material reviewed in the present paper: (a) pupils ascribe causes for their failures or successes on achievement tasks; (b) causal perceptions of pupils mediate between the antecedent factors and achievement-related behaviour, which means that pupils' attributions determine their achievement behaviour; and (c) teachers greatly influence pupils' use of causes to explain their successes or failures.

If we accept the evidence indicating that certain attributional patterns are more adaptive and, therefore, more desirable for educational achievement, then the influence of teachers has special meaning for applying the theoretical considerations and empirical findings to educational practices. The analysed attributional model indicates that pupils who tend to attribute success to internal, mainly stable or controllable, causes, and who attribute failure to internal-unstable-controllable causes, tend to exhibit adaptive, mastery-oriented achievement behaviour. That is, they tend to approach rather than avoid achievement tasks, tend to persist in the face of failure, and tend to perform achievement tasks with greater intensity. Pupils who tend to attribute success to external causes and failure to internal-stable-uncontrollable causes show a very different pattern. These pupils tend to exhibit maladaptive, helpless achievement behaviour. That is, they tend to avoid achievement tasks, tend to give up in the face of failure and do not perform achievement tasks with great intensity.

In view of the evidence regarding the behavioural consequences of pupils' attributional patterns, one educational objective should be to encourage pupils to use the adaptive pattern of causal perception of their success and failure. Within the framework of such an objective, teachers could play a major role. Their behaviour is one of the determinants of pupils' causal perception. Therefore, they can direct pupils to adaptive attributions. The primary objective should be to convince pupils that effort, as an unstable-controllable factor, is an important cause of achievement outcome. Hard trying might cause success, while lack of trying might cause failure. Pupils should be convinced that effort, which can take the form of preparation at home, paying attention during lectures, or trying hard during tests, can be changed by their will. Teachers should also direct pupils to attribute their successes to internal causes. Such a tendency increases satisfaction and feelings of competence and enhances the possibility of approaching achievement tasks. Teachers should also prevent attribution of failure to stable-uncontrollable causes, such as lack of ability, because this pattern facilitates the development of helplessness. It should be pointed out that teachers should not encourage in pupils an unrealistic perception which could imply that achievement depends only on effort. Pupils should be encouraged to establish realistic self-perceptions of ability. But, within the realistic perception, the importance of effort for achievement should be emphasized.

Several behavioural practices can be recommended to teachers, in order to facilitate the use of adaptive attributional patterns. Teachers should directly refer to effort attribution in the case of pupils' success or failure. In either case, pupils should be told that effort is the cause of their outcome. Such information should not be provided only as feedback, but also it should already be emphasized in the instructions that success on achievement tasks will depend on exerted effort. In addition, praise and criticism following pupils' performance should not be applied indiscriminately. Pupils should be especially praised after success on a difficult task, which implies that they tried hard and have ability. They should be criticized following failure when they did not try hard enough. Special precautions should be taken by teachers not to diffuse their negative and positive appeals, but to focus as much as possible on achievement behaviour. Frequent use of negative and positive appeals by teachers with regard to social, management and achievement problems discounts the appeals. Pupils interpret them as reflecting teachers' general attitudes toward pupils and not as feedback regarding their ability or exerted effort. Finally, it is suggested that competitive reward contingencies should not be used, since they facilitate self-derogatory attributions.

In order to affect teachers' behaviour in the described direction, there is the need to inform them of the importance of pupils' causal perception of success and failure, and to indicate to them their own influence on such perceptions. This might affect their behaviour. A stronger effect could be achieved by in-training procedures in which teachers would be able to learn how to interact with their pupils in order to facilitate the use of adaptive attributional patterns. In in-training sessions teachers can be exposed to attribution theory and its application to classroom situations. Moreover, they can learn the behavioural practices described above. It is important to recognize that although teachers may not be able to dramatically change everything about their pupils, their actions might be a significant determinant of pupils' achievement-related behaviour.

REFERENCES

Ames, C. and Felker, D. W. (1979). Effects of self-concept on children's causal attributions and self-reinforcement. *Journal of Educational Psychology* **71**, 613–619.

Ames, C., Ames, R. and Felker, D. W. (1976). Informational and dispositional determinants of children's achievement attributions. *Journal of Educational Psychology* **68**, 63–69.

Ames, C., Ames, R. and Felker, D. (1977). Effects of competitive reward structure and valence of outcome on children's achievement attributions. *Journal of Educational Psychology* **69**, 1–8.

Andrews, G. R. and Debus, R. L. (1978). Persistence and the causal perception of failure: modifying cognitive attributions. *Journal of Educational Psychology* **70**, 154–166.

Arkin, R. M. and Manuyama, G. N. (1979). Attribution, affect, and college exam performance. *Journal of Educational Psychology* **71**, 85–93.

Bar-Tal, D. (1974). *Causal schemata as a determinant of attributions of achievement-related behavior.* Unpublished doctoral dissertation, University of Pittsburgh.

Bar-Tal, D. (1978). Attributional analysis of achievement-related behavior. *Review of Educational Research* **48**, 259–271.

Bar-Tal, D. (1979). Interactions of teachers and pupils. In I. H. Frieze, D. Bar-Tal and J. S. Carroll (eds), *New approaches to Social Problems*, pp. 337–358. San Francisco: Jossey-Bass.

Bar-Tal, D. and Darom, E. (1979). Pupils' attributions of success and failure. *Child Development* **50**, 264–267.

Bar-Tal, D. and Frieze, I. H. (1976). Attributions of success and failure for actors and observers. *Journal of Research in Personality* **10**, 256–265.

Bar-Tal, D. and Frieze, I. (1977). Achievement motivation for males and females as a determinant of attributions for success and failure. *Journal of Sex Roles* **3**, 301–313.

Bar-Tal, D. and Goldberg, M. (1980). *How pupils form their causal perceptions of success and failure.* Unpublished manuscript. Tel-Aviv University.

Bar-Tal, D. and Guttmann, J. (1981). A comparison of pupils', teachers' and parents' attributions regarding pupils' achievement. *British Journal of Educational Psychology* **51**, 301–311.

Bar-Tal, D., Goldberg, M. and Knaani, A. (1980). *Causes of success and failure and their dimensions as a function of SES and gender: Phenomenological analysis.* Unpublished manuscript, Tel-Aviv University.

Beckman, L. J. (1976). Causal attributions of teachers and parents regarding children's performance. *Psychology in the Schools* **13**, 212–218.

Blumenfeld, P. C., Hamilton, L., Wessels, K. and Falkner, D. (1977). "You can", "You should', and "You'd better": teachers attributions regarding achievement and social behaviors. Paper presented in A. Kun (Chair), *Success and failure attributions and student behavior in the classroom.* Symposium presented at the meeting of the American Psychological Association, San Francisco, 1977.

Braun, C. (1976). Teachers expectation: sociopsychological dynamics. *Review of Educational Research* **46**, 185–214.

Brophy, J. E. and Good, T. L. (1974). *Teacher-student Relationships: Causes and Consequences.* New York: Holt.

Butkowsky, I. S. and Willows, D. M. (1980). Cognitive-motivational characteristics of children varying in reading ability: evidence for learned helplessness in poor readers. *Journal of Educational Psychology* **72**, 408–422.

Chapin, M. and Dyck, D. G. (1976). Persistence of children's reading behavior as a function of N length and attribution retraining. *Journal of Abnormal Psychology* **85**, 511–515.

Cooper, H. M. (1977). Controlling personal rewards: professional teachers' differential use of feedback and the effects of feedback on students' motivation to perform. *Journal of Educational Psychology* **69**, 419–427.

Cooper, H. M. (1979). Pygmalion grows up: a model for teacher expectation communication and performance influence. *Review of Educational Research* **49**, 389–410.

Cooper, H. M. and Burger, J. M. (1980). How teachers explain students' academic performance: a categorization of free response academic attributions. *American Educational Research Journal* **17**, 95–109.

Darom, E. and Bar-Tal, D. (1981). Causal perceptions of pupils' success or failure by teachers and pupils: a comparison. *Journal of Educational Research* **74**, 233–239.

Davis, W. L. and Davis, D. E. (1977). Internal-external control and attribution of responsibility for success and failure. *Journal of Personality* **40**, 123–136.

Diener, C. I. and Dweck, C. S. (1978). An analysis of learned helplessness: continuous changes in performance, strategy, and achievement cognitions following failure. *Journal of Personality and Social Psychology* **36**, 451–462.

Dusek, J. B. (1975). Do teachers bias children's learning? *Review of Educational Research* **45**, 661–684.

Dweck, C. S. (1975). The role of expectations and attributions in the alleviation of learned helplessness. *Journal of Personality and Social Psychology* **31**, 674–685.

Dweck, C. S. and Bush, E. S. (1978). Sex differences in learned helplessness: (I) Differential debilitation with peer and adult evaluators. *Developmental Psychology* **12**, 147–156.

Dweck, C. S., Davidson, W., Nelson, S. and Enna, B. (1978). Sex differences in learned helplessness: (II) The contingencies of evaluative feedback in the classroom and (III) An experimental analysis. *Developmental Psychology* **14**, 268–276.

Falbo, T. (1975). The achievement motivations of kindergarteners. *Developmental Psychology* **11**, 529–530.

Fitch, G. (1970). Effects of self-esteem, perceived performance, and choice on causal attributions. *Journal of Personality and Social Psychology* **16**, 311–315.

Friend, R. M. and Neale, J. M. (1972). Children's perceptions of success and failure. An attributional analysis of the effects of race and social class. *Developmental Psychology* **7**, 124–128.

Frieze, I. (1976). Causal attributions and information-seeking to explain success and failure. *Journal of Research in Personality* **10**, 293–305.

Frieze, I. H. and Bar-Tal, D. (1980). Developmental trends in cue utilization for attributional judgments. *Journal of Applied Developmental Psychology* **1**, 83–93.

Frieze, I. and Snyder, H. N. (1980). Children's beliefs about the causes of success and failure in school settings. *Journal of Educational Psychology* **72**, 186–196.

Frieze, I. and Weiner, B. (1971). Cue utilization and attributional judgments for success and failure. *Journal of Personality* **39**, 591–606.

Frieze, I. H., Bar-Tal, D. and Carroll, J. S. (eds), (1979). *New Approaches to Social Problems*. San Francisco: Jossey-Bass.

Fyans, L. J. and Maehr, M. L. (1979). Attributional style, task selection, and achievement. *Journal of Educational Psychology* **71**, 499–507.

Hargreaves, D. (1972). *Interpersonal Relations and Education*. London: Routledge.

Kelley, H. H. (1972). *Causal Schemata and the Attribution Process*. Morristown, N. J.: General Learning Press.

Krovetz, M. L. (1974). Explaining success or failure as a function of one's locus of control. *Journal of Personality* **42**, 175–189.

Kukla, A. (1972). Attributional determinants of achievement-related behavior. *Journal of Personality and Social Psychology* **21**, 166–174.

Kun, A. (1977). Development of the magnitude-covariation and compensation schemata in ability and effort attributions of performance. *Child Development* **48**, 862–873.

Kun, A. and Weiner, B. (1973). Necessary versus sufficient causal schemata for success and failure. *Journal of Research in Personality* **7**, 197–207.

Luginbuhl, J. E. R. Crowe, D. H., Kahan, J. P. (1975). Causal attributions for success and failure. *Journal of Personality and Social Psychology* **31**, 86–93.

McMahan, I. D. (1973). Relationships between causal attributions and expectancy of success. *Journal of Personality and Social Psychology* **28**, 108–114.

McMillan, J. H. and Sprat, K. F. (1980). *Causal attributions and affect in a real-life testing situation*. Paper presented at the annual convention of the American Educational Research Association, Boston, 1980.

Meyer, J. P. (1980). Causal attribution for success and failure: a multivariate investigation of dimensionality, formation and consequences. *Journal of Personality and Social Psychology* **38**, 704–718.

Meyer, W. U., Bachmann, M., Biermann, U., Hempelmann, M., Ploeger, F. O. and Spiller, H. (1979). The information value of evaluative behavior: influences of praise and blame on perceptions of ability. *Journal of Educational Psychology* **71**, 259–268.

Murray, S. R. and Mednick, T. S. (1975). Perceiving the causes of success and failure in achievement. Sex, race, and motivational comparisons. *Journal of Consulting and Clinical Psychology* **43**, 881–885.

Nichols, J. G. (1975). Causal attributions and other achievement-related cognitions: effect of task outcomes, attainment value, and sex. *Journal of Personality and Social Psychology* **31**, 379–389.

Raviv, A., Bar-Tal, D., Raviv, A. and Bar-Tal, Y. (1980). Causal perceptions of success and failure by advantaged, integrated, and disadvantaged pupils. *British Journal of Educational Psychology* **50**, 137–146.

Sohn, D. (1977). Affect-generating powers of effort and ability self-attributions of academic success and failure. *Journal of Educational Psychology* **69**, 500–505.

Valle, V. A. and Frieze, I. (1976). Stability of causal attributions as a mediator in changing expectations for success. *Journal of Personality and Social Psychology* **33**, 579–587.

Weiner, B. (1974). *Achievement Motivation and Attribution Theory*. Morristown, N. J.: General Learning Press.

Weiner, B. (1977). An attributional approach for educational psychology. *In* L. Shulman (ed) *Review of Research in Education*. Ithaca, II.: F. E. Peacock.

Weiner, B. (1979). A theory of motivation for some classroom experiences. *Journal of Educational Psychology* **71**, 3–25.

Weiner, B. and Kukla, (1970). An attributional analysis of achievement motivation. *Journal of Personality and Social Psychology* **15**, 1–21.

Weiner, B. and Sierad, J. (1975). Misattribution for failure and enhancement of achievements strivings. *Journal of Personality and Social Psychology* **31**, 415–521.

Weiner, B., Frieze, I., Kukla, A., Reed, L., Rest, S. and Rosenbaum, R. M. (1971). Perceiving the causes of success and failure. *In* E. E. Jones *et al.* (eds) *Attribution: Perceiving the Causes of Behaviour*. New Jersey: GLP.

Weiner, B., Heckhausen, H., Meyer, W. and Cook, R. E. (1977). Causal ascriptions and achievement behavior: the conceptual analysis of effort. *Journal of Personality and Social Psychology* **21**, 239–248.

Weiner, B., Nierenberg, R. and Goldstein, M. (1976). Social learning (locus of control) versus attributional (causal stability) interpretations of expectancy of success. *Journal of Personality and Social Psychology* **44**, 52–68.

Weiner, B., Russell, D. and Lerman, D. (1978). Affective consequences of causal ascriptions. *In* J. H. Harvey, W. J. Ickes, and R. F. Kidd (eds), *New Directions in Attribution Research*, (vol. 2). Hillsdale, N.J.: Lawrence Erlbaum Associates.

West, C. H. and Anderson, T. H. (1976). The question of preponderant causation in teacher expectancy research. *Review of Educational Research* **46**, 613–630.

11
Expectancy × Value: a Model of How Attributions Affect Educational Attainment

J. Mark G. Williams

A. INTRODUCTION

Malcolm is a 13-year-old boy attending an 1100-pupil comprehensive school. There are 27 other students in his mixed ability class. He is tall for his age, looking older than his 13 years, and is always very neatly dressed. His "problem" is that, although anxious to please his teachers, his writing, reading and spelling are very poor compared to his overall performance. If a task involves any of these skills, he puts in minimal effort from the outset, or gives up very easily. In general his work is characterized by apathy with occasional bursts of intense effort, during which he achieves good results. A disturbed home background, known to the teachers, causes some of them to attribute his behaviour to "anxiety due to family circumstances". Others think his behaviour is due to anxiety about failure, made worse by some members of staff expecting him to be "as bright as he appears".

In this chapter I hope to study something of the cognitive and motivational processes in this child and their effects on task performance. This will involve, firstly, the drawing together of some of the theories which have been proposed to explain the effects of anxiety on performance in achievement situations. Secondly, I shall consider the relevance of attribution theory in accounting for this behaviour, focusing on those variables which mediate between attribution and performance. Finally, the practical implications of understanding more about these mediating variables will be outlined.

B. ACHIEVEMENT MOTIVATION, TEST ANXIETY AND PERFORMANCE

The importance of achievement motive, anxiety and self-esteem in affecting performance on skilled tasks from the earliest days at school (e.g. Bridgeman and Shipman, 1978) right through to college and beyond (e.g. Alpert and Haber, 1960) cannot be overestimated. In Bridgeman and Shipman's study, measures of self-esteem and achievement motivation, taken in pre-school children, predicted performance (especially in maths) when they were nine years old. In Alpert and Haber's study, measures of test anxiety in college students predicted performance on a scholastic aptitude test and predicted the student's Grade Point Average.

Since the early 1950s a great deal of research has investigated these phenomena. The research has been conducted under the various headings of "achievement motivation theory" (Atkinson, 1958), "test anxiety theory" (Mandler and Sarason, 1952; Sarason, 1975), "cognitive-motivational theory" (Weiner, 1966; Weiner and Heckhausen, 1972), and more recently "attribution theory" (Kukla, 1972; Weiner, 1974, 1979). Despite their different terminology, they all seek to explain how certain individual differences (e.g. "test anxiety", "achievement motive", "fear of failure motive", "drive", etc.) combine with certain situational factors (task difficulty, amount of threat in the situation, IQ instructions or the amount of failure feedback, etc.) to determine performance. Such research has shown that subjects who are high test anxious do better on easy tasks than low test anxious subjects, but do worse than them if the task is difficult (e.g. Sarason and Palola, 1960; Sarason, 1975, gives a comprehensive review of this literature).

This pattern of results is found not only if the task is objectively more difficult, but if there are external stresses on the student such as (a) timing (high anxious do worse than low anxious if timed, better if untimed— Morris and Liebart, 1969); or (b) believing the task is a measure of IQ (high anxious do worse than low anxious under IQ conditions, better if neutral—Sarason and Palola, 1960; Sarason, 1961); or (c) believing that one is failing the task (high anxious do worse than low anxious if told they are failing, better if told they are succeeding—Weiner, 1966); or (d) seeing another subject failing (high anxious do worse than low anxious if they have seen another subject failing, better if they have not—Sarason, 1972).

A number of different theories have been proposed to account for these data. Mandler and Sarason (1952) hypothesize two types of "cognitive" task-orientated responses, the task-relevant and the task-irrelevant, which are elicited during task performance. Task-relevant responses are organizing self-talk responses which are helpful to performance (e.g. I must try harder, I must concentrate, go more slowly, etc.). Task-irrelevant responses are disorganizing self-talk responses which are unhelpful to performance (e.g. I can't do this task, etc.). High test anxious (or low achievement motivation) subjects tend to respond to tasks with task-irrelevant responses. The more difficult the task, the more necessary it is to concentrate, and the more task-irrelevant responses will interfere with performance.

The idea that task-irrelevant self-talk interferes with performance is consistent with many of the findings in the research literature. Morris and Liebart (1969) found that high anxious subjects did worse on timed tasks. When the test anxiety questionnaire responses were analysed into the Worry (self-talk) component and the Emotional (somatic signs of anxiety) component, it was found that it was the Worry component which was mainly responsible for debilitating performance.

An alternative model, not inconsistent with that of Mandler and Sarason, also viewed deficits in terms of anxiety-based response dis-organization. Spence et al. (1956), working within Hull–Spence Drive × Habit Theory, hypothesized that high anxious (high drive) subjects will do worst when the task is difficult because the correct response is relatively low in the Habit hierarchy, and incorrect responses are relatively high. They demonstrated that high anxious subjects did worse than low anxious subjects at a paired-associate learning task when the associations to be learned were remote and there was high intralist competition. The theory also predicted, and the experiment confirmed, that high anxious subjects did better than low anxious subjects on an easy list (associations not remote, and no intralist competition).

Weiner (1966) argued that Spence's results were consistent with a "cognitive-motivational" theory of performance. If high anxious subjects were very sensitive to failure feedback, then they would do worse at the difficult task simply because that task involved a great deal of failure feedback. Weiner repeated the experiment of Spence *et al.* but gave failure feedback on the (objectively) *easy* task and success feedback on the (objectively) *difficult* task. He found that highly anxious subjects did better than low anxious on the difficult task (with success feedback) and worse than low anxious on the easy task (with failure feedback). This result was not accounted for by the Spence model, but was consistent with a motivational theory—that the "fear of failure" was stronger than the "hope of success" in high anxious subjects—causing decreased motivation when faced with failure. By contrast, "hope of success" was stronger than "fear of failure" in low anxious subjects. Failure challenged the "Hope of Success" in these subjects, causing increased motivation to succeed. So Weiner's (1966) theory claimed that it was not anxiety-based irrelevant responses which interfered with performance, but anxiety-based "fear of failure" which undermined the motivation to strive for success. It predicted, and found, that if the fear of failure was reduced (by success feedback), then high anxious subjects did well, even on difficult tasks.

This research into test anxiety has several practical aspects. Reducing the stress of assessment procedures in general (Paul and Erikson, 1961) or in particular (e.g. by not timing items—Morris and Liebart, 1969) clearly helps the high test anxious student. Smith and Rockett (1958) found that high anxious students performed better when the test answer sheet had space for comments on it. Towle and Merrill (1975) found better performance by all students on a maths task if the sequence of items went from easy to difficult, rather than difficult to easy. Finally, Papay *et al.* (1975) assessed the response of high and low anxious students (six, seven-year-olds) to multi-age or traditional classrooms. (In the multi-age classrooms, children are assigned to groups on the basis of maturity and readiness to learn rather than chronological age. The children then receive individualized instruction programmes.) After six to eight months of differential teaching with the seven-year-olds they found that the high anxious performed better than low anxious in the multi-age class, but the low anxious performed better than the high anxious in the traditional class. Clearly, a pupil's anxiety level has to be taken into account when evaluating the effects of different teaching techniques on his or her performance.

C. ATTRIBUTIONAL MODELS OF PERFORMANCE

An attributional interpretation of the test anxiety/achievement motivation literature has been made by Weiner *et al.* (1972; Weiner, 1974, 1979). They have argued that performance is ultimately a function of expectancy of success multiplied by the incentive to succeed (for previous Expectancy × Value theories of performance see Lewin, 1946; Edwards, 1954; Tolman, 1955; Atkinson, 1958). Whether Expectancy or Value of success show trial-by-trial increases or decreases depends on a subject's attribution for past success or failure. Attribution to stable causes (task difficulty or ability) affects levels of expectancy of success for future trials more than does attribution to unstable causes (luck or effort during test). Attribution to internal causes (ability or effort) affects level of self-esteem following success or failure more than does attribution to external causes (task difficulty or luck). It is now generally accepted (see Bar-Tal, Chapter 9) that a major reason why test anxious or low achievement motivated subjects perform badly in the face of failure feedback is that they attribute failure to lack of ability—reducing expectancy of success for future occasions (Weiner, 1974) and lowering self-esteem (Weiner, 1979). By contrast, non-anxious subjects attribute failure to the unstable factor of lack of effort, which does not engender hopelessness about future performance. There are now remedial measures being used for persistently failing children based on changing maladaptive attributions (see Layden Chapter 4).

A development of attributional theory was proposed by Kukla (1972). He argued that the characteristic of high anxious/low achievement motivated subjects is their belief in their own lack of ability, their chronically low expectancy for achieving desired goals. Thus, when high anxious subjects come to estimate the difficulty of a task, it will always seem more difficult to them than it does to their low anxious colleagues, who have a greater belief in their own ability. It is this estimate of the perceived difficulty of a task which determines how much effort a subject thinks he will have to expend. As perceived difficulty increases, a subject will have to expend more effort to be sure of success, until a point is reached where the subject realises that further increases in effort are not making success any more probable, and gives up. The point at which the subject gives up will come sooner for high anxious individuals for whom perceived difficulty is always higher. So the facilitated performance of high anxious subjects on easy tasks as well as the delibitated performance of high anxious subjects on difficult tasks, are explained by the same process: the subjects underestimating their own competence, producing an overestimate of difficulty; this in turn leading to a greater estimate of the effort necessary to succeed at the lower end of the perceived facility/difficulty dimension, and leading to a lower threshold for giving up at the upper end of that dimension. Clearly, naturally occurring "low ability" estimates may be mimicked by situational cues which imply that a subject is incompetent (e.g. repeated failure).

D. SOME SHORTCOMINGS OF ATTRIBUTION THEORY

The fact that some treatment programmes for children who persistently under-achieve now explicitly or implicitly employ attributional concepts attests to the value of research in this field. However, attributional models have recently become much more complex, so that it is no longer clear what the links are between attributions for success and failure in one situation and performance in the next.

First, it has become clear that students make many more attributions for success and failure than ability, effort, task difficulty and luck. Frieze (1976) distinguishes between stable and immediate effort, and adds the attributional categories of "mood", and "other person". Bar-Tal and Darom (1977) add "interest in subject matter", "conditions in the home" and "home preparation". Cooper and Burger (1978) add "physical and emotional ability", "previous experience", "habits", "attitudes", "self-perception", "maturity", "attention", "directions", "instruction", "family", and "miscellaneous".

Secondly, it is unclear whether any attributional category always represents only one end of a particular dimension. For example, "mood" can be thought of as a temporary state or a relatively permanent trait, and "task difficulty" has sometimes been seen as an "unstable" attribute (Valle and Frieze, 1976). Clearly, in order to make accurate predictions for future performance, we need to know not only the attribution categories ("task difficulty", "mood", and so on) but at what end of what dimension they occur in that instance.

Thirdly, however, the picture has been complicated by the suggestion of at least two new dimensions (in addition to stability and internality) along which particular attributions may fall. Weiner (1979) adds a "controllability" dimension, and Abramson et al. (1978) add a "globality" (generalization across situations) dimension. With now four dimensions, even if each one of the four only has two discrete "ends" (e.g. either internal or external) there are 2^4 (16) possible combinations of the dimensions. If one quite reasonably allows each dimension to have a mid-point (e.g. either internal or external or in between) then there are 3^4 (81) possible combinations of the four dimensions. In the light of this, it is not surprising that attempts to experimentally manipulate college students' attributions for failure have resulted in a very confused picture. When subjects have been led to attribute their failure to task difficulty, facilitation (Tennen and Eller, 1977), debilitation (Klein et al., 1976) and no effects (Douglas and Anisman, 1975) in subsequent task performance have all been found. When subjects have been led to believe in their own personal incompetence, both debilitation (Klein et al., 1976; Douglas and Anisman, 1975; Tennen and Eller, 1977) and facilitation (Wortman et al., 1976; Hanusa and Schulz, 1977) have resulted.

Since attribution categories and dimensions are so numerous, and the task of relating them all directly to performance so complex, it may now

be time to simplify by focusing on the variables which actually mediate
task performance. Research into the effect of attributions on performance
has two distinct aspects which can be taken separately: first, investigation
of the impact of attributions on the mediating variables (expectancy,
value, etc.); second, investigation of the way these variables affect performance. Much has been made of the first question (see Weiner, 1974),
though the addition of new categories and dimensions provide scope for
much additional research. It is the second question to which a model
proposed recently by myself and John Teasdale is addressed (Williams
and Teasdale, 1982). This will now be described in some detail.

E. THE EXPECTANCY × VALUE MODEL

Williams and Teasdale follow Kukla (1972) in assuming that students'
expectancy of success for a skilled task is linked to the amount of effort
they intend to expend. Figure 1 shows this relationship for two anticipated tasks, one easy, the other difficult.

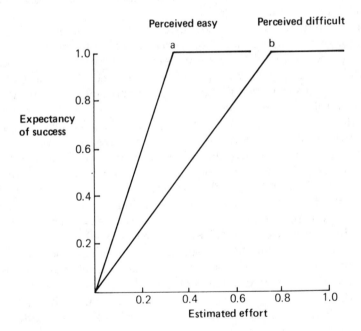

Fig. 1. Hypothetical relationship between expectancy of success and estimated
effort required for two tasks of different perceived difficulty levels.

As can be seen, students believe they will have to expend more effort on the task perceived as more difficult (relative to their own ability) to achieve the same expectancy of success, compared to the "easy" task. But "effort" or "work" has a cost—acts as a negative incentive. The more difficult the task, the more work is anticipated, and the greater the negative incentive. So unless the *positive* incentives to succeed are large enough to justify the extra effort, the negative consequences of trying at a task will outweigh the positive outcomes, and the subjects will give up. If the positive incentives are present, anticipation of a difficult task (whether realistic or not) will cause subjects to put in that great amount of effort they think is necessary to succeed. If the task then in fact turns out to be fairly easy, a better than average performance will be observed (the "facilitation" of the helplessness literature).

Level of positive incentive will not affect performance when the task is perceived as easy. Here subjects believe that success can be achieved with only moderate effort. The task outcome may be relatively unimportant, yet still be important enough to justify that moderate effort required to bring about success. With success assured for moderate effort, increases in the incentive value of the outcome will not make subjects expend any further (costly) effort.

These predictions have been tested in an experiment with college students, which manipulated both perceived difficulty and importance of success independently. Students were either told that only 5% of subjects typically succeed at the task or that 95% succeed. Within each group, students were either told that it was very important that they should be motivated to do well, or told that success or failure at the task was not important. In summary, there were 40 male and female subjects split into four groups (two levels of difficulty × two levels of importance). All subjects were tested individually. They were given the finger shuttlebox (Hiroto and Seligman, 1975) during which they could escape or avoid noise bursts by sliding a knob from one side to the other on top of the apparatus. Previous studies (Williams, 1979) had shown that the mean latency to escape the noise was very well correlated with how intense an effort the subjects expended in attempting to solve the task.

The results confirmed the predictions of the model (see Fig. 2). The performance on the test task showed that a belief that success was not important produced debilitation only if subjects expected a difficult task. The most effort was expended by those who thought the task was important and would be difficult. Importance level made no difference to performance for subjects who expected an easy task.

What happens if the expectancy of success of those showing facilitated performance is further reduced? A second experiment told all subjects that the task was important, and again told half the subjects that the task was difficult (5% succeed) and the other half that the task was easy (95% succeed). Within these two groups half the subjects received feedback that they were failing on the first eight of the 20 noise trials on the shuttlebox. The other half received no such feedback. In summary, there were 40 male and female subjects—all believing the task to be important and split into four groups (two levels of difficulty × two levels of feedback).

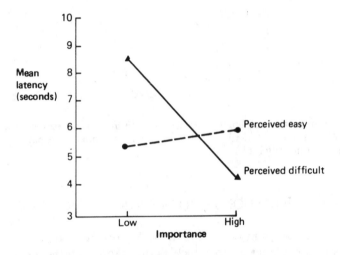

Fig. 2. Group means of latency to escape noise in the shuttlebox test task for two levels of perceived difficulty and two levels of outcome importance.

The results confirmed that the great effort of all who believed the task difficult and important, turned quickly into debilitation when these subjects thought they were failing (see Fig. 3).

The failure feedback made the students believe the task was even more difficult than they had thought, and required more effort than even the high importance level would justify, so they gave up. Note that the feedback did not affect subjects who expected an easy task. They started the task with only moderate effort, so that the fact that they were failing did not become as apparent to them as it had to those who were trying very hard from the outset.

Can the model explain how differences in test anxiety and achievement motivation lead to different levels of performance in the classroom?

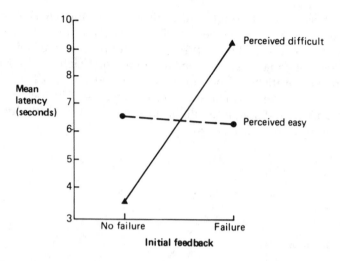

Fig. 3. Group means of latency to escape noise in the shuttlebox test task for two levels of perceived difficulty and two levels of initial feedback (outcome importance uniformly high).

F. IMPLICATIONS FOR EDUCATIONAL PRACTICE

There are two ways in which the model differs from the usual learned helplessness explanation in which performance deficits result simply from a lowered expectancy of success (e.g. Abramson *et al.*, 1978). Firstly, the model suggests that a person has not one expectancy for success for any given task, but an entire range of expectancies associated with different levels of anticipated effort expenditure. Secondly, the model assumes that effort has a cost which increases with the amount of effort expended.

In as much as laboratory studies succeed in making analogies of real-life conditions, the model would suggest that deficits in the classroom represent the effects of high perceived difficulty (low expectancy of success at most effort levels). If the task is perceived as unimportant, minimal effort will be expended from the outset. If, however, it is perceived as important, a student will choose to expend greater and greater effort levels, but beyond a certain point he will abruptly choose to expend minimal effort.

This abruptness of the transition from one level of effort to another deserves special attention. As seen above, slight changes in expectancy when a task is already seen as difficult (importance level constant) can make a large difference to amount of effort expended. Similarly, when a task is perceived as difficult very slight differences in the perceived importance of success may also lead to very large differences in effort level selected. In the light of this it is not surprising that, in previous experiments, apparently similar attributions have produced very different effects on task performance.

Can any of the phenomena talked about by the model be seen in practice? Malcolm, the 13-year-old boy referred to at the start of this chapter, is an example of a student who gives cause for concern to his tutors. In one lesson he had been given a project to do: to draw a poster, then write a short essay on the subject of the poster. Malcolm reckoned he could draw quite well, and the poster was soon completed. He did not, however, think he was any good at writing essays, nor could he see the value of it, so he sat looking out of the window for a while. When it became apparent that the other children had finished and were writing their essays he decided to do some more work on his poster. When the teacher came round, she found him drawing small lines of irrelevant detail on an apron on one small figure in the corner of the poster.

The case of Malcolm is an example of apathy for an anticipated task which is at once perceived as difficult and unimportant. But what practical suggestions can be made? Williams and Teasdale's experimental results suggest that effort may be increased by making the task look easier. Thus a teacher may attempt to change his perceptions, or change the task itself, for example by splitting up what was to him a complex assignment into more simple sub-parts. The important general point to note is that though the apathetic student looks as if all he needs is more incentive, this is not necessarily so. Williams and Teasdale's experiments demonstrated that if students believed that success was fairly easily attainable, lack of incentive did not by itself stop them expending some effort at the task.

In fact, for a student who is apathetic because tasks seem too difficult and unimportant, Williams and Teasdale's results would seem to caution against attempting only to increase incentive. The dangers of doing so may be illustrated by other events which happened to Malcolm. For a combination of reasons his headmaster decided to put him "on report". He had to carry around a timetable to be signed by every teacher whose lesson he attended. Each teacher had to closely monitor his work, lesson by lesson, and report on it. There was a sudden and dramatic increase in Malcolm's effort expenditure in all those subjects about which he had shown "apathy". His teachers were delighted, but were they right to be? The school's intervention had not brought about a gradual increase in effort which ended with moderate and appropriate levels of work, but a sudden switch from low to high effort expenditure. It seems that they had increased the incentives (albeit by increasing the scrutiny of the work) without changing the perceived difficulty of the tasks. The danger is that in this "high effort" state, as was seen in Williams and Teasdale's second experiment, the student is very vulnerable to failure feedback, which, if it occurs, will produce further debilitation and increased hopelessness. To avoid this possibility the remedial measures suggested in this book are clearly relevant. Any intervention which not only gradually increases positive incentive but also increases a student's expectancy of success for only moderate effort is predicted by the model to have beneficial consequences. One interesting aspect of this intervention is that pupils may have to be discouraged from trying too hard initially, so that, if failure occurs, it does not allow the child to conclude that he has failed after "giving all he can".

In Williams and Teasdale's experiment students who expected an important difficult task tended to put in a great deal of effort. However, if given failure feedback, they showed *below* average *persistence*. Thus, the model highlights the need to distinguish between intensity of effort, and degree of persistence. In attributional and achievement research, the type of test tasks used have been many and varied, and have not always made the distinction clear. Some tasks have emphasized the *intensity* aspect of performance (e.g. Digit Symbol Substitution tasks—Weiner *et al.*, 1972). Others have emphasised the *persistence* aspect (e.g. line tracing—Andrews and Debus, 1978). And still more tasks have emphasized the *quality* aspects of performance (e.g. reading, maths, Raven's Matrices—Bridgeman and Shipman, 1978). Only occasionally has more than one aspect of performance been examined—Lepper *et al.* (1973) not only looked at persistence in drawing pictures by 3 to 5-year-olds, but also examined the quality of the pictures.

The distinctions between the different aspects of performance are important, for there is evidence that children sometimes choose to trade off one aspect against another, e.g. to sacrifice more intense effort for increased persistence. Fisher *et al.* (1975) evaluated the effects of giving children choice on a Computer Aided Instruction (CAI) programme. The CAI consisted of a number of tasks varying in difficulty level. Half the children were allowed to choose the level of difficulty of the tasks presented, the other half were "yoked" so that they had equivalent difficulty levels but no choice. The results showed an increased persistence (time engaged in doing the tasks) for the pupils who had choice, but the tasks on which they spent most time were two grades lower than their pre-experimental achievement level—that is, they deliberately selected tasks on which they knew they could succeed and which thereby required less intense effort. One assumption of Computer Aided Instruction Programmes is that they keep the student on tasks whose difficulty level is optimally stimulating (neither too easy nor too difficult). Fisher *et al.* concluded that subjects given choice were not learning as much from their lessons as might be expected from the length of time they were engaged in the task. It seems that in order to maintain a sense of their own ability students were showing "low effort persistence" which is reminiscent of Malcolm's needlessly perseverative drawing of irrelevant detail on his poster.

Covington and Omelich (1979) have also pointed out how pupils act in ways to try and maintain a sense of their own ability. They point out a basic problem in the school system—that schools are both places to learn (where *effort* is most valued) and places where pupils are sorted out according to their *ability* to learn. They suggest alternative classroom reward systems featuring individual student goal-setting with absolute performance standards. In this system any number of students can achieve a given grade so long as their performance achieves a pre-arranged criterion. It is not clear, however, how much weight such a system would give to the achievement of the "individual goals" set by the student versus achievement of the "absolute performance standards". There is also some doubt, arising from the study of Fisher *et al.*, about whether completely free choice of goal actually maximizes learning. Nevertheless, the importance of re-attribution training so long as it is combined with teaching students to set realistic goals is evident. Together with an awareness of how such training is affecting the variables which directly mediate performance, such techniques suggest promising ways of making success at tasks (which are perceived as difficult) easier to achieve not only in the student's mind, but also in fact.

G. CONCLUDING REMARKS

Attempting to make sense of the factors influencing educational attainment is not easy. This chapter has outlined a possible way in which attribution may affect the amount of effort a student expends on a task. The argument has been that the particular attribution a student makes for past success and failure is not so important as the effect that attribution has on the perceived difficulty and outcome value of future tasks. As further research discovers more attributional categories and dimensions, so more work will be needed to establish the effects of these on perceived expectancy and value of future success. Williams and Teasdale's model offers one approach to understanding the next stage in the process—how

E and V then affect performance. The purpose of their model in the present context is to stimulate enquiry into the possible causes and remedies of children with learning difficulties—not to claim unique predictive power for particular variables. It is not known, for example, whether differences due to the age of pupils limit the generalizability of this or any other model. It is not known the extent to which children with learning difficulties differ qualitatively from subjects used in this or any other analogue studies. However, these are, at least, empirical questions for which further empirical enquiry will supply answers.

ACKNOWLEDGEMENT

I would like to thank Mrs Barbara Williams for her assistance in drafting parts of this paper.

REFERENCES

Abramson, L. Y., Seligman, M. E. P. and Teasdale, J. D. (1978). Learned helplessness in humans: critique and reformulation. *Journal of Abnormal Psychology* **87**, 49–74.

Alpert, R. and Haber, R. (1960). Anxiety in academic achievement situations. *Journal of Abnormal and Social Psychology* **61**, 207–215.

Andrews, G. R. and Debus, R. L. (1978). Persistence and the causal perception of failure: modifying causal attributions. *Journal of Educational Psychology* **70**, 154–166.

Atkinson, J. W. (ed.) (1958). *Motives in Fantasy, Action and Society*. Princeton: Van Nostrand.

Bar-Tal, D. and Darom, E. (1977). Causal perceptions of pupils' success or failure by teachers and pupils: a comparison. Unpublished manuscript. University of Tel-Aviv, Israel.

Bridgeman, B. and Shipman, V. C. (1978). Pre-school measures of self-esteem and achievement motivation as predictors of third grade achievement. *Journal of Educational Psychology* **70**, 17–28.

Cooper, H. M. and Burger, J. M. (1978). Internality, stability and personal efficacy: a categorisation of free response academic attributions. Unpublished manuscript. University of Missouri–Columbia.

Covington, M. V. and Omelich, C. L. (1979). Effort: the double-edged sword in school achievement. *Journal of Educational Psychology* **71**, 169–182.

Douglas, D. and Anisman, H. (1975). Helplessness or expectation incongruity: effects of aversive stimulation on subsequent performance. *Journal of Experimental Psychology: Human Perception and Performance* **1**, 411–417.

Edwards, W. (1954). The theory of decision making. *Psychological Bulletin* **51**, 380–417.

Fisher, M. D., Blackwell, L. R., Garcia, A. B. and Greene, J. C. (1975). Effects of student control and choice on engagement in a CAI arithmetic task in a low-income school. *Journal of Educational Psychology* **67**, 776–783.

Frieze, I. H. (1976). Causal attribution and information seeking to explain success and failure. *Journal of Research in Personality* **10**, 293–305.

Hanusa, B. H. and Schulz, R. (1977). Attributional mediators of learned helplessness. *Journal of Personality and Social Psychology* **35**, 602–611.

Hiroto, D. S. and Seligman, M. E. P. (1975). Generality of learned helplessness in man. *Journal of Personality and Social Psychology* **31**, 311–327.

Hull, C. L. (1943). *The Principles of Behaviour*. New York: Appleton-Century-Crofts.

Klein, D. C., Fencil-Morse, E. and Seligman, M. E. P. (1976). Depression, learned helplessness, and the attribution of failure. *Journal of Personality and Social Psychology* **33**, 508–516.

Kukla, A. (1972). Foundations of an attributional theory of performance. *Psychological Review* **79**, 454–470.

Lepper, M. R. Greene, D. and Nisbett, R. E. (1973). Undermining children's intrinsic interest with extrinsic reward. A test of the "overjustification" hypothesis. *Journal of Personality and Social Psychology* **28**, 129–137.

Lewin, K. (1946). Behaviour and development as a function of the total situation. In L. Carmichael (ed.) *Manual of Child Psychology*, pp. 791–844. New York: Wiley.

Mandler, G. and Sarason, S. B. (1952). A study of anxiety and learning. *Journal of Abnormal and Social Psychology* **47**, 166–173.

Morris, L. W. and Liebart, R. M. (1969). Effects of anxiety on timed and untimed intelligence tests: another look. *Journal of Consulting and Clinical Psychology* **33**, 240–244.

Papay, J. P., Costello, R. J., Hedl, J. J. and Spielberger, C. D. (1975). Effects of trait and state anxiety on the performance of elementary school children in traditional and individualised multi-age classrooms. *Journal of Educational Psychology* **67**, 840–846.

Paul, G. L. and Ericksen, W. W. (1961). Effects of test anxiety on "real life" examinations. *Journal of Abnormal and Social Psychology* **62**, 165–168.

Sarason, I. G. (1961). The effects of anxiety and threat on the solution of a difficult task. *Journal of Abnormal and Social Psychology* **62**, 165–168.

Sarason, I. G. (1972). Test anxiety and the model who fails. *Journal of Personality and Social Psychology* **22**, 410–413.

Sarason, I. G. (1975). Test anxiety, attention and the general problem of anxiety. In C. D. Spielberger and I. G. Sarason (eds) *Stress and Anxiety*, vol. II. New York: Wiley.

Sarason, I. G. and Palola, E. G. (1960). The relationship of test and general anxiety, difficulty of task and experimental instructions to performance. *Journal of Experimental Psychology* **59**, 185–191.

Solomon, R. (1948). The influence of work on behaviour. *Psychological Bulletin* **45**, 1–40.

Smith, W. and Rockett, F. (1958). Anxiety and test performance. *Journal of Educational Research* **52**, 138–141.

Spence, K. W., Farber, I. E. and McFann, H. H. (1956). The relation of anxiety (drive) level to performance in competitive and non-competitive paired-associate learning. *Journal of Experimental Psychology* **52**, 296–305.

Tennen, H. and Eller, S. J. (1977). Attributional components of learned helplessness and facilitation. *Journal of Personality and Social Psychology* **35**, 265–271.

Tolman, E. C. (1955). Principles of performance. *Psychological Review* **62**, 315–327.

Towle, N. J. and Merrill, P. F. (1975). Effects of anxiety type and item difficulty sequencing on maths test performances. *Journal of Educational Measurement* **12**, 241–249.

Valle, V. A. and Frieze, I. H. (1976). Stability of causal attributions as a mediator in changing expectations for success. *Journal of Personality and Social Psychology* **33**, 579–587.

Weiner, B. (1966). The role of success and failure in the learning of easy and complex tasks. *Journal of Personality and Social Psychology* **3**, 339–343.

Weiner, B. (1974). An attributional interpretation of Expectancy × Value Theory. *In* B. Weiner (ed.) *Cognitive Views of Human Motivation*. London and New York: Academic Press.

Weiner, B. (1979). A theory of motivation for some classroom experiences. *Journal of Educational Psychology* **71**, 3–25.

Weiner, B. and Heckhausen, H. (1972). Cognitive theory and motivation. *In* P. C. Dodwell (ed.) *New Horizons in Psychology*. Penguin Books.

Weiner, B., Heckhausen, H., Meyer, W. and Cook, H. E. (1972). Causal ascriptions and achievement behaviour. *Journal of Personality and Social Psychology* **21**, 239–248.

Williams, J. M. G. (1979). Factors mediating the after-effects of failure in relation to models of depression. Unpublished D.Phil. thesis. University of Oxford, 1979.

Williams, J. M. G. and Teasdale, J. D. (1982). Facilitation and helplessness: the interaction of perceived difficulty and importance of a task. *Behaviour Research and Therapy* (in press).

Wortman, C. B., Panciera, L., Shusterman, L. and Hibscher, J. (1976). Attributions of causality and reactions to uncontrollable outcomes. *Journal of Experimental and Social Psychology* **12**, 301–316.

12

An Attributional Approach to Hyperactive Behavior

Lee A. Chaney and Daphne Blunt Bugental

A. INTRODUCTION

The concern of this paper is the application of attribution theory to the understanding and control of hyperactive behavior in children. The attributional focus is on the extent to which people feel that they have personal control over their successes and failures. Hyperactivity, the behavior of concern, involves an impulsive style that tends to be outside the control of the children themselves and the adults in their environment.

In the last few years, Bugental and her colleagues have conducted a series of studies involving impulsive children in both naturalistic and laboratory settings. Of primary concern was the degree to which impulsive behavior is related in a meaningful way to the perceptions of control held by children and their caregivers. One line of investigation explored the differential effectiveness of two interventions on the behavior and attributions of hyperactive children. A second concerned the control efforts employed by adults interacting with these children. The central concerns addressed in these studies can be subsumed under the following questions:

(1) Is there a relationship between the attributions of children commonly seen as hyperactive and their actual behavior? The particular concern was whether these children believe they have low control of their own successes and failures.

(2) What is the best attributional strategy to use in altering hyperactive

behavior? Specifically, is there a differential effectiveness of interventions emphasizing internal v. external controls?

(3) Finally, are adults with high perceived control better able to cope with the impulsive behavior of hyperactive children than those with low perceived control?

B. RESEARCH VARIABLES

Hyperactive Behavior

Although originally attributed to some sort of minimal brain dysfunction, "hyperactivity" has subsequently become understood as multiply caused (Schmitt *et al.*, 1973). "Hyperactive" and "impulsive" are used interchangeably here to describe this style of functioning, reflecting our belief that "hyperactivity" is best understood as a description of behavior rather than the result of some specific organic condition. Children labeled hyperactive (through a variety of mechanisms) tend to be impulsive, easily distracted, and intractible. Their behavior is a particular source of concern in the classroom environment and they are often behind academically. Adults in a position of responsibility for these children commonly find them frustrating and aversive to work with.

In the research to be described, hyperactive behavior was defined in terms of (a) low ability to maintain attention on an externally imposed task, and (b) a high incidence of off task behavior. This behavior was measured in two ways. First, ratings of classroom behavior were obtained on the Conners Abbreviated Teacher Rating Scale (Conners, 1973). This measure is frequently employed in hyperactivity research and involves teacher ratings of behaviors in the classroom. The instrument asks the teacher to assess the frequency of such behaviors as "fidgeting," "impulsivity," and "low task persistence." Second, scores on the Porteus Mazes were computed on the basis of number of qualitative errors. This measure is generally accepted as a good indicator of impulsivity (O'Keefe, 1975), and involves the degree to which a child makes careless errors (e.g. going outside lines or cutting corners) while solving mazes.

Attributions

Our central interest was in attributional styles that imply high versus low self-perceived control. That is, we were interested in measuring the extent to which individuals see successes or failures as caused by factors under personal control. This attributional construct finds its roots in the work of a variety of theorists. For example, it overlaps Rotter's (1966) construct of "internal" versus "external" locus of control (IE). Rotter defined externals as attributing the cause of reinforcing events to environmental factors, or luck, and internals as perceiving reinforcement as contingent upon personal factors. He believed these perceptions to be the result of learning and to influence future expectations. The construct of self-perceived control also has origins in Heider's theoretical notions, as later applied by Weiner (1974) to the achievement domain. Weiner developed a two-dimensional taxonomy encompassing four major causal attributions, including ability (internal, stable), effort (internal, unstable), task difficulty (external, stable), and luck (external, unstable). In addition, and like Elig and Frieze (1975), our construct was applied in both the *social* as well as the academic domain.

The research of Bugental and her colleagues incorporated aspects of the variety of measures employed by the aforementioned theorists. For children, the Child Attribution Measure (CAM) was developed to assess causal perceptions along four axes: (a) internal v. external, (b) stable v. unstable, (c) success v. failure, and (d) the social v. academic domain. Children were asked to rate the importance they assigned to effort, ability, relevant others, and luck. The internal–external and stable–unstable dimensions was equivalent to those employed by Weiner, with the exception that "relevant others" (e.g. the teacher) was substituted for "task difficulty" as a measure of a stable, external factor. In doing so, this definition of externality approaches that of Rotter (i.e. luck + powerful others). Of particular interest was the children's perceived control in the academic domain, that is, the extent they felt their own efforts as opposed to luck or teacher preference influenced their grades. (As a communication convenience, we will often refer to individuals with high self-perceived control as "internal".) This can also be referred to as a belief in effort-outcome covariation. Ability ("being smart") was not included in our perceived control measure because it could not be clearly specified as high or low in controllability. Children who attributed their success to "being smart" also attributed their failures to "*not* being smart." This correlational pattern made the use of ability conceptually awkward.

For adults, two attributional measures were employed. Originally, the Levenson Locus of Control Scale (Levenson, 1974) was used. This instrument can be understood as assessing the extent to which individuals make attributions to ability and effort (the internal scale) as opposed to luck or powerful others (the external scales). Later the Parent Attribution Test (PAT) was developed to measure internal v. external and stable v. unstable attributions for both success and failure. It was designed with the specific purpose of measuring adult attributions in their interactions with children.

Pilot tests of the PAT revealed that, as causes of social success, attributions to ability and luck (as a negative factor) reliably predicted adult assertiveness (Bugental et al., 1980b; Shennum et al., 1980). Confident or assertive communication styles were positively correlated with the belief that social success reflects ease or comfort in the interaction. Assertion was not predicted by attributing importance to effort (i.e. acting friendly) or the characteristics of the other person. It may be that high self-perceived control in the social domain is defined by the belief in one's own ability (and that luck will have little influence) rather than in the belief in effort. As a result of these pilot test findings, our measure of perceived social control retained only the dimensions of ability and luck.

C. RESEARCH QUESTIONS

Is there a relationship between the attributions of children commonly seen as hyperactive and their actual behavior?

Given that hyperactive children differ markedly from others in their school behavior, it was of interest to determine whether there is a parallel difference in their perceptions of causality in an academic domain. To answer this question, the CAM was administered to a group of hyperactive boys in elementary school and an unselected comparison group of same age boys. A significant difference was found in the attributions made by the children in these two groups. Hyperactive boys perceived relatively less control over their academic outcomes, that is, they were less likely to attribute success and failure to effort than were boys in the comparison group. For both groups, there was also a significant difference in perceived control as a function of age. Older children had a greater sense of perceived control, due mostly to their reduced belief in luck as a causal factor. Although not included in the measure of perceived control, hyperactive boys were also less likely to perceive ability as a causal agent in academic outcomes.

Using a slightly revised version of the CAM, Pearl et al. (1979) found similar attributional differences in their comparisons of learning disabled and non-disabled children. Learning disabled children made lower attributions to lack of effort as a cause of academic failure. No differences were found, however, between these two groups in their attributions to academic success. The two lines of investigation thus agree on the relatively lower attributions to effort for children who had experienced learning problems, but disagree on the extent to which these differences are limited to failure. Pearl et al. also found that younger children assign significantly greater importance to luck as a causal factor than do older children.   .

Using different attributional measures, other investigators have found results consistent with those described above. For example, Dweck and Repucci (1973) found low levels of perceived control in children with low task persistence. Bachrach *et al.* (1977) found a similar pattern in young children. It is probably reasonable to suppose that the attributions of hyperactive, learning disabled, and younger children are to some extent veridical in that they reflect their inexperience with effort-outcome covariation.

What is the best attributional strategy to use in altering hyperactive behavior?

In recent years, there has been an increasing trend towards the use of behavior management interventions as opposed to medication in the treatment of hyperactivity. Because of the difficulty hyperactive children have monitoring their behavior and sustaining attention on externally imposed tasks, behavior management techniques emphasizing self-control skills are intuitively appealing, and they have had reasonable success in reducing behavioral impulsivity (Palkes *et al.*, 1968; Meichenbaum and Goodman, 1971). Success has also been obtained using more conventional behavior modification techniques (O'Leary, 1980).

An attributional rationale can be developed to explain the success of either a self-control or a contingent reinforcement manipulation (i.e. an intervention in which the child is given a reward contingent upon the performance of a particular behavior). Interventions that provide contingent reinforcement can be understood as matching the predominantly external attributional style of hyperactive children. There is a body of evidence to support the efficacy of manipulations whose control mechanisms match the motivational or attributional orientation of the child. For example, in exploring the relationship between reinforcement systems and motivational orientations, Switsky and Haywood (1974) found intrinsically motivated children performed better under self-reward conditions (i.e. the right to set their own performance goals and administer their own rewards) while extrinsically motivated children did better when rewarded from an external source. Baron and his colleagues (Baron *et al.*, 1974; Baron and Ganz, 1972) found the performance of internal children to be better under intrinsic feedback conditions while external children worked better with extrinsic feedback.

An equally valid attributional argument can be made supporting the success of self-control manipulations. Because hyperactive children appear to have a low sense of personal control, an intervention designed to enhance their self-control would appear to directly address the problem. Both direct attributional manipulations and self-instruction techniques can be seen as providing a greater sense of control, resulting in more controlled behavior. For example, Meichenbaum and Goodman (1971) designed a self-instruction intervention in an effort to reduce impulsivity in hyperactive children. Their intervention (described in greater detail later) involved teaching children to use self-directed speech to monitor and control task performance. As a result of this manipulation, impulsivity was significantly reduced on laboratory measures (e.g. Matching Familiar Figures, Porteus Mazes). Other investigators have employed more direct attributional manipulations in an effort to influence behavior. For example, Dweck (1975) used a manipulation on children with low task persistence in which she attempted to teach them to reattribute failure to a lack of effort. Following this, these children were found to be less likely to give up after failure and to have improved performance on a problem solving task.

Although both self-control and contingent reinforcement interventions have had beneficial short term effects, little is known of their long term consequences. Perhaps they differ in durability of changes produced. Additionally, their utility may vary between different types of children or between different types of behavior. In order to assess the utility of intervention strategies emphasizing either self-control or contingent reinforcement, an investigation was designed to measure both their short and long term consequences (Bugental et al., 1977, 1978). Specifically, two predictions were made. First, it was hypothesized that an intervention matching the predominant attributional style of the child should produce more immediate gains than one that does not. Internal children should benefit more from a self-control manipulation and external children from one employing contingent reinforcement. Second, it was predicted that a self-control manipulation should have greater durability than one using external controls. The resulting behavior change should be more stable in that it does not require maintenance from external sources.

To test these two predictions, the effects of both a self-control and contingent reinforcement manipulation were compared for a group of hyperactive boys. For purposes of discussion, these manipulations will be referred to as "internal" and "external," respectively. The internal manipulation was based on Meichenbaum and Goodman's (1971) self-instruction training. The goal of this intervention was to teach the children to monitor and reward their own behavior in a way similar to that normally provided by external sources, such as teachers and parents. The children learned to provide their own "internal" feedback. This manipulation was applied by a group of "trainers," undergraduates who had received instruction on the interventions employed. These trainers were instructed to first model self-controlling speech and self-reinforcement to the children while performing a task such as handwriting or coloring. Meichenbaum and Goodman provide an example of the type of speech modeled:

> Okay, what is it I have to do? You want me to copy the picture with the different lines. I have to go slow and be careful. Okay, draw the line down, down, good, then to the right, that's it, now down some more and to the left. Good, I'm doing OK so far. Remember, go slow. Now back up again. No, I was supposed to go down. That's okay. Just erase the line carefully. . . . Good. Even if I make an error, I can go on slowly and carefully. Okay, I have to go down now. Finished. I did it. (p. 117)

The child was then asked to imitate the adult's self talk, first covertly, then by whispering, and finally only to himself. At this point, the trainer provided him with additional input or corrections by occasionally asking the child to repeat out loud what he was saying to himself. Once the self-instruction technique was mastered, the child was asked to apply it to his regular classroom assignments.

The external intervention employed conventional contingent social reinforcement techniques. The trainers were instructed to provide attention and praise when the child was on task and to ignore inappropriate or inattentive behavior. Instruction to trainers was provided by graduate students experienced in behavior modification techniques.

The interventions were administered to two groups of hyperactive boys. Our sample was restricted to boys because of the infrequency of hyperactivity among girls (too few hyperactive girls could be located to allow an adequate comparison). Children ranged in age from 7–12 ($\bar{x} =$ 10). Thirty-two children were in regular classrooms and five were in classrooms for learning disabled children. Half the boys were selected on the basis of medication status (i.e. currently receiving methylphenidate) and half were selected on the basis of teacher ratings of classroom impulsivity (Conners Abbreviated Teacher Rating Scale). Children selected on the basis of teacher ratings were not receiving medication at the time of the interventions. Within each of these two groups, children were randomly assigned to receive either the internal or external intervention. Our comparison, correspondingly, was for the *relative* success of the two interventions for different kinds of children. Both interventions have already been shown to be effective; our interest was in their relative suitability for different children and their relative effectiveness in changing different kinds of behavior. For these reasons, a control group was not employed.

A variety of measures were taken before the interventions began. To assess impulsivity, the Conners and Porteus Mazes were administered. The CAM was used to measure attributions, and the Peabody Picture Vocabulary Test provided an estimate of intelligence. There were no significant differences between the groups on any of the pretest measures. A median split was made on CAM "perceived control" scores. As mentioned earlier, children in this sample were *relatively* "external" ($\bar{x}$ = 1·02, S.D. = 1·24) in comparison with a sample of 38 same-aged non-hyperactive boys ($\bar{x}$ = 1·69, S.D. = 1·06). Scores ranged from +3 (high perceived control) to −3 (low perceived control). The "internal" group ($\bar{x}$ = 2·03) was only slightly higher than the non-hyperactive sample and may be more accurately described as normative with respect to their attributions.

After the pretests were completed, each student was seen by a trainer two hours a week for six weeks. In an effort to facilitate generalization, tutoring occurred in the pupil's regular classroom whenever possible. The week after the interventions ended, each pupil was again measured on the Conners, CAM, and Porteus Mazes. Follow-up measures were taken six months later on the boys and their new teachers.

The first prediction, that an intervention matching the causal perceptions of the child would be more effective (in terms of immediate gains), was confirmed for impulsivity as measured by the Porteus Mazes. Children who were more internal showed greater improvement under the self-instruction manipulation; external children improved more when receiving contingent social reinforcement. Boys in the non-congruent attribution-intervention pairings showed either lower gains (internal children, external intervention) or increased errors (external children, internal intervention). Changes on the Conners and CAM administered directly after the interventions consisted only of non-significant trends.

In addition, an unexpected interaction was found between medication status and type of intervention. Similar to the "match" effects described above, error scores on the Porteus Mazes decreased more for medicated children receiving contingent social reinforcement and non-medicated children receiving self-instruction. Even though medicated children were no more external on the CAM, it may be that medication produces an expectation of external control over behavior. Contingent social reinforcement can therefore be seen as congruent with their past history.

The effects of the match between intervention and attributions (and medication status) were found only for the immediate post-test scores. These differential changes had washed out by the time of the six month follow-up. It appears that the advantage of matching attributions and interventions is short lived. Even so, the findings suggest that *quicker* gains in behavior can be expected using an intervention strategy congruent with the causal attributions of the child in an academic environment. Attributions can thus be understood as contributing to a child's initial receptivity to a behavior change strategy.

In terms of the second prediction, the interventions did lead to differential long-term changes. But the observed changes differed somewhat from that which was anticipated. Six months later, boys who received the internal intervention had indeed increased in internality, an increase that did not occur for boys given contingent social reinforcement. Boys in the "internal" condition, increased from an initial CAM score of 0.94 to a follow-up score of 1·57. This is equivalent to the mean CAM score of non-hyperactive boys (1·69). Boys in the "external" condition showed a *decrease* in their CAM score from 0·99 to 0·53. The shift in attributions demonstrated by children in the internal intervention failed to produce the expected changes in behavior, however. Instead, both interventions were equally effective in producing stable changes on the Mazes, and the *external* intervention was more effective in reducing impulsivity as measured by the Conners.

It appears that both interventions produced stable changes, but the differential changes were dependent upon the behavior targeted. The internal manipulation targeted self-control and self-monitoring, and correspondingly, this is where long-term gains occurred. Contingent social reinforcement focused on the child's behavior as directed and responded to by an adult and resulted in long-term gains in behavior as perceived by adults. Changes in classroom behavior (Conners) for children receiving the external intervention were dramatic; ratings on hyperactive behaviors dropped down to a level found for non-hyperactive children. Children in the internal condition showed no change in the high levels of impulsivity initially shown in the classroom.

Are adults with high perceived control better able to cope with the impulsive behavior of hyperactive children than those with low perceived control?

In the course of the aforementioned study, some trainers appeared to have more influence than others on the behavior of the children. There is little question that impulsive behavior is often very disturbing to adults in positions of responsibility, but some people appear more devastated by its erratic and intractible style than do others. Some undergraduates, for example, reported they were glad to have worked in the experiment because they had learned that a career with problem children was not for them. Others were substantially less affected. There is an emerging body of literature demonstrating the role of attributions in the effects of uncontrollable experiences (Abramson *et al.*, 1978). Individuals whose attributions imply low self-perceived control are more likely to give up in the face of difficult situations (e.g. Dweck, 1975). Typically, empirical investigation of the debilitating effects of uncontrollable or difficult situations on individuals with low self-perceived control have focused on behavior in the *task* domain. The focus in the research described here was on the relationship between attributional style and response to an uncontrollable or difficult *social* situation. To the extent impulsive children provide an uncontrollable stimulus, there should be a relationship between the attributions of adults and their behavior towards hyperactive children. Adults with low self-perceived control were expected to show a decline in their non-verbal assertiveness when interacting with the relatively uncontrollable behavior of impulsive children.

In a pilot investigation, Shennum and Bugental (1978) explored the role of attributions in parental assertiveness with their impulsive children. Voice intonation was employed to assess assertiveness because it is a relatively nonreactive yet sensitive measure (Holzman and Rousey, 1966). Speakers have little awareness of how they sound. Moreover, voice intonation is an excellent source of information about internal states of the speaker (Scherer, 1980) and has a large impact on the listener (Bugental, 1974). Voice assertion was assessed by judgements made of content-free speech (tape recordings were routed through a band-pass filter to remove high frequencies carrying intelligibility); judges were asked to rate how strong or assertive these filtered voices sounded. Different patterns of voice assertiveness were found for internal and external parents. Externals lowered their voice assertion while making affective (as compared to neutral) statements while internals showed the opposite pattern. This latter pattern is typical of parents of non-impulsive children, while the former has been found to be more prevalent in families with emotionally disturbed children (Bugental and Love, 1975). It may be that the style of communication employed by external parents is less effective in that it limits the potential impact of social reinforcement.

Much of the research relating attributional patterns to parenting is limited by its correlational nature, providing no secure way to establish direction of effects. The behavior of external parents may be to some degree a cause of hyperactivity or the effect of it. Moreover, attributions may follow rather than precede behavior. That is, they may be the result of behavioral experiences rather than their cause.

In order to clarify the causal relationship between adult attributions and behavior, a study was designed (Bugental *et al.*, 1980a) to measure the effect of impulsive behavior on the communication patterns of adults as moderated by their perceptions of control. To allow more clear causal inferences, child confederates were employed to demonstrate specific behavior patterns and to interact with women with whom they were not acquainted. In this way, the communication effects produced could be seen as a function of the child's particular behavior pattern rather than the history of a particular dyad. It was expected that external adults would have relative decrements in voice assertion for affective statements made to an impulsive child. The opposite pattern was predicted for internals.

The adults employed were asked to interact on a tinker toy task with one of four boys aged 7–9 trained to enact both impulsive and non-impulsive behavior patterns (as "actors"). Impulsive behavior included being slow to respond, spending little time "on task" (building an as-signed object), and engaging in a lot of extraneous activities with the tinker toys. Non-impulsive behavior involved the opposite responses. The following is a sample interaction between an adult and child stooge enacting the impulsive role:

> *Mother*: O.K. I think I need some help again. . . We've got to put things on the end here. C'mere.
> (Child jumps over car she is building with a gun he has made from the tinker toys.)
> *Mother*: Oh, I bet you know how to do this. I bet you could do it. C'mere. . . Billy. . . Don't you think you could do it? . . . Can't you make this good car and then you could make the other one? C'mere. . . What are you doing?
> *Child*: Playing with guns.

After these videotaped interactions were obtained, sample messages were selected on the basis of verbal content (affectively pleasant, un-pleasant or neutral). Judges were asked to rate the various speech samples, filtered to remove content clues yet leave voice intonation intact. Consistent with earlier correlational studies, there was a relationship between attributions and vocal patterns in response to an impulsive child. Women with a relatively high perception of their own control elevated their voice assertion while making pleasant and unpleasant statements. External women responded to impulsive behavior with the opposite pattern, speaking with relatively less assertion while making these statements. No difference in communication patterns were found when these adults were interacting with a child acting non-impulsively. Both groups showed the "usual" pattern of elevated voice assertion while making affective statements to these children.

It should be noted that it is a *pattern* of intonational shift rather than an absolute level of voice assertion that was found. An external speaker can be as or more assertive than an internal one, but maximum assertion is more likely for neutral (typically consisting of minor directions) rather than affective or evaluative statements. Externals are more assertive when making statements such as "Pass me the green stick" than when saying "Oh, that looks good" or "No, you didn't put that in right."

In this study, as in other research (Bugental *et al.*, 1976, 1980b), the difference in communication patterns between internal and external adults occurs in stressful, hard-to-control interactions. It appears, then, that adults with low perceptions of control are most likely to alter their communication patterns in response to the behavior of impulsive children. Moreover, they show changes that could have clear consequences for their impact on the child by weakening the effects of potential verbal reinforcement. By demonstrating relatively low non-verbal assertion during evaluative statements, they may be less likely to obtain either attention or response from the child. In earlier research (Bugental, 1972) parents of disturbed children (prone to the communication pattern being discussed) were observed to have to repeat themselves more than parents of well-functioning children—in order to get a response from the child. Low responsiveness on the part of the child may, in turn, exacerbate the parent's perception of low control—creating a maladaptive feedback loop.

D. CONCLUSIONS AND DISCUSSION

In review, it seems safe to draw the following conclusions. First, the attributions of hyperactive children appear to differ from those of other children. Relative to others, they have a low sense of effort-outcome covariance, that is, the belief that effort makes a difference. Second, it appears that the most effective intervention for changing the behavior of impulsive children is one using contingent social reinforcement (of the two strategies compared). Self-instruction training seemingly alters attributions but not behavior. This is an interesting finding to be discussed more fully below. Third, there is an apparent relationship between adult attributions and their reaction to children who behave impulsively. Adults with a low sense of (social) control seem less well equipped to deal with these children.

Inferences can be drawn as to the differential effect of the internal and external interventions. It is surprising that the self-instruction manipulation did not result in beneficial effects on classroom behavior, especially since the attributions of children receiving this intervention were altered to a level of internality comparable to that found in a group of non-hyperactive boys of equivalent ages. One can only speculate as to why this shift in attributions was not accompanied by a corresponding shift in behavior. The attributional shifts observed may only reflect expressed notions of causality in response to an intervention stressing self-control. That is, children may have answered the follow-up measure in a way consistent with what they thought their tutoring was about. It may also be that changes in causal perceptions are limited in their effect by the degree of actual change in the environment. Unless the perception of control is supported by changes in the child's world (i.e. from his or her family, teachers, and friends), the effect on behavior may be minimal. Changes in behavior may require greater environmental support than we were able to induce.

The implications for the success of the social reinforcement intervention are clearer. Over the years, there has been a general concern over the stability of gains produced through the application of behavior modification techniques. O'Leary (1980) has noted the paucity of evidence regarding the long term effectiveness of behavioral treatment programs with hyperactive children. It is gratifying, then, that significant long term gains in the behavior of these children were produced on the basis of an intervention using social reinforcement.

As to what is the most effective type of intervention to employ with hyperactive children, several considerations must be taken into account. Practically, it appears that behavior of these children can be changed using social reinforcement. In doing so, they can be provided with a repertoire of useful behaviors. The value of this approach seems therefore unquestionable. However, there is a cost paid if a child is primarily dependent on external agents for the rewards in his or her life. Behavior performed for the approval of others can be either "good" or "bad," depending on the individual's social network. Moreover, such reward is but one factor influencing behavior, and as such it may conflict with individual needs. As social animals we must act on the evaluations of others, but as individuals we must have a sense of ourselves as agents as well as objects of change. Children who received the social reinforcement intervention retained their low perceptions of control in the six month follow-up. In that sense, the intervention was not completely successful.

On the basis of these considerations and the research discussed, we suggest the optimal strategy for working with hyperactive children may include three components. First, it is necessary to provide the child with the basic skills and behaviors needed to begin to deal with the world in a competent fashion. This goal is perhaps best achieved through the systematic application of social reinforcement (or some other system employing contingent rewards). Once the child has begun to learn new behaviors, an effort should be made to enhance and emphasize the causal connections between his or her behavior and the outcomes produced, that is, to provide a sense of effort-outcome covariance. This second component is not meant to preclude the use of social reinforcement, but to be used in conjunction with it. Finally, it is important that the child's sense of control be supported in the real world. It is of little value to enhance a sense of personal control if that perception is negated by external events.

Finally, it appears there is an optimal attributional style for adults hoping to effect changes in impulsive children. Adults with a low sense of control react to hyperactive children (as opposed to other children) by adopting a communication style that may decrease their effectiveness. As suggested earlier, the voice assertion decrements shown by these adults may increase the unresponsiveness of the child—leading to a debilitating feedback loop in the adult–child interaction. We anticipate, however, that it is not enough for adults to have a strong sense of personal control. They also need the ability to perceive and communicate the causal connections between a *child's* efforts, abilities, and outcomes. It is our belief that adults who generally believe in the competence of children are more likely to elicit effective behavior. Ongoing research is concerned with adult perceptions of child competence, and the effects of these attributions on adult–child communication.

REFERENCES

Abramson, L. Y., Seligman, M. E. P. and Teasdale, J. D. (1978). Learned helplessness in humans: critique and reformation. *Journal of Abnormal Psychology* **87**, 49–75.

Bachrach, R., Huesmann, L. R. and Peterson, R. A. (1977). The relation between locus of control and the development of moral judgment. *Child Development* **48**, 1340–1352.

Baron, R. M. and Ganz, R. L. (1972). Effects of locus on control and the type of feedback on the task performance of lower-class black children. *Journal of Personality and Social Psychology* **28**, 124–130.

Baron, R. M., Cowan, G., Ganz, R. L. and McDonald, M. (1974). Interaction of locus control and type of performance feedback: considerations of external validity. *Journal of Personality and Social Psychology* **30**, 285–292.

Bugental, D. E. (1972). Inconsistency between verbal and nonverbal components in parental communication patterns: its interpretation and effects. *In* P. Zimbardo (Chairman) *Consistency as a Process and a Problem in Psychology.* Symposium presented at the Meetings of the International Congress of Psychology, Tokyo.

Bugental, D. B. (1974). Interpretation of naturally-occurring discrepancies between words and intonation: modes of inconsistency resolution. *Journal of Personality and Social Psychology* **30**, 125–133.

Bugental, D. B. and Love, L. R. (1975). Nonassertive expression of parental approval and disapproval and its relationship to child disturbance. *Child Development* **46**, 747–752.

Bugental, D. B., Henker, B. and Whalen, C. K. (1976). Attributional antecedents of verbal and vocal assertiveness. *Journal of Personality and Social Psychology* **34**, 405–411.

Bugental, D. B., Whalen, C. K. and Henker, B. (1977). Causal attributions of hyperactive children and motivational assumptions of two behavior-change approaches: evidence for an interactionist position. *Child Development* **48**, 874–884.

Bugental, D. B., Collins, S., Collins, L. and Chaney, L. A. (1978). Attributional and behavioral changes following two behavior management interventions with hyperactive boys: a follow-up study. *Child Development* **49**, 247–250.

Bugental, D. B., Caporael, L. and Shennum, W. A. (1980a). Experimentally-produced child uncontrollability: effects on the potency of adult communication patterns. *Child Development* **51**, 520–528.

Bugental, D. B., Hubbard, J., Lund, L., Mantyla, S. and Shennum, W. A. (1980b). The influence of speaker social attributions and partner responsiveness on the assertiveness of speech patterns. Unpublished paper.

Connors, C. K. (1973). Rating scales for use in drug studies with children. *Psychopharmacology Bulletin* (Special Issue: Pharmacotherapy of children), pp. 24–84.

Dweck, C. S. (1975). The role of expectations and attributions in the alleviation of learned helplessness. *Journal of Personality and Social Psychology* **31**, 674–685.

Dweck, C. S. and Repucci, D. (1973). Learned helplessness and reinforcement responsibility in children. *Journal of Personality and Social Psychology* **25**, 109–116.

Elig, T. W. and Frieze, I. H. (1975). A multi-dimensional scheme for coding and interpreting perceived causality for success and failure events. *JSAS Catalog of Selected Documents in Psychology* **5**, 313 (ms. no. 1009).

Holzman, P. S. and Rousey, C. (1966). The voice as a percept. *Journal of Personality and Social Psychology* **4**, 78–86.

Levenson, H. (1974). Activism and powerful others: distinctions within the concept of internal–external control. *Journal of Personality Assessment* **38**, 377–383.

Meichenbaum, D. H. and Goodman, J. (1971). Training impulsive children to talk to themselves: a means of developing self-control. *Journal of Abnormal Psychology* **77**, 115–126.

O'Keefe, E. J. (1975). Porteus Maze Q score as a measure of impulsivity. *Perceptual and Motor Skills* **41**, 674–678.

O'Leary, K. D. (1980). Pills or skills for hyperactive children. *Journal of Applied Behavioral Analysis*, Spring.

Palkes, H., Stewart, W. and Kahana, B. (1968). Porteus maze performance of hyperactive boys after training in self-directed verbal commands. *Child Development* **39**, 817–826.

Pearl, R., Bryan, T. and Donahue, M. (1979). Learning-disabled children: attributions for success and failure. Unpublished paper, University of Illinois at Chicago Circle.

Rotter, J. B. (1966). Generalized expectancies for internal versus external control of reinforcement. *Psychological Monographs* **80** (1, Whole No. 609).

Scherer, K. R. (1979). Personality markers in speech. In K. R. Scherer and H. Giles (eds) *Social Markers in Speech*. London: Cambridge University Press.

Schmitt, B. D., Martin, H. P., Nellhaus, G., Cravens, J., Camp, B. W. and Jordon, K. (1973). The hyperactive child. *Clinical Pediatrics* **12**, 154–169.

Shennum, W. A. and Bugental, D. B. (1978). Effects of child impulsivity on material communication patterns. Paper presented at the meeting of the Western Psychological Association, San Francisco, California.

Shennum, W. A., Bugental, D. B. and Lund, L. A. (1980). Social attributions as predictors of time spent alone. Paper presented at the meeting of the Western Psychological Association, Honolulu, Hawaii.

Switzky, H. N. and Haywood, H. C. (1974). Motivational orientation and the relative efficacy of self-monitored and externally imposed reinforcement systems in children. *Journal of Personality and Social Psychology* 30, 360–366.

Weiner, B. (1974). Achievement motivation as conceptualized by an attribution theorist. *In* B. Weiner (ed.), *Achievement Motivation and Attribution Theory.* Morristown, New Jersey: General Learning Press.

13
The Contribution of Attribution Theory to Educational Research

Colin G. Rogers

A. INTRODUCTION

In this chapter I shall try to set attribution theory in the context not only of other social psychological theories that have found their way into educational research, but also of educational research itself, and what it chooses to look at in the classroom. I shall examine what attribution theory has to offer us both as a description, and also as an explanation, of pupils' perceptions of their teachers, and vice versa. I shall use some examples from the work done on sex differences in attributions to draw out some points to qualify any premature enthusiasm for the theory as a complete answer to our problems. Throughout the chapter I shall be concerned to make links between attribution theory and its stablemates in educational research, and I hope that by juxtaposing different sorts of theories I shall be clarifying the context of educational questions for any intended application of attribution theory.

B. PERCEPTIONS IN THE CLASSROOM

A number of studies conducted over the last ten to fifteen years have demonstrated clear links between the ways in which teachers perceive their pupils and the nature of the interactions that take place between teacher and pupil (e.g. Silberman, 1969; Brophy and Good, 1974; Sharp and Green, 1975). Varying claims have been made as to the significance of these perceptions for the development of a pupil's educational career. Some of the strongest claims have been made by those working within the framework of "expectancy effects" where, for example, Rist (1970) argues that the initial classifications made of pupils by a teacher on the basis of his or her impressions of their potential can establish what is virtually an educational caste system. Pupils who are deemed to be of low promise find it increasingly difficult to escape the implication of such a label. Other researchers (e.g. Jackson *et al.*, 1969) have been more cautious, limiting themselves to the claim that it will be impossible for a teacher to maintain the standards of objectivity and detachment in all judgements that the profession sets for him or her.

Only more recently, and still to a much lesser extent, have researchers concerned themselves with the effects of pupils' perceptions of their teachers (e.g. Meighan, 1978; Marsh *et al.*, 1978). Such a relative lack of interest in the effects of pupils' own perceptions upon their own educational career has two separate causes. The first stems from within social psychology where, for further reasons that cannot be gone into here, research into the development of person perception processes has received only limited and relatively unsystematic attention (see Livesley and Bromley, 1973; Rogers, 1978). While those interested in the perceptions of pupils by teachers have a well developed body of social psychological theory and data to support their efforts, those concerned with perceptions of teachers by pupils have no such advantage.

The second cause for this lack of attention to the pupil lies within educational research itself where the assumption is generally made, and usually only at an implicit level, that the teacher has the power to determine what happens within her or his class and therefore the perceptions of the pupil are relegated to a level where they are seen to have only a curiosity rather than an explanatory value.

This inbalance of research attention is regrettable. Whatever model of interpersonal perception one may wish to adopt in an examination of classroom processes it seems clear that it is *inter*personal perception that one should be studying. Teachers' perceptions of their pupils have become a subject of interest to educational researchers with a social psychological or sociological orientation primarily due to the links believed to exist between these perceptions and teacher behaviour. Given that the ultimate concern of most educational researchers is with aspects of pupil behaviour, an examination of the effects of pupils' perceptions upon their own behaviour is desirable. Throughout this paper attempts will be made to illustrate points with reference to research concerning pupils' perceptions of the school setting wherever this is appropriate.

This paper seeks to examine some of the strengths and limitations of attribution theory as applied to the study of interpersonal perception within the classroom. In the past it has frequently been the case that social scientific knowledge has been applied to the study of educational processes in a way that gives little consideration to the actualities of classroom practice (see Desforges and McNamara, 1977; McNamara and Desforges, 1978). It has also been the case that discussions of the application of particular models of theoretical systems within the social sciences have given little or no attention to the relevant bodies of educational research. As one of the more important theoretical systems within social psychology attribution theory is currently "being applied" to a wide variety of different issues (see for example Frieze *et al.*, 1979 and this volume). Due primarily to the development of Weiner's attributional theory of achievement motivation (Weiner, 1974 and see Chapter 1 for the difference between theories of attribution and attributional theories), education has been one of the major areas to which these applications have been made.

However, as with previous attempts to apply social scientific theories to educational problems, most of the discussions of these applications (e.g. Weiner, 1976) have developed the concerns of the attributional theorist rather than those of the educationalist. It is not claimed that this paper will halt, let alone reverse this trend, but it is hoped that it will serve to illustrate some of the issues drawn from educational research to which attribution theory may be applied. Given that the problems are being defined outside of attribution theory itself it is to be expected that the "fit" between attribution theory and these problems will be far from perfect. This should not be taken as an indication of the author's belief in the general inadequacy or inappropriateness of attribution theory for a study of educational processes but as an indication that attribution theory must accommodate itself to the demands of the "real world" rather than to expect to assimilate the "real world" into its own relatively neat and orderly framework.

The next section of this paper will begin an outline of the nature of existing research into teacher and pupil perceptions of each other. Following sections will go on to highlight the problems and difficulties inherent in this work and the potential contribution of attribution theory to the resolution of these difficulties.

As discussed in the introductory chapter to this book the term "attribution" has come to take on a fairly general and wide-ranging meaning that includes far more than the attribution of specific causes to specific events. In this particular chapter an attempt is to be made to relate work on causal attributions to the wider body of existing research into teacher–pupil perceptions. The early stages of the following discussion will therefore primarily refer to the broader issue of teacher–pupil and pupil–teacher perceptions. Once this context has been established, attention will be focused on studies that are representative of those concerned more directly with causal attributions *per se*. It is only within this more general context that the role of attributions *per se* can be properly understood. The process of causal attribution can be considered to be one of the processes contributing to the final perception that one person will have of another while at the same time the existing perception will have a role to play in determining particular causal attributions.

C. EXISTING RESEARCH INTO TEACHERS' PERCEPTIONS
OF THEIR PUPILS

Research into teachers' perceptions of their pupils has followed a similar path in terms of its historical development as that taken by the "pure" social psychological study of person perception in general, (see Hastorf *et al.*, 1979). This in itself serves as an illustration of the typical process involved in applying social psychology to education. An early concern was with the problem of accuracy in teachers' perceptions. The main questions asked concerned the extent to which teachers' impressions of pupils matched some criterion measure of relevant pupil characteristics and the extent to which teachers of different types would differ in the accuracy of their perceptions.

As is the case in the "pure" research these questions still lack a clear answer primarily due to the inadequacy of the questions themselves. The work of Jackson (1968) illustrates the nature of some of the problems that were encountered in the educational context. Jackson used as his criterion measure of pupil characteristics the pupils' own responses on a question-naire designed to assess their attitudes to school. Teachers of these pupils had to attempt to predict the responses given. This the teachers were able to do, but with a degree of accuracy that varied not so much as a function of characteristics of the teachers but of the characteristics of the relation-ship that existed between the teachers and the pupil.

Similar results obtained from studies in social psychology led to the large-scale abandonment of such research in favour of studies concerned more with the processes underlying impression formation (although it should be noted that this shift in research attention, while perhaps now best understood in terms of theoretical developments, that is changing views about the nature of person perception, was at the time attributed more to methodological problems). A similar shift in the focus of attention has also taken place in educational research.

A recent theoretical paper (Hargreaves, 1977) is for the most part concerned with the processes involved in the development of a teachers' impressions (or typifications) of her or his pupils ranging from initial impressions based upon the extent to which an individual pupil matches a teacher's view of a typical pupil of this sort, through to a fully fledged, stabilized impression that is best understood in its entirety as a construction of the researcher. The teacher at this stage will be responding to the pupil in ways related to the particular context and purposes of each meeting. Underlying this process can be discerned a concern on the part of the teacher with constructing an impression of the pupil that enables him or her to work with the child.

Such an emphasis on the underlying functions of teachers' impressions of pupils is seen more clearly in the work of Sharp and Green (1975). Their detailed study has been open to a number of somewhat different interpretations. The major point of the study for present purposes is its examination of the functions of teachers' perceptions (or ideologies). For example,

> Our analysis might suggest the functionality of an ideology which looks at working class pupils in terms of a deprivation and pathology model, in that it legitimizes the use of concepts like "odd", "disturbed", "peculiar" as explanations of pupils' failure which could be seen as militating against a sense of failure on the teachers' part. (Sharp and Green, 1975, p. 188)

In other words, a teachers' perceptions of a pupil serve not only to aid the teacher in making necessary educational decisions with respect to that pupil but may also, under certain conditions, serve a self protecting function for her or his self esteem. Sharp and Green are at pains to point out in several parts of their analysis that functions of this latter sort may well not be part of the teacher's own conscious realization of the nature of her or his impressions of the pupils. As was mentioned above, Hargreaves (1977) has claimed in a different context that the fully elaborated impression of a pupil held by a teacher may only exist as the creation of the researcher.

The relevance of such research for an understanding of attributions within the classroom follows from the intimate link seen to exist between a teacher's (or pupil's) ideology and the attributions made to produce causal explanations of particular events. The quotation from Sharp and Green given above shows how they see one particular teacher ideology (the "deprivation and pathology model") leading to the use of a certain explanatory vocabulary, e.g. "odd", "disturbed" and "peculiar". If the teacher's general perceptions and ideology are to be seen as having some self-enhancing function, then so too, to some extent, will the causal attributions made in connection with those perceptions and ideology.

Current approaches to the study of interpersonal perception within the school classroom are best understood as having an equal concern with the processes underlying impression formation and the functions of the impressions once formed. While it is clearly the case that if some degree of normality is to be maintained in the interactions that take place within the classroom, the perceptions of pupils by teachers, and vice versa, must demonstrate some degree of accuracy, accuracy itself is not the main criterion against which to assess these perceptions. Rather they should be examined in terms of the functions that they serve for the teacher and the effects that they have upon the behaviour of both teacher and pupil.

The Problems of Classroom-based Interpersonal Perception Research

Research into classroom processes of any type is rarely, if ever, simple, and in the case of interpersonal perceptions and their effects the researcher is confronted with some particular difficulties. Some of these difficulties are held in common with many other types of cognitive psychological research. The researcher is faced with the task of gaining access to cognitions and cognitive processes that are not usually, or even ever, objects of conscious awareness. There are however a number of particular problems that are relevant to the development of this paper.

The first of these can be termed the problem of spatial context. Teachers and pupils interact with each other over a wide range of different settings. In many respects this reflects the breadth and complexity of the teacher's role. She or he is part instructor, part child-minder and part socialization agent. The effects of this on the nature of teacher–pupil perception are largely unknown as it has been largely ignored by researchers. Researchers have for the most part striven to produce generalizable descriptions of the impressions that teachers and pupils hold of each other (e.g. Hallworth, 1962; Hallworth and Morrison, 1964) while only a few have given any attention to the possible effects of contextual variables (e.g. McIntyre et al., 1966).

The second problem refers to the type of relationship between teacher and pupil. While there are many ways in which teacher–pupil relationships can be classified, a useful approach to classification is to be found in the distinction between contemporary and consociate relationships. Originating in the writings of Schutz (1932, 1973) this dimension has been utilized in an educational framework by Sharp and Green (1975) and Hargreaves (1977). It is not intended to elaborate any of the details here. It is sufficient for present purposes to point out that the claim has been made that only in consociate relationships with pupils does the teacher respond to the immediacy of the unique characteristics of the other person. In contemporary relationships it is the impression itself rather than the person that the individual responds to. Hargreaves (1977) has argued that these two types of relationships will characterize the nature of the interactions between any given teacher and pupil at different times and is primarily concerned with pointing out the implications of this for research methodology. The researcher will generally only have access to the impressions relevant to contemporary relationships but has typically used this data to make claims for consociate ones. Sharp and Green (1975) use the term in essentially the same way but are more concerned with investigating the possibility that some pupils will nearly always have relationships of a contemporary nature with their teachers and will rarely, if ever, achieve consociate status. Whatever model is taken of the nature of teacher pupil relationships it is clear that associated methodologies and explanations must be able to account for these possible differences across situations.

The third problem facing the educational researcher is that of historical context. Educational research literature is rich with examples, usually anecdotal in nature, of the way in which particular remarks or gestures can have marked effects upon the behaviour of the members of a class that appear to be quite unwarranted to the outsider. A remark once made by a teacher in a moment of anger can be used over and over by her pupils as a way of letting her know that they have not forgotten. Anyone unfamiliar with the original incident would miss the significance of later referrals to it. Anyone attempting to explain the nature of interpersonal judgements in an educational environment must be sensitive to the effects of the historical context of the setting that they happen to visit.

Finally, the educational researcher has to acknowledge that there are likely to be substantial differences between the class comprised of one adult and 30 five-year-olds and that comprised of one adult and 30 sixteen-year-olds. Unfortunately, as has been mentioned above, the effects of the pupils' perceptions upon classroom life have been given only scant attention. Perhaps one reason for this is the self-evident absurdity of assuming that comments can be made about the typical pupil. When the oldest pupil in one school may be legally an adult while the youngest in another may be under five it is obvious that the researcher interested in the perceptions made by pupils will have to be concerned with the nature of developmental processes (this is not to deny that developmentally oriented studies of the life span of the teacher are not also called for).

Any theoretical system that is to be used to help make sense of the nature of interpersonal perception within the classroom will have to be able to contend with the difficulties caused by these basic problems inherent in the nature of classrooms. The extent to which attribution theory will be able to do this will be the subject of further discussion below. However, before discussing the promise and limitations of the application of attribution theory to this research area there are two further difficulties that need to be discussed.

Particular Problems with Attributional Research in the Classroom

These particular problems differ from those outlined above in that while they naturally have their origins in the nature of classroom life they have been further exaggerated by the approaches adopted hitherto by class-room researchers. Both concern the nature of the various judgements that teachers make and the relationship between these types.

Research into teachers' judgements of their pupils has been dealt with in two fairly distinct domains, that of teacher decision-making and that of teacher–pupil impression formation. The first of these equates closely to what social psychologists have come to refer to as episodic judgements while the second relates to dispositional judgements (Warr and Knapper, 1968). In a similar manner teachers are faced from moment to moment with having to explain the past actions of their pupils and also with predicting their future behaviour. Attribution theory, as presently articulated, seems well equipped to help bring together the first of these two sets of areas, but some problems can be seen to exist with respect to the second.

(a) *Episodic and dispositional judgements.* From the earliest days attri-bution theorists (e.g. Jones and Davis, 1965) have been concerned with elaborating the links between the momentary attributions made to explain and account for individual actions and the long term dispositions that are later attributed to the actor. In this respect attribution theory would seem to be well equipped to aid educational researchers concerned with classroom-based interpersonal perceptions. This seems to be par-ticularly the case in the light of evidence obtained by Miller *et al.* (1978) demonstrating that under certain circumstances observers will distort the information available to them to enable them to attribute dispositions to others. Miller *et al.* argue that these distortions arise from the individual's need to maintain the belief that they have effective control over the interactions in which they engage. So, in their study, individuals who believed that they would be having future interactions with the person they were observing were more likely to attribute dispositions than those who did not have such a belief. The attribution of dispositions here is believed to assist in maintaining a belief in effective control as one can then assume that the same disposition will be producing a consistent effect upon the other's behaviour, rather than that behaviour varying with the vagaries of situational circumstances. Of further interest, Miller *et al.* report that these distortion effects can take place even if the observer is informed of the likelihood of future interactions after the person's behaviour has been observed. In other words, the process of inferring dispositions from observed actions is one that is subject to continual updating. As the individual's motivational states vary so too will the nature of the inferences made.

Findings such as these are neatly in accord with the claims made by educational researchers like Murphy (1974) who has argued that teachers' impressions of pupils are likely to be variable and flexible and that the caste-like systems suggested by Rist (1970), if they occur at all, will not occur due to any rigid and fixed perceptions of pupils by teachers. At present, however, there is no systematic research into the processes involved in teachers' attributing dispositions to pupils that draws directly upon attribution theory principles. One has to continually guard against too readily assuming that the processes unearthed in the laboratory by people like Miller and his colleagues will also be found in the hurly-burly of the everyday classroom. At a later point in this paper research within an attribution theory framework relevant to the reverse of the above process, that is the way in which dispositions that have already been attributed to an individual help to determine the interpretations of particular actions, will be discussed.

(b) *Predictive and explanatory judgements.* However, before going on to examine these more specific issues a final general point needs to be made. This arises from a consideration of the second difficulty alluded to above. In the course of their business teachers make interpersonal judgements of a number of kinds. The present author has elsewhere (Rogers and Antaki, 1980) drawn attention to one particular distinction between types of judgements that teachers are required to make, which has particular relevance to an application of attribution theory to classroom processes.

Teachers, in making judgements about pupils, will typically be doing one of two things. They will either be attempting to explain why a certain event has taken place or they will be attempting to predict what will happen under given circumstances. As the teacher, formally at least, is the individual within the classroom with the power to decide what type of activities will be made available, and as the teacher is generally charged with the responsibility of reaching certain objectives, it is suggested here that the teacher will be primarily concerned with making predictive judgements. "What will happen if I attempt to teach X to these pupils using this method?" would seem to be the type of question most often found to be uppermost in the minds of practising teachers. Attribution theory however is concerned with the making of explanatory judgements, making decisions regarding the causes of events that have already taken place.

It is the case, however, that these two types of judgements, predictive and explanatory, cannot be considered to be independent of each other. The type of predictive questions a teacher will be confronted with, and the type of answers that she or he will consider to be acceptable will depend to a large extent on the answers obtained to previously asked explanatory questions. The things that have to be explained will in turn depend, in part, on the decisions that have followed the asking and answering of predictive questions. While attribution theory itself may not be directly concerned with the type of judgements that a teacher is perhaps most concerned with, that is, predictive judgements, its relevance will come through its close connections with the chain of judgements that teachers will be making (predictive–explanatory–predictive–explanatory).

The teacher's predictive judgements, and her or his explanatory judgements also, will be strongly influenced by the educational ideology to which the teacher subscribes. The things that appear to be problematic and the things that are acceptable as solutions to those problems are defined by the working ideology developed by a particular teacher. So too will be the teacher's view of how teaching ought to be. While it has now been suggested by many that attribution theory has a potentially significant part to play with respect to the articulation of an investigative theory and an accompanying methodology (see Weiner, 1976, 1979, and Bar-Tal, 1979 and in this volume) it has yet to play much of a part in the development of an educational ideology. Given that attribution theory has been developed as a social-psychological theory and not an educational one this is unremarkable, but it is claimed here that unless attribution theory is able to play some part in the articulation of an educational ideology then its potential application to the study of educational processes will be severely limited.

D. THE ROLE OF ATTRIBUTION THEORY:
PROMISES AND LIMITATIONS

The remainder of this paper will attempt to illustrate the extent to which attribution theory, as it is presently articulated, is able to deal with the various problems outlined above. While it would be possible to illustrate these arguments by using a number of different studies, those employed here will be primarily taken from the body of attribution theory research that has concerned itself with the problem of underachievement in female school pupils. What follows is not in any way intended to be an exhaustive review of this part of the "sex differences" literature, and is an expansion of part of the picture of attributional analysis drawn in Bar-Tal's chapter.

It has been clear for some time that attribution theory is capable of at least demonstrating, if not yet accounting for, some of the functional features of teachers' and also pupils' classroom perceptions. This is perhaps seen most clearly in the making of "defensive" attributions, some examples of which are given below. The point, which these examples illustrate, is that while the general perceptions of a class held by a teacher or a pupil can be interpreted and understood in terms of self-defensive functions of the type discussed by Sharp and Green, it will often be through the causal attributions made for particular events that these functions will actually be fulfilled. Beckman (1970) reports a study in which teachers were asked to make attributions for the causes of successful and unsuccessful teaching experiences. Teachers' judgements showed that they assumed a greater personal responsibility for the performance of those pupils who got better during the duration of the study than they did for those that got worse. Observers of the teachers, however, made the opposite assumption. Such self-defensive attributions have also been found in pupils making attributions for their own successes and failure. Covington and Omelich (1979), in a test of Weiner's (1974) attributional model of achievement motivation, found little support for a strict information-processing interpretation of the model, but did find support for an attributional model that assumed that pupils were motivated to do what they could in their attributions to protect their levels of self-esteem.

In research on sex differences in achievement levels it is possible to find evidence to support both the view that the attributions of boys and girls represent the straightforward application of the same set of information-processing rules but to different sets of data, and the view that the differences in attributions are due to motivational systems closely allied to the pupils' self-concepts. Attempts to test between these two different approaches in attribution theory—the assumption on the one hand that a more or less universal set of information-processing rules can account for all attributions and, on the other, the assumption that these information-processing rules will be constantly affected in operation by self-serving motivational forces—are likely to become crucial in determining the nature of attribution theory's contribution to an understanding of educational processes. A strict information-processing approach would imply a more passive role on the part of the pupil. A view of attribution theory that acknowledges the existence of self serving biases gives some credit to the pupil in helping to create the psychological world that he or she inhabits at school—even if the created world is one that does not operate to the advantage of the pupil.

Research associated with Weiner's attributional analysis of achievement motivation has shown that the tendency to attribute failure to lack of effort rather than to a lack of ability is associated with high levels of achievement motivation. Given evidence showing that the differences in attainment between boy and girls, particularly from early adolescence onwards where the performance of girls goes into a relative decline, cannot be readily accounted for in terms of different levels of ability (see Maccoby and Jacklin, 1974, for a comprehensive review) researchers have directed their attention towards motivational variables. For those working within attribution theory this has meant a search for sex-related differences in attributions for success and failure particularly those relating to the perceived role of effort. A number of studies have succeeded in showing that girls are more likely than boys to neglect a lack of effort as a possible cause of their failures (e.g. Nicholls, 1975) while others have also shown that girls are more likely than boys to show a decrement in performance following an instance or instances of failure (e.g. Dweck and Gilliard, 1975; Veroff, 1969).

Dweck *et al.* (1978) investigated the relationship between these sex-related differences in attributions made by pupils and the feedback that they received from teachers. Essentially their results show that criticism from teachers directed at girls is nearly all concerned with actual academic aspects of the pupils' work. In the case of boys, however, teachers' criticisms were more diffuse. Some 45% of the criticism directed at boys was concerned with things other than the academic content of their work—for example, classroom misbehaviour. This, it is suggested by the authors, leads to boys and girls making different attributions for their failures. For a boy, criticism of a particular piece of work is seen against a background of criticism for many aspects of his behaviour. As such, the single work-related criticism is relatively uninformative with respect to a boy's ability. For a girl, however, the single piece of work-related criticism is seen against a background of an absence of other forms of criticism and is therefore relatively more likely to be interpreted as an indication of a lack of ability on the part of the girl.

Such differences between the sexes become more pronounced when particular subject areas are examined. Several studies (Duckworth and Entwistle, 1974; Maccoby and Jacklin, 1974) have shown that girls are likely to perceive mathematics as being a particularly difficult subject. This will be further examined below, but at present it can be pointed out that research by Leinhardt *et al.* (1979) has shown that teachers will give more attention to boys in subjects in which they are generally believed to excel (e.g. mathematics) and less in subjects in which girls are believed to be superior. Furthermore the same study showed that while there were no actual differences between the sexes along these lines initially, by the end of the school year differences had emerged that were in keeping with the amount of teacher attention made available to each sex.

Studies such as the above indicate that sex-related differences in attributions for success and failure may be explicable solely in terms of the different sets of information that boys and girls have available. However, other research reports results that are not in keeping with this view. Crandall (1963) and Veroff (1969) provide evidence supporting the view that boys are trained for greater independence and are therefore more likely than girls to be able to ignore any items of unfavourable feedback. However, Dweck and Bush (1976) have shown that when peers rather than the more typical adult is used to provide the feedback, it is boys rather than girls who are more susceptible to the possibly damaging consequences of negative feedback. Such results indicate that the attributions of both boys and girls for their successes and failures are mediated by motivational and value systems. To understand the attributions we must also seek to understand the motivational and value systems.

The studies above help to illustrate the way in which research guided by attribution theory can help to demonstrate the functional utility of the judgements made by various classroom participants and also the extent to which attributions are influenced by the contexts within which they are made. However, these same studies also go some way toward illustrating the nature of some of the limitations of attribution theory as applied to an analysis of classroom processes.

Primarily, it is clear even from the very brief outline above of a small number of studies that research into attributions alone will be quite inadequate. It is necesary also to have available information regarding, for example, the style and frequency of teacher–pupil interactions. This really refers back to the points made above concerning the need, invariably, to investigate closely the effects of context upon the nature of the interpersonal judgements that might be made within the classroom. Attribution theory has been developed primarily under laboratory conditions in which it is usually assumed that the context in which subjects make their attributions will be the same for all subjects at least within one particular treatment group. Within a classroom this is not necessarily so. The contexts in which boys and girls make their attributions for success and failure have been seen to vary as a function of the type of evaluative feedback they are receiving, the source of that feedback, the particular subject being studied and the behaviour of the teacher towards pupils of either sex which in turn varies as a function of the subject being studied. Closer investigations, for example, of the subject based differences in teacher–pupil interaction would reveal a whole complexity of factors related in part to the contemporary–consociate distinction discussed above.

A second limitation is that the studies discussed above for the most part do not tell us much about the meaning of particular attributions for those who have made them. Reference is being made here to the ideological component contained in the effects of research upon educational practice. Attribution theory itself does not contain any prescriptions concerning the values that are to be attached to certain types of cognitive activities.

E. FROM ATTRIBUTIONS TO VALUES

The final section of this paper will seek to demonstrate that attribution theory, while it may not contain within it prescriptions for an educational value system, contains within it the means to explore the often implicit value systems of the participants, both teachers and pupils, within the educational system itself. That is, rather than providing a value system for education from "outside", attribution theory leads to an examination of the "naive" value systems already being put into operation by the various insiders.

A study by Rogers (1980) was concerned not so much with the attributions made by boys and girls for their successes and failures, but more with the evaluations that they made of the successes and failures of others both as a function of pupil characteristics (age and sex), and as a function of the relative importance of three elements of the performance to be evaluated (degree of success, level of effort expended and the level of ability usually displayed by the pupil to be judged on this particular task). The results of this study bear a close relationship with those discussed above as the performance to be evaluated in this study was the results obtained on a test of mathematics. In essence the results showed that while girls evaluated the performance of both other girls and boys according to the same criteria, boys, especially those aged 12 years and over, did not. These results demonstrate that between the ages of 12 and 15 the value systems of these boys with respect to educational success and failure in girls undergoes change. Furthermore, as argued by Rogers (1980) these value changes can be seen to be detrimental as far as the continuation of high levels of achievement motivation in girls is concerned. In essence, in the case of mathematics, girls in middle adolescence not only have to contend with teachers who may give them less time, but also, and this may well prove to be more significant, they have to contend with male peers who undervalue their successes in this subject while also making light of their failures. Reports of successful school-based (and school-sponsored) trials of single-sex mathematics sets in co-educational schools would seem to support this view (Smith, 1980).

Research into teachers' attributions for pupils' behaviour has so far been limited to a study of the explanations they give for success and failure, concentrating for the most part on the pre-determined causes of ability, effort, task difficulty and, to a lesser extent, luck. In these studies (Ames, 1975; Bar-Tal and Guttman, 1978; Darom and Bar-Tal, 1977) teachers' views on the importance of effort as a covariant of success are clearly demonstrated. A knowledge of these attributional patterns and the circumstances under which they will obtain will greatly aid our attempts to assess the significance of certain teacher impressions or typifications of pupils. For a teacher to conclude that a particular pupil is lazy will be of substantial significance if that teacher typically attributes success to high effort and failure to a lack of effort.

Mention was made above of the cyclic nature of the judgements that teachers make of their pupils. Predictive judgements play their part in giving rise to new situations some elements of which may prove to be problematic and need explanation. These explanations will provide the basis for the next set of predictive judgements. The role of attribution theory in helping to provide an account of the way in which the explanatory judgements are made is relatively clear. Attribution theory is, after all, a theoretical system designed to account for the making of explanatory judgements. It is suggested here that attribution theory will also have a role to play in the development of an understanding of predictive judgements through an analysis of the value systems that teachers', and pupils', causal attributions can be seen to reveal.

The potential applications of attribution theory to research into the nature of teacher–pupil interpersonal perceptions and relationships is at present still limited by the laboratory origins of the theory. The initial limiting effects of these origins were to be seen in the rigid application of methodologies that had been developed in a laboratory settings to deal with very specific questions. There are now increasing signs (e.g. Bar-Tal, 1979) that the need for more open-ended and flexible methodologies is being recognized.

More importantly, however, it is still the case that the limited educational research that has been carried out under the aegis of attribution theory has been directed more by the already established patterns of attribution research than by the actual degree of educational significance that particular issues might have. All of the above examples concerning attribution-related studies of sex differences within the educational system were concerned with attributions made for instances of success and failure, and the attributions themselves primarily concerned with the causal factors of effort and ability. This quite accurately reflects the emphasis within current applications of attribution theory concepts to educational issues where the theoretical formulations of Weiner and his colleagues (1974) have been particularly influential.

Clearly one would not wish to deny that teachers' perceptions of the causes of their pupils' successes and failures will be of particular significance for the determination of the nature of the relationships and the interactions that will exist and take place between teacher and pupil. However, such attributions are by no means the only ones of any educational importance.

Recent research into the "teacher expectancy effect" (Crano and Mellon, 1978) has shown that it is the social expectations rather than the academic ones that teachers, particularly of young children, have for their pupils that are likely to have a causal influence upon those pupils' later levels of academic performance. In another area of research, but still closely related to teachers' impressions of their pupils, Algozzine (1977) reports that pupils, particularly girls, who were perceived by their teachers as having a high degree of facial attractiveness engaged in more positive interactions with their teachers. Such a finding may well be related to the earlier findings of Dion (1972) who showed that the misdeeds of the physically attractive were, relative to those of the unattractive, unlikely to be attributed to an underlying negative disposition.

These two examples serve to illustrate the point that straightforward judgements of ability and effort will be only a part of the universe of judgements that teachers make about their pupils. The same can also be said of pupils and their perceptions of the school setting and of themselves within it. The research gathered together by Meighan (1978) demonstrates that pupils also show a high degree of concern with their social relationships within school, their opportunities for developing social skills and their teachers' ability to maintain effective discipline within the classroom. The claim made here, stemming from the earlier comments about the importance of considering the various contexts of classroom interpersonal perception, is that the full promise of attribution theory for the study of classroom processes will not be realized until fuller attention is given to educational research drawing on other theoretical systems, and until attribution theory principles are applied to a wider variety of problems than those that have been of concern so far. Until this happens attributional studies of educational processes will continue to be examples of applied social psychology and will fail to become pieces of educational research. This distinction may be a subtle one but it is of considerable importance.

REFERENCES

Algozzine, B. (1977). Perceived attractiveness and classroom interactions. *Journal of Experimental Education* **46**, 207–213.

Ames, R. (1975). Teachers' attributions of responsibility: Some unexpected non-defensive effects. *Journal of Educational Psychology* **67**, 668–676.

Bar-Tal, D. (1979). Interactions of teachers and pupils. In I. H. Frieze, D. Bar-Tal and J. S. Carrol (eds) *New Approaches to Social Problems*. London: Jossey-Bass.

Bar-Tal, D. and Guttman, J. (1978). Unpublished manuscript, Tel-Aviv University.

Beckman, L. J. (1970). Effects of students' performance on teachers' and observers' attributions of causality. *Journal of Educational Psychology* **61**, 76–82.

Brophy, J. E. and Good, T. L. (1974). *Teacher-Student Relationships: Causes and Consequences*. New York: Holt, Rinehart and Winston.

Calderhead, J. (1979). Teachers' classroom decision making: its relationship to teachers' perceptions of pupils and to classroom interaction. Unpublished Ph.D. thesis, University of Stirling.

Covington, M. V. and Omelich, C. L. (1979). Are causal attributions causal? A path analysis of the cognitive model of achievement motivation. *Journal of Personality and Social Psychology* **37**, 1487–1504.

Crandall, V. J. (1963). Achievement. *In* H. W. Stevenson (ed.) *Child Psychology: the sixty-second year book of the National Society for the Study of Education*. National Society for the Study of Education: Chicago.

Crano, W. D. and Mellon, P. M. (1978). Causal influence of teachers' expectation on children's academic performance: a cross-lagged panel analysis. *Journal of Educational Psychology* **70**, 39–49.

Darom, E. and Bar-Tal, D. (1977). Unpublished manuscript. Tel-Aviv University.

Desforges, C. and McNamara, D. (1977). One man's heuristic is another man's blindfold: some comments on applying social science to educational practice. *British Journal of Teacher Education* **3**, 27–39.

Dion, K. K. (1972). Physical attractiveness and evaluation of children's transgressions. *Journal of personality and Social Psychology* **24**, 207–213.

Dweck, C. S. and Bush, E. S. (1976). Sex differences in learned helplessness: (1) Differential debilitation with peer and adult evaluators. *Developmental Psychology* **12**, 147–156.

Dweck, C. S. and Gilliard, D. (1975). Expectancy statements as determinants of reactions of failure: sex differences in persistence and expectancy change. *Journal of Personality and Social Psychology* **32**, 1077–1084.

Dweck, C. S., Davidson, W., Nelson, S. and Enna, B. (1978). Sex differences in learned helplessness: II The contingency of evaluative feedback in the classroom and III An experimental analysis. *Developmental Psychology* **14**, 268–276.

Duckworth, D. and Entwistle, N. J. (1974). Attitudes to school subjects: a repertory grid technique. *British Journal of Educational Psychology* **44**, 76–78.

Frieze, I. H., Bar-Tal, D. and Carroll, J. S. (eds) (1979). *New Approaches to Social Problems*. London: Jossey-Bass.

Hallworth, H. J. (1962). A teacher's perceptions of his pupils. *Educational Review* **14**, 124–133.

Hallworth, H. J. and Morrison, A. (1964). A comparison of peer and teacher personality ratings of pupils in a secondary modern school. *British Journal of Educational Psychology* **34**, 285–291.

Harvey, J. H., Ickes, W. and Kidd, R. F. (1978). *In* J. H. Harvey, W. Ickes and R. F. Kidd, (eds) *New Directions in Attribution Research*. Vol. 2. Lawrence Erlbaum Associations, New Jersey.

Hargreaves, D. H. (1977). The process of typification in classroom interaction: models and methods. *British Journal of Educational Psychology* **47**, 274–284.

Hastorf, A. H., Schneider, D., and Ellsworth, P. (1979). *Person Perception*, 2nd Ed., Reading, Mass.: Addison-Wesley.

Jackson, P. W. (1968). *Life in Classrooms*. New York: Holt, Rinehart and Winston.

Jackson, P. W., Silberman, M. L. and Wolfson, B. J. (1969). Signs of personal involvement in teachers' descriptions of their students. *Journal of Educational Psychology* **60**, 22–27.

Jones, E. E. and Davis, K. E. (1965). From acts to dispositions: the attribution process in person perception. *In* L. Berkowitz (ed.) *Advances in Experimental Social Psychology*, Vol. 2. New York and London: Academic Press.

Kallos, D. and Lundgren, U. P. (1975). Educational psychology: its scope and limits. *British Journal of Educational Psychology* **45**, 111–121.

Leinhardt, G., Seewald, A. M. and Engel, M. (1979). Learning what's taught: sex differences in instruction. *Journal of Educational Psychology* **71**, 432–439.

Livesley, W. J. and Bromley, D. B. (1973). *Person Perception in Childhood and Adolescence*. London: Wiley.

McIntyre, D., Morrison, A. and Sutherland, J. (1966). Social and educational variables relating to teachers' assessments of primary school pupils. *British Journal of Educational Psychology* **36**, 272–279.

McNamara, D. and Desforges, C. (1978). The social sciences, teacher education and the objectification of craft knowledge. *British Journal of Teacher Education* **4**.

Maccoby, E. E. and Jacklin, C. N. (1974). *The Psychology of Sex Differences*. Stanford: Stanford University Press.

Marsh, P., Rosser, E. and Harré, R. (1978). *The Rules of Disorder*. London: Routledge and Kegan Paul.

Meighan, R. (ed.) (1978). The learners' viewpoint. Explorations of the pupil perspective on schooling. *Educational Review* Special Number, (10) **30**.

Miller, D. T., Norman, S. A. and Wright, E. (1978). Distortion in person perception as a consequence of the need for effective control. *Journal of Personality and Social Psychology* **36**, 598–607.

Murphy, J. (1974). Teacher expectations and working class under-achievement. *British Journal of Sociology* **25**, 326–344.

Nicholls, J. G. (1975). Causal attributions and other achievement related cognitions: effects of task outcome, attainment value and sex. *Journal of Personality and Social Psychology* **31**, 379–389.

Rist, R. G. (1970). Student social class and teacher expectations. The self-fulfilling prophecy in ghetto education. *Harvard Educational Review* **40**, 411–451.

Rogers, C. (1978). The child's perception of other people. *In* H. McGurk (ed.) *Issues in Childhood Social Development*. London: Methuen.

Rogers, C. (1980). The development of sex differences in evaluations of others' successes and failures. *British Journal of Educational Psychology* **50**, 243–252.

Rogers, C. and Antaki, C. (1980). An introduction to basic attribution theory and its potential application to education. Paper presented at the British Psychological Society (Education Section) Conference. Lancaster University.

Schutz, A. (1932). *The Phenomenology of the Social World*. London: Heinemann.

Schutz, A. (1973). *The Structures of the Life-World*. London: Heinemann.

Silberman, M. L. (1969). Behavioural expression of teachers' attitudes towards elementary school students. *Journal of Educational Psychology* **60**, 402–407.

Sharp, R. and Green, A. (1975). *Education and Social Control*. London: Routledge and Kegan Paul.

Smith, S. (1980). Should they be kept apart? *Times Educational Supplement*, 18.7.1980. No. 3344.

Veroff, J. (1969). Social comparison and the development of achievement motivation. *In* C. P. Smith (ed.) *Achievement-related Motives in Children*. New York: Russell Sage.

Warr, P. B. and Knapper, C. (1968). *The Perception of People and Events*. London: Wiley.

Weiner, B. (1974). *Achievement Motivation and Attribution Theory*. Morristown, N.J.: General Learning Press.

Weiner, B. (1976). An attributional approach for educational psychology. *Review of Research in Education* **4**, 179–209.

Weiner, B. (1979). A theory of motivation for some classroom experiences. *Journal of Educational Psychology* **71**, 3–25.

Subject Index